AMERICANS IN WAITING

AMERICANS IN WAITING

The Lost Story of Immigration and Citizenship

in the United States

HIROSHI MOTOMURA

OXFORD
UNIVERSITY PRESS

2006

OXFORD

UNIVERSITY PRESS

Oxford University Press, Inc., publishes works that further
Oxford University's objective of excellence
in research, scholarship, and education.

Oxford   New York
Auckland   Cape Town   Dar es Salaam   Hong Kong   Karachi
Kuala Lumpur   Madrid   Melbourne   Mexico City   Nairobi
New Delhi   Shanghai   Taipei   Toronto

With offices in
Argentina   Austria   Brazil   Chile   Czech   Republic   France   Greece
Guatemala   Hungary   Italy   Japan   Poland   Portugal   Singapore
South Korea   Switzerland   Thailand   Turkey   Ukraine   Vietnam

Copyright © 2006 by Oxford University Press, Inc.

Published by Oxford University Press, Inc.
198 Madison Avenue, New York, New York 10016

www.oup.com

Oxford is a registered trademark of Oxford University Press

Library of Congress Cataloging-in-Publication Data

Motomura, Hiroshi, 1953–
Americans in waiting : the lost story of immigration
and citizenship in the United States / Hiroshi Motomura.
    p.   cm.
Includes bibliographical references and index.
ISBN-13 978-0-19-516345-2
ISBN 0-19-516345-1
1. United States—Emigration and immigration—Government policy.
2. Immigrants—United States.   3. Citizenship—United States.   I. Title.
JV6483.M67   2006
325.73—dc22   2005036788

9   8   7   6   5   4   3   2   1
Printed in the United States of America
on acid-free paper.

For Linda and Amy,
and for Akira
and our parents

ACKNOWLEDGMENTS

This book has been a long time in coming. It began with a short essay that I prepared for a Workshop on Citizenship and Naturalization at the Terry Sanford Institute of Public Policy at Duke University in October 1997. That tentative exploration appeared as a short essay, "Alienage Classifications in a Nation of Immigrants: Three Models of Permanent Residence," in *Immigration and Citizenship in the Twenty-First Century* (ed. Noah Pickus, 191–220).

Some of the material in this book has appeared in various articles and essays that I have published over the past sixteen years, but virtually nothing has remained in its original form or its original context, nor kept its original purpose. The most satisfying aspect of writing this book has been gradually coming to understand how my prior work was part of a larger project, whose outlines have emerged slowly and through much effort. Pursuing this larger project has forced me to disassemble and rethink prior writing, and then to synthesize it with a great deal of new material in an entirely new conceptual framework, and for a broader audience.

Many friends and colleagues have blessed me with their tremendous generosity on the long and sometimes winding path from that conference to this book. For very helpful conversations and comments on ideas and drafts, I am grateful to Alex Aleinikoff, Linda Bosniak, Curt Bradley, Lynn Calder, Paul Campos, Adrienne Davis, Max Eichner, Ann Estin, Linda Greenberg, Kay Hailbronner, Clare Huntington, Barbara John, Kevin Johnson, Jerry Kang, Sarah Krakoff, Jay Krishnan, Steve Legomsky, Carol Lehman, David Martin, Nancy Morawetz, Amy Motomura, Gail Musen, Gerry Neuman, Krista Perreira, Scott Peppet, Noah Pickus, Victor Romero, Ruth Rubio Marin, Lucy Salyer, Amy Schmitz, Peter Schuck, Linda Spiegler, Peter Spiro, Margaret Taylor, Dan Tichenor, Art Travers, Leti Volpp, Phil Weiser, Deborah Weissman, Mimi Wesson, Nadine

Wettstein, and Frank Wu, as well as participants in the 1998 biennial Immigration Law Workshop at the University of California at Berkeley, and in colloquia, symposia, and workshops at the Albany Law School, the American Academy in Berlin, Ruprecht-Karls-Universität Heidelberg, the New York Law School, the University of California at Los Angeles, the University of Chicago, the University of Colorado, the University of Iowa, the University of North Carolina, the University of Virginia, and Wake Forest University. For excellent research and comments on drafts, I thank Kerry Burleigh, Jessica Catlin, Heather Corbin, Melissa Decker, Paige Gardner, Katy Lewis, Traci Massey, Sean McAllister, Tracy Nayer, Kate Noble, Vini Nuon Gopal, Sarah Robson, Justin Stein, and Danielle Urban. I also owe thanks to my editors: Dedi Felman, for her encouragement, suggestions, and faith in this project, and Linda Donnelly, for transforming this book from manuscript to bound volume with poise and efficiency.

As the length of the previous paragraph shows, I could not have written this book without the help of many people. I have also been lucky enough to enjoy the steadfast support of three great institutions. Two are the law schools on whose faculties I have served—the University of Colorado School of Law and the University of North Carolina School of Law. The third is the American Academy in Berlin, where a Lloyd Cutler Fellowship gave me the time to mold this project into its near-final shape.

I owe an incalculable debt to many friends and colleagues whose scholarship has laid the foundation for what I say here—even if in the end they disagree with me—and who have profoundly shaped my thinking for as long as I have been writing about immigration and citizenship. Peter Schuck's 1984 article *The Transformation of Immigration Law* has been both a model for my writing as a whole and the conceptual catalyst for this book. And since 1994, my friendship and collaboration with my casebook coauthors, Alex Aleinikoff and David Martin, has been my most constant source of intellectual encouragement and stimulation. Our work together also has been my most constant reminder that scholarship is a way of teaching, that teaching is a form of scholarship, and that both are essential if ideas are to make a difference.

Most of all I want to thank Linda and Amy. I could never have done this without you.

CONTENTS

AMERICANS IN WAITING

INTRODUCTION

Immigrants in America

★

My family came to America in 1957, when I was three years old. We lived in an apartment on Bush Street in San Francisco, a ten-minute walk from the traditional Japantown first settled by Japanese immigrants a half-century before us. The 1950s were a time when not many immigrants came to America, at least as compared to today. My family arrived long after the early waves of Asian and European immigrants around the turn of the twentieth century. We arrived before the resurgence of immigration that would start in the late 1960s and still continues, so the America of my childhood wasn't quite the nation of immigrants that preceded or followed it. Even in the rich diversity of a San Francisco childhood, kids with "foreign" names—like Ziad, Juanita, and Hiroshi—found that the early 1960s world of *Ozzie and Harriet*, *Leave It to Beaver*, and *American Bandstand* prompted deep and unsettled questions about what it means to come to America, and what it means to say that America is a nation of immigrants.

These questions seemed to have little to do with the legal issues that years later I would come to call immigration and citizenship law. The distinctions that mattered most in my family, as in immigrant families everywhere, had to do with generations and language. My parents came to America in their late twenties, while my brother, Akira, and I grew up in San Francisco. My parents learned English imperfectly, while English became the mother tongue for Akira and me.

I later learned that the line between citizens and noncitizens can make a big difference, and that in my family, too, legal status was a complex question. The law treated each of us differently. Though my father came to America as a young man, he had been born in San Francisco in 1925 and was a U.S. citizen by virtue of birth on U.S. soil. His parents moved back to Japan in 1930. He grew up there, and in the 1950s he was able to return to the United States. Immigration law treated him simply as coming home, yet he felt, acted, and was treated as an immigrant. My mother was the one in our family whose legal status most clearly matched how she felt. She was born in Japan in 1924, which happened to be the same year that U.S. law made her ineligible on account of race to immigrate to the United States. We were allowed to come to San Francisco only to join my father (who had preceded us to America by several years, also a typical immigrant story), because we were coming as the spouse and child of an American.

Young children who immigrate to the United States with their parents usually have their parents' nationality, but my own citizenship status was more complicated. A child born outside the United States with one citizen parent may be a U.S. citizen at birth, but only if the citizen parent fulfills a U.S. residency requirement, which my father had not. So I was stateless until I became a naturalized U.S. citizen at the age of fifteen. Akira was born in San Francisco three years after my mother and I immigrated. He and I were both children of immigrant parents, but as a citizen, he had a legal status quite different from mine.

My family history shows that the law makes distinctions of various kinds, most prominently by drawing a line between citizens and noncitizens, but that this line between "us" and "them" often does not match up with the ways in which families come to this country. Perhaps because the law cannot capture, let alone freeze, the ways that immigrants think about what it means to come to America, immigrants have crossed the line between us and them. Over the course of American history, families like ours have started as "them" and ended up—at least in part—as "us," even if that process has taken time, sometimes even generations.

Just four years before my family came to America, the U.S. Supreme Court held in *Brown v. Board of Education* that public schools segregated by law are unconstitutional.[1] *Brown* stands for the idea in the law that all persons are equal and should be treated accordingly. The Court's decision is widely celebrated today as a landmark of national commitment to the equality that is central to any democracy. But thinking about *Brown* as a symbol of equality reveals how hard it is to apply the lessons of *Brown* to immigration and citizenship, where the idea of equality is elusive.

Citizens and noncitizens are not always equal. Among the noncitizens, some will be admitted to the United States, while others will not be. Citizens can insist on being treated as the equals of other citizens and on having the same rights. But noncitizens are not always treated like citizens. Noncitizens generally cannot vote. Noncitizens can be deported. In short, "all men are created equal" only if those "men" are not noncitizens.

The reason for these differences between citizens and noncitizens—between those who are members and those who are not—is that a democracy must have the power to shape and preserve itself as a community of individuals who share interests and values. In order to do so, a democracy must have the power to grant or refuse membership to newcomers, as well as the power to say that members can do some things that nonmembers cannot. And yet, the line between citizens and noncitizens and the concept of equality in immigration are highly fluid and dynamic notions. As my own family history shows, the line between us and them has never been fixed or impermeable. The question is not just when "we" and "they" are equal, but also: when and how do "they" become part of "us."

To start answering these questions, consider the imaginary but typical Juan and Rosalita Garcia, who came to the United States from Mexico six years ago. They are lawful immigrants, or "permanent residents" in legal parlance.[2] Permanent residents are noncitizens who have been admitted to the United States for an indefinite period of time. They have what are often called "green cards," although the cards have been off-white rather than green for some years.

Juan works in a small factory in the San Francisco Bay Area that makes cardboard boxes. Rosalita works taking care of elderly residents of an assisted living center nearby. Their son, Jesus, and their daughter, Maria, were born in the United States, which automatically makes the children U.S. citizens. Juan and Rosalita work hard and are saving what they can for a down payment on a house. They pay taxes and are active in their church and in several community organizations. They speak only halting English, but their heavy work schedules and the demands of parenting leave them no time for language classes. They have thought about becoming U.S. citizens, but they have heard that the paperwork takes a long time, and they are wary of cutting ties to Mexico.

How should we in America treat lawful immigrants like Juan and Rosalita? Should they be allowed to vote? Under current law, they may not vote in state or national elections, and only a few scattered communities would allow them to vote in local elections. Juan and Rosalita have no health insurance and no money to pay for medical care. What if Rosalita is diagnosed with a rare blood disorder that requires continuous medical monitoring and leaves her too weak to work regularly? Under current law, lawful immigrants pay taxes, but a complex array of rules governs their eligibility for various public benefits. What if Juan is convicted of shoplifting? Under current law, some crimes can make a lawful immigrant deportable. But how serious a crime should—or should *any* crime—lead to deportation? These questions probe what it means for lawful immigrants in the United States to be something less than the equal of U.S. citizens.

Here are three considerations that might influence lawmakers as they decide how to treat lawful immigrants. First, it might matter that Juan and Rosalita have worked hard in their jobs and have paid taxes and have children who are both U.S. citizens. Second, a lawmaker might think that an immigrant who commits a crime has breached some form of trust implicitly bestowed when this country admitted him. Third, a lawmaker might be troubled that Juan and Rosalita recently became eligible to become U.S. citizens but have done nothing about it.

I recognize that the Garcia family story implicitly raises this question: Who should be allowed to immigrate lawfully to the United States in the first place? But public debate on this threshold admission question often reaches an impasse precisely because we have not thought enough about how we treat lawful immigrants after they get here. This boundary between lawful immigrants and citizens is the line of greatest intimacy but also of most pointed exclusion between outsider and insider. What the United States does with this line tells us most about what it means to be a nation of immigrants. Our treatment of lawful immigrants is the key to debating intelligently who should be let into the United States in the first place.

Lawful Immigrants: A Brief Overview

The legal concept of permanent residence first emerged in the 1920s. Before then, various laws barred many categories of immigrants—for example those with contagious diseases or unacceptable political views—but the *number* of immigrants was not limited. Starting in 1921, however, federal immigration law capped how many immigrants would be admitted to

permanent residence in the United States, and it distinguished such immigrants from nonimmigrants, who are admitted lawfully but only for a
limited duration and a particular purpose, for example, to study or to
work in a certain job. (Of course, permanent resident status also contrasts
with undocumented noncitizens, who are unlawfully present.) Since 1921,
the terms "lawful immigrant" and "permanent resident" have meant the
same thing, and I use them interchangeably.[3]

There are five basic ways to become a lawful immigrant. Family ties
account for the largest number—about a half million annually, or over
63 percent of the total. Most favored are spouses and unmarried children
of U.S. citizens, and parents of adult citizens. Other relatives qualify but
must wait longer, sometimes much longer. Employment qualifies more
than 16 percent of lawful immigrants, who must meet various education
and experience requirements. Almost 12 percent of lawful immigrants are
refugees fleeing persecution, either chosen for admission from outside
the United States, or getting asylum at or inside the U.S. border. Four percent are winners of an annual lottery open to noncitizens from countries
that have not sent many immigrants to the United States recently. Finally,
4 percent of lawful immigrants use ad hoc exceptions that allow noncitizens to legalize their status.[4]

The number of lawful immigrants to the United States in any given
year has varied greatly by historical period. The highest numbers were
admitted in the period from 1900 to 1915, when the annual number of
new immigrants routinely approached or exceeded one million. Immigrant admissions dropped to a trickle during World War I, rose to half
of prewar levels during the 1920s, then dropped again during the Great
Depression and World War II. After 1945, the flow steadily increased
from decade to decade. Since 1980, annual lawful immigrant admissions
have sometimes exceeded one million and thus approached the historically high numbers of the early 1900s, but as a lower percentage of the
total U.S. population.

The source countries for lawful immigrants to the United States have
changed dramatically over the past century. European countries dominated
the flow in the period 1901–10, but Mexico had emerged as a significant
source by the 1920s. That mix prevailed through the 1950s, with a high percentage of lawful immigrants coming from Mexico, Canada, and a few European countries. The source countries changed dramatically after 1965, so
that by the 1980s the largest numbers came from Latin America (especially

Mexico) and Asia. In 2004, 57 percent of lawful immigrants came from twelve countries—Mexico, India, the Philippines, China, Vietnam, the Dominican Republic, El Salvador, Cuba, Korea, Colombia, Guatemala, and Canada. Of the twelve, Mexico accounted for the most by far, with India a distant second, and the Philippines third. In 2004, more than a third of all lawful immigrants came from one of these three countries.

Permanent residents are not U.S. citizens. All countries divide persons into those who are citizens and those who are not. I will refer to the latter group as noncitizens; federal law almost always calls them "aliens." Almost everyone born on U.S. soil is a citizen, regardless of his parents' citizenship or immigration status. (The only exception is for children of foreign diplomats.) A child born outside the United States may also be a citizen, if one or both of his parents are citizens. A noncitizen who wants to become a U.S. citizen must generally become a permanent resident first. Then, after a waiting period—generally five years—and satisfying other requirements, he may become a citizen by a process called naturalization.[5]

In 2003, about 11.5 million permanent residents lived in the United States, about 7.9 million of whom had lived here long enough to become citizens through naturalization. Of those noncitizens who have been permanent residents long enough to naturalize, about 60 percent do so—an average of about 550,000 new U.S. citizens each year from 1991 through 2004. But nothing requires lawful immigrants to naturalize. Unless they become deportable, they may stay indefinitely in the United States as permanent residents.[6]

The Lost Story: Americans in Waiting

This book tries to recover a lost story that once was central to American thinking about immigration. The story is that for much of its history, America treated lawful immigrants as future citizens, and immigration as a transition to citizenship. Lawful immigrants—or as I will outline later, *some* lawful immigrants—could become "intending citizens." For more than a century and a half—from 1795 to 1952—every applicant for naturalization had to file a declaration of intent several years in advance.[7] This declaration gave any noncitizen who was eligible to naturalize a precitizenship status that elevated him, even from his first day in America, well above those who had not filed declarations and therefore were not seen as on the citizenship track. Many statutes throughout this period expressly

preferred intending citizens. The Homestead Act of 1862, the key to set-
tling the western frontier, made noncitizens eligible for grants of land
once they filed declarations.[8] The U.S. government sometimes extended
diplomatic protection to intending citizens who got into trouble overseas.
And until the early twentieth century, many intending citizens could vote.

Today, the declaration of intent is optional, and few are filed. Intending
citizens do not enjoy U.S. diplomatic protection. In 1926, Arkansas repealed the last state law allowing noncitizen voting.[9] The significance of
this shift goes well beyond the demise of the declaration of intent as a formal document and of intending citizen as a formal status. In the century
from the mid-1800s to the mid-1900s, the basic idea that new immigrants
should be treated as future citizens faded from prominence.

To capture this way of viewing immigration, I have coined the term *immigration as transition*. It treats lawful immigrants as Americans in waiting, as if they would eventually become citizens of the United States, and
thus confers on immigrants a *presumed equality*. In a broad range of ways,
we Americans no longer view immigration as transition, nor do we think
of immigrants as Americans in waiting. In fact, the opposite is true; we
treat new immigrants as outsiders until shown otherwise. They may later
become citizens, but we no longer treat them as if they will. This book ex-
amines how this happened, why this has undermined the very idea of a
nation of immigrants, and why it is important to once again treat lawful
immigrants as Americans in waiting.

Three Views of Immigration

It is striking that a view of immigration and immigrants that was important for much of American history would largely fade from sight. To explain understand how this story was lost and how it might be recovered,
this book reinterprets the evolution of U.S. immigration and citizenship
law—especially its treatment of lawful immigrants—as a set of tensions
among three ways of viewing immigration. Immigration as transition is
only one of the three views, and it is less evident because the other two
have eclipsed it.

One of these other two views of immigration is what I call *immigration
as contract*. The Garcias may be lawful immigrants, but perhaps they have
"promised" to stay out of trouble with the law, on pain of deportation. Or
even if they do not commit any crimes, their admission to this country

may be just a temporary grant of permission that the government can revoke at any time. Or perhaps the Garcias promised to support themselves financially. On the other hand, the U.S. government may have promised not to change the rules governing their vulnerability to deportation, or the rules governing their access to public benefits. These similar ideas appear frequently in the making of law and policy, past and present.

By "contract" I do not mean a formal, legally binding document marked by the parties' signatures. Nor do I mean an agreement after back-and-forth bargaining in the marketplace between two sides that both have enough power to negotiate terms. Immigrants from poor backgrounds are especially likely to accept any terms of admission, as long as they think coming here is better than staying home. Nor do I mean a more modern view of a contract among legal scholars, as a set of social obligations that may evolve well beyond the parties' original understanding.

Rather, by contract I mean a certain way of making immigration decisions. The offer that immigrants accept by coming to America may be a take-it-or-leave-it proposition. Their bargaining power is very weak, and there is no real negotiation. And yet, immigration as contract is accurate to describe this view of immigration because it adopts ideas of fairness and justice often associated with contracts. The core idea is thinking about coming to America as a set of expectations and understandings that newcomers have of their new country, and their new country has of newcomers.

Underlying this way of talking about fairness and justice in our treatment of lawful immigrants is a certain way of thinking about equality in immigration and citizenship. Immigration as contract is based on the sense that fairness and justice for lawful immigrants does not require us to treat them as the equals of citizens. Though immigration as contract is a model of justice, it is a model of *unequal justice* that turns not on conferring equality itself, but on giving notice and protecting expectations.

One reason that immigration as transition waned is that immigration as contract assumed a prominent role, especially in the immigration law decisions of the U.S. Supreme Court in the late 1800s. Over time, however, immigration as contract also had to share influence with other views of immigration. One was the idea that simply being present in the United States bestows certain minimum rights on lawful immigrants and other noncitizens. This is what I call *territorial personhood*.

Gradually, territorial personhood evolved into a third view of immigration alongside transition and contract, which I call *immigration as affiliation*.

This is the view that the treatment of lawful immigrants and other noncitizens should depend on the ties that they have formed in this country. Newcomers put down roots. Immigration as affiliation is the foundation for the argument that lawful immigrants like the Garcias should be treated just like citizens, now that they have paid taxes, have children who are U.S. citizens, and have shown themselves to be reliable and productive workers.

As a way of thinking and talking about fairness and justice in immigration, affiliation drives arguments that lawful immigrants—though convicted of crimes that make them deportable—should be allowed to stay in the United States, if they have been here for a long time and have strong family and community ties. The longer they are here, and the more they become enmeshed in the fabric of American life, the more these lawful immigrants and citizens should be treated equally. This view of immigration is not based on the justice without equality of immigration as contract, nor on the presumed equality of immigration as transition, but rather on an *earned equality*.

"Immigration as contract" and "immigration as affiliation" are new terms, but they capture ways of thinking and talking that have become commonplace in discussions of immigration and citizenship. For example, the law's recognition of noncitizens' ties in America is a key part of our self-perception as a nation of immigrants. And the law's insistence that immigrants adhere to the conditions of their admission reflects immigration as contract. The prevailing account of immigration and citizenship in the United States reflects a combination of immigration as contract and immigration as affiliation. But this account is incomplete, for it neglects immigration as transition as a third way that America has thought about immigration and immigrants.

These three ways of talking and thinking about immigration—as transition, contract, and affiliation—are not mutually exclusive. All three have important roles to play. No one who adopts an attitude toward any aspect of law or policy needs to choose one view of immigration and reject the other two. Any attitude or decision will likely reflect a blend, but typically not by conscious choice. When a legislator or the person on the street takes a position on an immigration issue—for example, that the Garcias should be allowed to vote—she is quite unlikely to say to herself, "Oh, I'm viewing immigration mainly as affiliation," but the differences between immigration as contract, affiliation, and transition help us understand her position and how it differs from alternatives. In an area as complex as immigration and citizenship, this way of assessing choices clarifies a great deal.

It is precisely because this book is concerned with ways of viewing immigration and citizenship that my focus is immigration *law*, not just as a set of legal principles, but as something that reflects broader patterns of thought and debate. Though I am not engaged in the traditional archival work of historians, this book is archival in a different sense. Whether in the form of court decisions, statutes, or agency regulations, law typically reveals our society's values and attitudes in concrete, crystallized, and accessible terms. Even if the language of court decisions or the legislative history of statutes does not convincingly explain their holdings or rules, court decisions and statutes reflect influential thought about immigration and immigrants.

Constitutional law concerning immigration and immigrants is especially worth examining. In any area of government activity, there is a body of court decisions that uphold or strike down government decisions as consistent or inconsistent with the Constitution. For example, the U.S. Constitution plays an important role in saying how far government can go in displaying religious symbols on public property. The Constitution sets limits on interrogation of suspected criminals and on searches of their homes and cars. The Constitution also helps define the power of the federal government to enact gun-control laws. In immigration law, however, it speaks volumes about our attitudes toward noncitizens and their role in American society that courts often will not even listen to claims by noncitizens that the government's immigration decisions violate the Constitution.

Even when no court issues a ruling on the constitutionality of a government decision, constitutional ideas crystallize the public values that permeate everyday discussions involving everyday people on topics of public significance. These values also guide legislators and government agency officials when they draft, debate, enact, and administer new laws. Consider the constitutional idea that unfair procedures may violate someone's rights to notice and a fair hearing. A legislator may draft a bill with strong procedural protections, thus anticipating and allaying these concerns. A bill without those protections will likely draw the charge that it is unfair. Drafting choices and objections of this sort will not produce a court ruling on constitutionality, or on anything else for that matter, but it is still constitutional law at work, shaping the content of the law.

What it would take to revive the idea of Americans in waiting, and why it is important to do so? Here is a quick sketch of my proposal: new lawful immigrants should be treated like U.S. citizens until they fulfill the residency requirement (generally five years) to be eligible to apply for citizenship. This would mean that new lawful immigrants could sponsor their close relatives for immigration as if they were citizens. They would be eligible for public benefits just like citizens, and vote just like citizens. The only exception to equal treatment for new lawful immigrants is that they could be deported for serious crimes. In sum, new lawful immigrants would be treated not like noncitizens, but rather as Americans in waiting.

This is not a proposal to erase the line between lawful immigrants and citizens. If a lawful immigrant does not apply for citizenship as soon as he is eligible, his status would be only the status that a lawful immigrant has today. He would no longer have the same ability as a citizen to sponsor a family member for immigration. He would have only the limited welfare eligibility for lawful immigrants under current law, and he could no longer vote. The essence of my proposal is to treat a new lawful immigrant more generously, but also to use that extra generosity to help him take full advantage of the opportunity to integrate into America. If he chooses not to naturalize, he would lose that better treatment.

Some parts of this proposal are less politically viable than others, but I am offering not just a legislative recommendation, but also a way of understanding the basic tensions in immigration and citizenship over the past two hundred years. I want this proposal and its underlying rationale to help us understand and assess the choices that we face now and in the future.

This entire inquiry reflects my hope that national citizenship in the United States can be a viable context for a sense of belonging and for participation in civic, political, social, and economic life that is inclusive and respectful of all individuals. There are certainly other models of belonging, including transnational models that reflect a sense of belonging to more than one nation, and postnational models that think beyond national citizenship entirely. But the apparent inclusiveness of these other approaches to belonging can mask other modes of exclusion. If national citizenship matters less, ties of religion, race, class, and other groupings that are less cosmopolitan or democratic than national citizenship will matter even more than they do already. The result may be a world without national walls but also a world of a "thousand petty fortresses," as political philosopher Michael Walzer once put it.[10]

Making national citizenship into an inclusive vehicle is not easy. It requires a welcome of immigrants—crystallized in the idea of Americans in waiting—that has faded from law and policy in the United States. Although this idea has weakened and is in danger of weakening further, it should be restored to prominent influence because it captures this basic truth: a sensible we/they line must reflect the understanding that many of them will become part of us. This understanding was the conceptual engine for integrating generations of immigrants—mostly those from Europe. With much of this understanding gone, we should not be surprised if more recent waves of immigrants, especially immigrants of color, seem more reluctant to cross the we/they line into American society. Recovering the lost story of immigrants as Americans in waiting is thus crucial not only to giving immigrants their due, but also to recovering the vision of our national future that is reflected in the phrase "a nation of immigrants"—that America is made up of immigrants, but still one nation.

CHAPTER 1

Contract and Classical Immigration Law

★

Chae Chan Ping was a Chinese laborer who came to the United States and settled in San Francisco in 1875, near the end of the first great wave of Chinese immigration. Twelve years later, he took a trip to China to visit his family, who had stayed behind in typical fashion. By the time Chae left on his journey, the Chinese Exclusion Act of 1882 had put a moratorium on the new immigration of laborers from China. Returning Chinese laborers would be readmitted only if they had a U.S. government certificate to prove they had been in America before the ban took effect. Chae left in 1887 with a certificate in hand, issued by the collector of customs in San Francisco.

A year later, while Chae was still away, Congress passed the Scott Act, whose chief sponsor was Congressman William Scott of Pennsylvania. This law tightened Chinese immigration restrictions still further by barring the *return* of all Chinese laborers, stranding even the twenty thousand Chinese who had left with certificates. Just one week after the Scott Act became law, Chae arrived in San Francisco Bay, where he remained confined aboard ship for months. He sought readmission by challenging the Scott Act in court, and by insisting on the validity of his return certificate notwithstanding its purported revocation. The U.S. Supreme Court ultimately rejected his challenge in what is commonly called the *Chinese Exclusion Case*.[1]

Chae Chan Ping's case is a prime example of the view of immigration that I am calling immigration as contract. The Court's decision invoked the idea of contract by explaining that the U.S. government had originally admitted Chae and other Chinese immigrants by granting them a permit.

According to the Court, one of the conditions of the permit was that the government could revoke it at any time, and this is precisely what the Scott Act did. What mattered was the terms of an implied agreement between Chinese immigrants and the U.S. government that allowed the government to override any rights that Chae might have acquired by his return certificate.

Coming to Gold Mountain

Chinese immigrants first came to America in large numbers starting with the California Gold Rush in 1849, so drawn by the prospect of riches that among them California came to be called Gold Mountain. Few would find that dream of quick wealth, but the growing economy in the western United States needed cheap labor. At first, most Chinese worked in mines; later they toiled to build the transcontinental railroad. The Central Pacific Railroad's workforce was 90 percent Chinese. Many were enticed by the allure of wages far surpassing what they could earn in China. During the 1860s, a worker could earn $30 per month on the railroad, six times what he could earn in southern China. In 1852, somewhere between 12,000 and 25,000 Chinese were in California. By 1870, this number had grown to about 63,000, and it exceeded 105,000 by 1880, when the U.S. Census reported the total population of California as 865,000. About 250,000 Chinese immigrated to the United States from 1850 until the 1882 Chinese Exclusion Act.[2]

The U.S. government first addressed Chinese immigration when it negotiated and signed the Burlingame Treaty with China in 1868. At the time, the United States was interested in cheap labor and trade with China. By signing the treaty, the U.S. government accepted Chinese immigration, and the Chinese government accepted emigration, which would still remain a crime theoretically punishable by death until 1893. The treaty declared the "inherent and inalienable right of man to change his home and allegiance, and also the mutual advantage of free migration and emigration of [American and Chinese] citizens . . . for purposes of curiosity, of trade or as permanent residents."[3]

Even when tens of thousands of Chinese workers were needed to lay the rails, anti-Chinese sentiment was strong throughout the West. "Anti-coolie" clubs depicted Chinese workers as indentured servants not unlike the slaves who had just been freed in the Southern states. There were also boycotts of Chinese-made goods, anti-Chinese newspaper editorials, and licensing requirements for Chinese miners and merchants. In 1852, California enacted a tax on Chinese miners to force them into other employment.[4]

When the completion of the transcontinental railroad in 1869 put some ten thousand Chinese laborers out of work, they spread out into new occupations, depressing wages throughout the western United States. A severe recession from 1873 to 1878 further provoked popular sentiment in California and elsewhere in the American West to blame Chinese workers for American joblessness. During the 1870s, a rising tide of anti-Chinese fervor swept over the western states and gradually influenced national politics.

In 1876, a special joint congressional committee urged renegotiation of the Burlingame Treaty to curb Chinese immigration.[5] In 1879, Congress passed a bill limiting arriving ships to only fifteen Chinese passengers, but President Rutherford Hayes vetoed it on the ground that it conflicted with the Burlingame Treaty. By the 1880 presidential election, however, both the Democratic and Republican Party platforms called for restrictions on Chinese immigration. That year, the two countries entered into a supplemental treaty that allowed the United States to "regulate, limit or suspend" immigration of Chinese laborers whenever their entry or residence in the United States "affects or threatens to affect the interests of that country, or to endanger the good order of [the United States] or of any locality within the territory thereof." But the supplemental treaty allowed those Chinese already in the United States in November 1880 to continue "to go and come of their own free will and accord."[6]

The supplemental treaty did not quiet the crescendo of calls for further limits on Chinese immigration, and some states, impatient and unwilling to wait for federal action, acted on their own. An 1879 California statute required incorporated towns and cities to remove Chinese from their city limits. But did the U.S. Constitution allow states and localities to control immigration, or was the regulation of immigration exclusively a federal power?

Immigration and Citizenship Law Before the Chinese

Perhaps it is curious that the U.S. Constitution never mentions immigration. At the Philadelphia convention and during ratification, the framers vigorously debated the desirability of immigrants, in particular whether they should be eligible for federal elective office. The framers limited the presidency to "natural born" citizens but did not address government power to regulate immigration itself.[7]

The Constitution authorizes Congress "to establish a uniform Rule of Naturalization." Perhaps power to naturalize includes power to regulate immigration, but the Constitution does not say this. The Constitution gives Congress the power "to regulate Commerce with foreign Nations, and among the several States." Immigration may be a form of commerce, but commerce refers to much more than the movement of people. Another part of the Constitution addresses "migration or importation," but historical sources make clear that this was a thinly veiled reference to the slave trade. Evidently the framers could not bring themselves to mention slavery in a document that spoke of the inalienable rights of man and the liberty and autonomy of the individual.[8]

History may explain why the framers never addressed immigration explicitly. Immigration was a part of daily life, as European newcomers came to tame what they considered wilderness, and slaves were brought to the New World against their will. The national government's power to allow or limit the arrival of newcomers may have seemed so basic, not just to the founding of the United States but also to the very concept of nationhood, that the founding document did not need to mention it. But this does not diminish the basic fact that immigration and citizenship were important issues from the very beginning of the nation, and that immigration and citizenship law reflected an evolving sense of who belonged and who did not. The Chinese exclusion laws would be one result, but there were many precursors.

Two of the earliest federal statutes—enacted in 1798 as part of what are often called the Alien and Sedition Acts—would be understood today as immigration laws. One of them, the Alien Friends Act, reflected fear of foreign influences in the wake of the French Revolution. This law authorized the president to order any alien "dangerous to the peace and safety of the United States" to leave the country without a hearing. The Alien Friends Act expired after two years without being extended. The other 1798 law—the Alien Enemies Act—remains on the books today and provides that "natives, citizens, denizens, or subjects" of enemy nations, upon presidential proclamation during declared wartime, are "liable to be apprehended, restrained, secured, and removed as alien enemies" without a hearing.[9]

These two early federal laws stood out in an era when the federal government left immigration virtually untouched, and states and localities addressed immigration but not comprehensively. Attitudes early in the 1800s favored a sustained flow of immigrants, at least the northern and western Europeans who dominated the flow. The reasons were largely economic, with immigrant labor badly needed to settle the new land: first to farm it, then to mine it, and later to work the factories and mills as industrialization spread. The expansion of railroads provided the transportation necessary to reach and settle areas previously inaccessible to white people. Many states and territories recruited immigrants with advertisements both overseas and at ports of entry in America, sometimes with tax breaks and other financial incentives. Many Americans believed that it was part of the nation's essence to take in immigrants seeking a better life. An abiding faith assumed not only that America could absorb these newcomers, but also that they would fortify the nation. In this climate, the main role for government in immigration was to encourage it.[10]

At mid-nineteenth century, American public opinion and national self-image began to harden as the immigrant population changed. Before 1830, most white newcomers had been Protestants from Great Britain or elsewhere in western Europe, but in the next two decades newcomers also came from a wider array of countries. Catholic immigrants from Ireland and Germany came for the first time in substantial numbers. Given the understandings of race that prevailed in that era, the fact that many Europeans immigrants in this new wave were not Anglo-Saxon was enough to cast them as belonging to another race and unsuitable for self-government. This was especially true for the Irish, who made up almost half of all immigrants to the United States in 1847, one of the worst years of the Irish Famine.[11]

Another reason for growing opposition to immigration was that the sheer size of the flow rose dramatically. The causes included rapid population growth in Europe, as well as major spurs to emigration like the revolutions of 1848 and the Irish Famine of 1845–49. The foreign-born portion of the total U.S. population held steady at around 14 percent, as compared to the historical low of about 5 percent in 1970 and 11.7 percent in 2003. But then as now, the tendency of immigrants to cluster in a few cities exaggerated their apparent numbers. In 1870, immigrants accounted for more than 40 percent of the population in New York, Chicago, San Francisco, and six other cities. In a cycle to be repeated over and over again, many Americans feared the arrival of too many newcomers who were different from them.[12]

Popular reaction against immigration soon turned into an organized political force: nativism. Historian John Higham's classic study, *Strangers in the Land*, defined nativism as "intense opposition to an internal minority on the ground of its foreign (i.e., 'un-American') connections." In the 1850s, the nativist movement became firmly established with the rise of the American Party, formed by the secret Order of the Star-Spangled Banner. This was a Protestant fraternal order whose members were sworn to secrecy about its internal workings, and who hence came to be called the Know-Nothings. The popularity of the Know-Nothing movement reflected not only nativism, but also the emergence of anti-Catholicism as a major force in American society and politics. Political turmoil in Europe also brought German immigrants under an additional umbrella of suspicion for their perceived radical politics. The Know-Nothings and their allies backed bills in Congress to limit naturalization, for example by raising the residency requirement from five to twenty-one years. They also sought to bar immigrants who had criminal records or who were poor, blind, or mentally infirm, and to disqualify naturalized citizens from election to all but minor local offices.[13]

Opposition to immigration and immigrants during this period was an organized force, but not a dominant one. Business interests generally favored unrestricted immigration to maintain a continuous source of cheap labor. The Free-Soil Party, later absorbed into the Republican Party, based its platform on continued immigration. The Republican platform of 1864 included a plank that immigration "should be fostered and encouraged by a liberal and just policy." The nativism that had emerged in the 1850s receded with the Civil War, which, like other wars in American history, was an intense time of immigrant integration and acceptance. Almost a quarter of the Union Army was foreign-born.[14]

After the Civil War, with the westward expansion of settlement, the ideology of immigration was largely one of enlightened Europeans fulfilling their destiny by subjugating other peoples and thus civilizing the land. In this setting, nativism was not just the ideology of longtime residents trying to keep out newcomers that it had been before the Civil War. It became an ideology of conquest, invoked not only to defend established homelands, but also to settle newly acquired territory in the western United States.

Nowhere was this racial nativism more evident than in California, where it drove a political juggernaut that targeted the growing Chinese population. Unclear at the time, however, was how this rising tide would lead to anti-Chinese laws. The principal uncertainty was whether the lobbying would focus on Sacramento or on Washington, D.C., and thus whether the laws would be state or federal. This, too, is an important part of the story that led to the Chinese exclusion laws, and in turn to the U.S. Supreme Court's ultimate defense of those laws in contract-based terms.

From State to Federal Immigration Law and Chinese Exclusion

It is a common myth that immigration to the United States was unregulated before 1875 and that the federal immigration statutes that then emerged (including the Chinese exclusion laws) were the first immigration laws. Many states regulated immigration both before and after the Civil War, as legal scholar Gerald Neuman has amply documented. Many of these laws are not immediately recognizable as immigration laws because they addressed migration by citizens and foreigners alike. Some state laws barred criminals, or restricted the movement of free blacks, or quarantined anyone with a contagious disease. Other state laws limited migration of the poor, often reflecting the notion that indigence was evidence of personal failure. Some laws required shipmasters to post bonds to guarantee that their passengers would be financially self-sufficient after arrival. Other laws imposed a head tax on immigrants, paid into a welfare fund for those who became indigent. Restrictionists urged that states enforce and expand these laws to keep out various undesirables.[15]

For much of the 1800s, it was generally accepted that states could regulate immigration as long as they did not conflict with federal regulation of commerce or foreign affairs. One important early episode in the courts did not directly involve immigration, but a monopoly on steamboat travel on waterways in the state of New York, principally concerning travel up the Hudson River from New York City to the state capital in Albany. The state had granted the monopoly to a group of investors that included Aaron Ogden and Robert Fulton, the inventor of the *Clermont*, the first steam-powered vessel to travel any significant distance.

Gibbons, the owner of a rival company, challenged the monopoly as unconstitutional. In its 1824 decision in *Gibbons v. Ogden,* the U.S. Supreme Court found that the New York statute that authorized the monopoly unconstitutionally conflicted with the federal power to regulate interstate and foreign commerce. While the decision stands as an early landmark in the Supreme Court's interpretation of the Constitution's Interstate Commerce Clause, it also has particular significance for immigration law. The Court acknowledged that states have a general authority called "police power" to enact laws regulating the movement of persons. As an example the Court mentioned health quarantine laws.[16]

Another New York statute required masters of ships sailing from outside the state to the port of New York to report on all passengers or pay a $75 penalty for each unreported passenger. In 1837, the U.S. Supreme Court ruled in *City of New York v. Miln* that this requirement was constitutional under the state's police power. Taken together with *Gibbons,* this decision reflected a general understanding during this period that states could regulate immigration. Yet the source and scope of state power remained tantalizingly vague at just the point in history when waves of new immigrants would prompt intense public reaction from some quarters.[17]

The scope of state power to regulate immigration was especially important in this period because there were almost no federal immigration statutes. An exception was an 1819 federal law that capped the number of passengers on any ship bound for America. The same law also required shipmasters to record passenger information and provide basic necessities, including "at least sixty gallons of water, one hundred pounds of salted provisions, one gallon of vinegar, and one hundred pounds of wholesome ship bread for each and every passenger on board." There were other federal laws between 1798 and 1875 that might fairly be called immigration laws. An 1803 statute barred the entry of free blacks and slaves in violation of state laws. The 1862 Coolie Trade Law prohibited the transportation of "the inhabitants or subjects of China, known as 'coolies,' . . . for any term of years or for any time whatever, as servants or apprentices, or to be held to service or labor."[18] But it was not until 1875 that Congress began to enact federal measures that would be immediately recognized today as immigration statutes.

Starting at mid-nineteenth century, several U.S. Supreme Court decisions established that federal power over immigration displaced any state immigration power. The first key decisions involved state requirements that shipmasters pay taxes or post bonds for every immigrant. Massachusetts required shipmasters to post a bond for immigrants deemed likely to become indigent, and to pay a head tax of $2 on all others. The state of New York imposed a head tax on immigrants for the support of the marine hospital. In 1849, the Supreme Court struck down these two state laws in the *Passenger Cases*, holding five to four that regulating immigration is exclusively a federal responsibility. It is hard to discern a majority rationale among the eight different opinions, but four justices reasoned that the federal commerce power displaced any state power over immigration.[19]

A few states tried to squeeze new statutes within the state immigration power acknowledged in *Gibbons* and *Miln* but restricted in the *Passenger Cases*. New York required shipmasters arriving at the port of New York to report all immigrants on board, and either pay $1.50 each or post a $300 bond to indemnify states and localities if a new arrival sought public assistance within four years. This was a logical development in this period, for although the *Passenger Cases* had narrowed state power to address immigration, direct federal regulation was still absent.

On the other side of the continent, the California legislature adopted a $50 head tax in 1855, as part of "an act to discourage the Immigration to this state of persons who cannot become citizens thereof." This unmistakably referred to Asian immigrants, who, as chapter 3 will explain, were barred from naturalization until the mid-1900s. In 1857, the California Supreme Court struck down this tax as exceeding state immigration authority in a terse opinion that did little more than cite the *Passenger Cases*. The state legislature tried again with a blunter law designed to "discourage the immigration of the Chinese into the State of California," but the California Supreme Court voided this statute as well.[20] The state legislature next gave state inspectors discretion to refuse admission to new arrivals unless the shipmaster or owner either posted a $500 support and maintenance bond or paid a sum to be set by the state inspector, who would then keep 20 percent.

In two cases decided on the same day in March 1876, the U.S. Supreme Court invalidated the New York and California statutes, as well as a similar Louisiana statute. In *Henderson v. Mayor of the City of New York*, the Court held that the New York and Louisiana statutes infringed upon the federal power to "regulate commerce with foreign nations." New York had encroached in particular on the federal policy to recognize that "immigrants . . . come among us to find a welcome and a home," and that "they bring . . . the labor which we need to till our soil, build our railroads and develop the latent resources of the country in its minerals, its manufactures and its agriculture." The second decision, *Chy Lung v. Freeman*, struck down the California bond requirement as unconstitutionally interfering with the federal government's conduct of foreign affairs. Having twice struck down state immigration laws, the Supreme Court confirmed federal power to regulate immigration in 1884, when its decision in the *Head Money Cases* upheld a 50-cent federal head tax on ship owners for all arriving immigrants to defray processing costs and for "the relief of such as are in distress."[21]

While *Henderson, Chy Lung,* and the *Head Money Cases* combined to move toward an exclusive federal immigration power, they left the door ajar for some state immigration laws. The Court did not repudiate the state police power that *Gibbons* and *Miln* had recognized before the Civil War. The Court continued to acknowledge some state immigration power, rejecting arguments that state health quarantine laws unconstitutionally encroached on the federal commerce power.[22] States continued to enforce their own public health immigration laws even after 1875, when Congress began to enact a series of federal immigration statutes. New York was the last state to surrender its international quarantine functions, in 1921.

States also helped to administer and enforce the new federal immigration laws. In 1882, Congress set up a joint federal-state system that vested federal immigration authority in the secretary of the treasury, who delegated day-to-day administration to the states. States then set rules for their own officials to inspect new arrivals and grant or deny them landing. In New York City, the state government ran a large immigration station at Castle Garden at the southern tip of Manhattan, a stone's throw from the pier where today's tourists and pilgrims can board ferries to tour Ellis Island.[23]

The shift to federal immigration laws (including the Chinese exclusion laws) reflected several main factors. The first, pivotal but often overlooked, was the Civil War and the end of slavery. This established the primacy not only of the national government over the states, but also of national over state citizenship. Moreover, the federal government could regulate migration without having to deal with the intractable question of the movement of slaves and free blacks. Second, concerns about immigration from China prompted demands for diplomatic initiatives by the federal government, for example to renegotiate the Burlingame Treaty.

A third factor behind the shift to federal regulation was federal preemption, which is the complex process by which federal law can displace state law. An area of law may be so inherently federal that states may not address it at all, even absent federal laws. Or if there is a federal law that conflicts with state law, the federal law preempts the state law. Once *Henderson*, *Chy Lung*, and the *Head Money Cases* made clear that state immigration statutes would pose hard preemption issues and federal statutes would not, the political pressure to curtail immigration—especially Chinese immigration—targeted Washington and set off a cycle of lobbying and legislation. Much of the demand for federal legislation came from the states themselves, including state agencies like the New York Board of Emigration Commissioners and the New York Board of Charities. These efforts presaged the modern-day pleas of states for the federal government to do more about illegal immigration. As more federal immigration laws were enacted, they preempted state laws even more clearly. In the space of several decades, the U.S. Congress became the logical forum for restrictionists.[24]

In 1875, the anti-Chinese lobbying in Washington bore fruit with the Page Act, named after its chief sponsor, California Congressman Horace F. Page. Page hailed from Placerville in the heart of the gold country and had himself engaged in mining. Though this statute was drafted in general terms to bar convicted criminals and prostitutes, the legislative history shows that the exclusion of prostitutes was meant to keep out Chinese women. Seven years later, in the spring of 1882, Congress enacted a twenty-year moratorium on immigration of Chinese laborers, but President Chester Arthur vetoed it with a call for a shorter ban. Two months later, wide margins in both houses enacted a ten-year moratorium, which President Arthur signed into law—the first Chinese Exclusion Act. Congress declared that "the coming of Chinese laborers to this country endangers the good order of certain localities." Chinese exclusion was renewed several times and extended indefinitely in 1904, remaining the law of the land until 1943.[25]

The Chinese Exclusion Act was hard to enforce, partly because it was not clear who was exempt as a returning Chinese immigrant who had originally arrived in the United States before the effective date of the ten-year moratorium. The act appeared to require Chinese laborers who were returning from China to show certificates, obtained from the U.S. government when they departed, to prove that they had first come to America before November 17, 1880. Chinese arriving in the United States were also exempt if they were merchants, teachers, students, or travelers. To prove this, they had to show a certificate to that effect, issued by the Chinese government.[26]

At each port, a collector of customs decided whether a Chinese immigrant was barred or exempt. Working before the use of photographs became ordinary in processing, immigration inspectors relied on the certificates, which included "physical marks or peculiarities, and all facts necessary for . . . identification." Even after photographs came into widespread use by the end of the nineteenth century, government inspectors measured numerous body parts in great detail.[27]

The collector often denied reentry even if the immigrants had certificates, but federal judges in San Francisco overturned many of these decisions and sometimes even allowed Chinese laborers to prove pre–November 1880 residency without a certificate at all. Federal judges also relaxed the entry requirements for Chinese merchants. In 1884, Congress reacted to these court decisions by making the certificate the "only evidence permissible to establish his right of re-entry." However, federal judges continued to show flexibility in the proof that they demanded, especially of Chinese who claimed to have left the United States before the certificate requirements took effect.[28]

In 1888, Congress responded by changing the law yet again with the Scott Act, which barred a Chinese immigrant's return even with a certificate. This was the law that stranded Chae Chan Ping, who had a return certificate but was not allowed to land. Chae brought his lawsuit with considerable help from San Francisco's Chinese community, whose social organization and experience with bureaucracy would enable it to challenge a number of government decisions excluding or deporting Chinese immigrants.[29]

Plenary Power and Immigration as Contract

The U.S. Supreme Court's rejection of Chae Chan Ping's arguments in the *Chinese Exclusion Case* turned ultimately on the larger question of whether the courts would apply the U.S. Constitution in immigration cases. As a general matter, the Constitution limits the government's ability to act.

Congress cannot pass laws that abridge freedom of speech, that impose cruel and unusual punishment, or that discriminate in ways that violate equal protection of the laws. The traditional understanding is that courts will intervene and strike down unconstitutional laws and policies.

Of course, courts often decide that a statute or a government act does not violate the Constitution. But courts usually give careful consideration to constitutional challenges by U.S. citizens, and in this sense citizens enjoy the Constitution's protections. What about noncitizens and the Constitution? Can noncitizens argue that an immigration decision by the government violates their constitutional rights? What if they believe the government has barred them from the United States by applying rules that unconstitutionally discriminate against them because of their race or gender?

The Supreme Court's 1889 decision in the *Chinese Exclusion Case* is usually cited as a source of the so-called plenary power doctrine. When used in the immigration law context—by which I refer to the admission and deportation of noncitizens—plenary power means that Congress and the executive branch have exclusive decision-making authority without judicial oversight for constitutionality. Courts may be more willing to intervene on other issues concerning noncitizens, as later chapters will discuss. But courts, citing the plenary power doctrine, have been reluctant to ask seriously if immigration law decisions by Congress and the executive are unconstitutional. With some exceptions, courts have ceded decision making to Congress and the executive branch of government.

There are two ways that one might understand the plenary power doctrine. One is that the Constitution applies differently (or not at all) to immigration law cases. The other is that the Constitution applies to immigration law cases, but that the courts as a matter of institutional self-restraint will not fully enforce constitutional requirements, leaving Congress and the executive branch to police themselves. Because Congress and the executive branch seldom if ever inquire seriously into the constitutionality of their immigration decisions, both understandings of plenary power leave noncitizens with only limited constitutional protection if the government decides to bar or deport them. [30]

The *Chinese Exclusion Case* rejected Chae Chan Ping's two main arguments. The first argument was that the Scott Act was invalid because its provision that barred laborers who held reentry certificates conflicted with the

1880 supplemental treaty's guarantee that Chinese laborers already in the United States could leave and return. Justice Stephen Field, writing for a unanimous Court, acknowledged the conflict but found that the Scott Act prevailed because it was later in time.

Second, Chae Chan Ping argued that the Scott Act was "beyond the competency of Congress" under the U.S. Constitution. He raised three arguments based on his individual constitutional rights, the first being that the Scott Act violated the Fifth Amendment's due process guarantee to him as a "person." He also argued that the act was an unconstitutional bill of attainder—legislation that punishes an individual without a judicial trial. Third, Chae argued that the act was an unconstitutional ex post facto law in that it retroactively imposed criminal punishment for an act committed when it was not a crime.[31]

Suppose laws like those in the *Chinese Exclusion Case* were enacted today. Imagine a law barring new immigrants only from predominantly Arab or Muslim countries, but allowing any already in the United States to leave and return as long as they first get certificates. Imagine further that a subsequent law voids these certificates, barring the return of those who have them. Lawsuits would surely allege that both laws discriminate by race, religion, or nationality, and that the second law violates due process by undermining reliance on the certificates.

As later chapters will explain, plenary power has eroded in various ways over the past century, so it is not at all clear how courts today would respond to these sorts of constitutional challenges to this imaginary law. But it is not at all surprising for the era that Chae Chan Ping did not allege racial, ethnic, or nationality discrimination. Just a few years later, the U.S. Supreme Court would declare: "Given in congress the absolute power to exclude aliens, it may exclude some and admit others, and the reasons for its discrimination are not open to challenge in the courts." And the Court would soon rule in *Plessy v. Ferguson* that the U.S. Constitution allowed "separate but equal" treatment of blacks and whites. And although the Fourteenth Amendment's Equal Protection Clause provides, among other things, that no state shall "deny to any person within its jurisdiction the equal protection of the laws," only well into the mid-twentieth century did it become clear that the equal protection guarantee applies to the federal government as well.[32]

In rejecting Chae's constitutional challenge, Justice Field did not expressly respond to Chae's three arguments or address how individual constitutional rights might limit the federal immigration power. Instead,

Field first reasoned that a sovereign nation has the inherent power under international law to exclude noncitizens from its territory as a matter of sovereignty, national security, and self-preservation. Second, this immigration power belongs to the federal government, not the states. And within the federal government, immigration regulation is for Congress and the executive branch, not the courts. "[If Congress] considers the presence of foreigners of a different race in this country, who will not assimilate with us, to be dangerous to its peace and security . . . its determination is conclusive upon the judiciary." According to Justice Field, the Chinese government might seek remedies for its citizens from the U.S. Congress and the executive branch, but noncitizens here have no remedy in the courts for constitutional violations. This limitation on the judicial role in immigration decision making by the government was the essence of plenary power.[33]

Justice Field emphasized national sovereignty coupled with national security and self-preservation, but these themes were only a thin veil for the Court's more basic premise. The *Chinese Exclusion Case* and similar Supreme Court decisions were premised on Anglo-Saxon racial superiority at a time of expanding American empire in the Caribbean and the Pacific. Prevailing notions of national sovereignty were descended from the nativism that had served as an ideology of conquest and subjugation as the American frontier moved westward. For Justice Field to call the Chinese a "different race . . . who will not assimilate with us" was not exceptional. In another of the Court's plenary power decisions from this period, even a dissenter who urged constitutional protection for Chinese deportees spoke of "the obnoxious Chinese" and "this distasteful class." When Justice Harlan dissented from the Court's approval of "separate but equal" for blacks in *Plessy v. Ferguson*, he compared them favorably to the Chinese, "a race so different from our own that we do not permit those belonging to it to become citizens of the United States." As troubling as Chinese exclusion may seem to the modern observer, it was only the precursor of many other laws that would limit immigration to the United States by race or ethnicity.[34]

While Anglo-Saxon racial superiority may have been the core of the *Chinese Exclusion Case*, other aspects of the decision fit into ways of thinking about fairness and justice in immigration and citizenship that have greater currency today. The plenary power doctrine still has judicial and political vitality because the national sovereignty rationale in the *Chinese Exclusion Case* appeals to notions of fairness and justice based on a nation's power to define the terms of admission. This fits squarely within what I call immigration as contract.[35]

Justice Field's opinion invoked contract-based reasoning by stressing that the Chinese laborers' right to return was grounded in a type of agreement. The U.S. government had granted to immigrants an entry permit or license that the government could revoke at will. The concept of a license often surfaces in the law of property, where it signifies a private agreement that grants a right to use property for a specific purpose, like parking a car or staging a concert. It does not matter much whether this is a term that technically belongs to the law of property or contracts. In the immigration setting, contract is the idea of an agreement rooted in notions of promises, notice, and expectations, and this idea appears clearly in Justice Field's reasoning: "Whatever license . . . Chinese laborers may have obtained . . . to return to the United States after their departure, is held at the will of the government, revocable at any time, at its pleasure."[36] In short, immigrants are guests to be let in, but only on the condition that they are easily evicted.

Nor was it just the government whose reasoning reflected immigration as contract. One of Chae Chan Ping's arguments in the lower federal court was that the return certificate was a contract between him and the United States, and that Congress's decision to void the certificate violated the constitutional clause that forbids laws impairing the obligation of contracts. While the lower court rejected this argument, both sides framed their arguments as a matter of the understandings that can be inferred from coming to America, even if they differed on what those understandings were.[37]

Let me reemphasize that when Chae Chan Ping came to the United States, or when he obtained his certificate and left for China, he did not necessarily enter into a contract enforceable in court. It may even offend modern notions of contract to something as one-sided as any "agreement" between Chae Chan Ping and the U.S. government, which many would view as fictional. And lawyers can quibble about whether this was technically a contract, a license, or yet another form of legal relationship. What really matters in assessing the *Chinese Exclusion Case* is something more fundamental. The Court's decision embodied an appeal to the essence of what one hears in defense of contractual obligations: the value of promises, notice, and expectations, even if these notions mask deeper motivations or assumptions. In turn, this implies the core of immigration as contract: that fairness and justice in immigration and citizenship may be attained without treating noncitizens as the equals of citizens.

Japanese Immigration and the Entrenchment of Contract

Immigration as contract continued to serve as the conceptual basis of the plenary power doctrine in several Supreme Court decisions after the *Chinese Exclusion Case*. The first involved immigration from Japan, which began in earnest around 1891. Until the 1880s, the Japanese government severely limited emigration, but it let laborers emigrate to work on Hawaiian sugar plantations starting in 1884, and the next year it let them go to the continental United States. Once exit restrictions were lifted, Japanese emigration grew rapidly, not just to the United States but to other destinations, notably in Latin America. Although 2,270 Japanese came to the United States from 1881 to 1890, almost 26,000 came from 1891 to 1900, and almost 130,000 from 1901 to 1910.[38]

Unlike the Chinese, the Japanese were not specifically excluded by U.S. immigration laws in this period. From mid-1892 to 1910, the U.S. government denied admission to only about 7 percent of the tens of thousands of Japanese immigrants who applied. Healthy Japanese faced only one significant legal obstacle to immigration: the bar that Congress first enacted in 1882 to keep out "any person unable to take care of himself or herself without becoming a public charge."[39] Moreover, the many Japanese who were in Hawaii gained lawful access to the mainland when the U.S. annexed the islands in 1898.

Hostility to Japanese immigrants grew with their numbers, largely paralleling the earlier resentment of the Chinese. Many white Americans came to see the Japanese as an even greater menace, especially as they bought land in the western states and established themselves as farmers. Japan's victory in the Russo-Japanese War of 1905 also raised the specter of a rival for power in the Pacific. That year, the San Francisco School Board required Japanese immigrant children to attend a segregated school that it operated in Chinatown for Chinese children. Another sign of growing native alarm was the founding in 1905 of the Japanese and Korean Exclusion League, later renamed the Asiatic Exclusion League, which claimed 100,000 members.

The absence of exclusion laws like those aimed at China reflected Japan's stronger international stature, which in turn fortified its diplomatic protests over insults like the San Francisco school segregation order. But lobbied by anti-Japanese restrictionists, the U.S. government pressured Japan to curtail emigration, though by executive order rather than statute. In 1907, President Theodore Roosevelt issued an order barring Japanese and Korean immigration from Hawaii to the mainland. Later the same year, Japan and the United States entered into the so-called Gentlemen's Agreement, under which Japan limited emigration by no longer issuing passports that would allow immigrant laborers to travel to the U.S. mainland. In exchange, the U.S. government allowed Japanese immigrants to join parents, spouses, or children already in the United States. After proxy marriages in Japan, "picture brides" could still come to the United States to join new husbands whom they had never met. This allowed the Japanese-American community to grow and maintain gender balance, in contrast to the bachelor society created by Chinese exclusion.[40]

Around this time, two major criticisms of federal immigration administration prompted changes that would lead to the Supreme Court's next major plenary power decisions. Some charged that the federal government had lost control over immigration by delegating administration to the states. In 1890, the federal government responded by revoking its contract with the state of New York for inspecting immigrants, replacing it with direct federal administration. A year later, Congress ended all state contracts and placed administration of the immigration laws with a federal superintendent of immigration within the Department of the Treasury (except for immigration from China, which remained under the Chinese Bureau within the Customs Service until 1903). Having assumed control over immigration through the port of New York, the federal government began to build the immigration depot at Ellis Island, which opened in 1892.[41]

The second criticism was that federal judges too readily overturned exclusion orders issued by immigration officials, letting in Chinese who fraudulently claimed to be merchants or students to avoid the ban on laborers, or to be U.S. citizens to avoid immigration restrictions altogether. Congress responded in 1891 with an immigration law that made any decisions by federal officials to admit or exclude arriving immigrants "final," subject only to review by the superintendent of immigration and the secretary of the treasury. Lower federal courts then refused to entertain arguments by immigrants that agency decisions denying them admission had erroneously interpreted statutes or were unconstitutional.[42]

Much as the new law's backers had hoped, admission to the United States became more difficult. On May 7, 1891, Nishimura Ekiu, a twenty-five-year-old Japanese immigrant, arrived in the port of San Francisco after having sailed from Yokohama aboard the steamship *Belgic* with $22 in her pocket. An immigration officer refused to admit her, invoking the 1882 bar to "any person unable to take care of himself or herself without becoming a public charge." If this gender-neutral reference seems oddly modern for 1882, the reason was that it followed the 1875 Page Act in targeting unmarried immigrant women, who were believed to be paupers or prostitutes.[43]

Nishimura sued for admission. The case ultimately reached the U.S. Supreme Court, which rejected her challenge in an 1892 decision that answered two key questions left open in the *Chinese Exclusion Case*. First, how might the constitutional rights of an individual noncitizen limit the federal immigration power? Second, would courts hear constitutional challenges not to *categories* of barred immigrants as had been at issue in the *Chinese Exclusion Case*, but rather to the *procedures* for applying those categories? The decision in *Nishimura Ekiu v. United States* answered these questions in ways that broadened plenary power and reaffirmed its grounding in immigration as contract.

The *Nishimura* decision framed the issue as involving the constitutional right of an individual noncitizen—whether the procedures were unfair and therefore violated Nishimura's constitutional rights. The Supreme Court rejected this individual rights claim, relying on the *Chinese Exclusion Case* to reaffirm that courts would not examine the constitutionality of admission and exclusion decisions by Congress or the executive branch. *Nishimura* also extended the plenary power doctrine by insulating the procedures for applying an immigration statute. At least for immigrants seeking admission for the first time (as opposed to returning residents), "the decisions of executive or administrative officers, acting within powers expressly conferred by Congress, are due process of law."[44]

To reach these conclusions, the *Nishimura* Court adopted the contract-based rationale that immigrants agree to certain conditions of admission, no matter how unfavorable. Sovereign nations have the inherent and essential power "to forbid the entrance of foreigners within its dominions, or to admit them only in such cases and upon such *conditions* as it may see fit to prescribe."[45] In this way, immigration as contract figured prominently in *Nishimura*, much as it had in the *Chinese Exclusion Case*.

This emphasis on the conditions of admission and the conceptual basis in immigration as contract persisted when the Supreme Court issued another major plenary power decision one year later. This next case involved the application of the U.S. Constitution not to admission to the United States, but rather to *deportation* of a noncitizen who had been lawfully admitted.

The matter arose under the Geary Act of 1892, named after Congressman Thomas J. Geary of Santa Rosa, California. The Geary Act extended the 1882 immigration ban on Chinese laborers for ten more years. It also made any Chinese laborer deportable unless he had a certificate proving he had been in the United States before 1892. The stated reason for requiring the certificate was that Chinese names and faces were all alike. Consistent with this official skepticism, the government issued these certificates only upon registration with the "affidavit of at least one credible witness," which was defined to mean a white witness. Chinese laborers without certificates were deportable unless they could show both good cause for not getting a certificate and "at least one credible white witness" to prove pre-1892 residency.[46]

The Geary Act's white-witness rule reprised a traditional practice of barring nonwhites from testifying in court. There had been many similar statutes before the federal Civil Rights Act of 1870 effectively overrode them. An 1850 California statute, apparently adapted from Southern slave codes, provided that "no black or mulatto person, or Indian, shall be permitted to give evidence in favor of, or against any white person." The chief justice of the California Supreme Court, who also was a member of the Know-Nothings, wrote the decision for the court that interpreted this statute to bar Chinese witnesses. The Chinese, he explained, were a "distinct people . . . a race of people whom nature has marked as inferior and who are incapable of progress or intellectual development beyond a certain point."[47]

The case that tested the constitutionality of the Geary Act involved Fong Yue Ting and two other Chinese laborers named Wong Quan and Lee Joe. They were arrested in New York City, where they had lived since before 1892. Fong and Wong refused to register to get certificates, and Lee tried to register but had no white witness. Theirs was a test case carefully planned by the Chinese Six Companies, a community council led by merchant leaders and made up of family and district associations in San Francisco. The Six Companies urged Chinese immigrants to protest the act by refusing to register and asked them to contribute $1 each for litigation costs to challenge the law. Less than 2 percent registered in San Francisco, home to more than one-third of Chinese immigrants in the United States, and less than 20 percent registered nationwide.

The Six Companies' lawyers challenged the Geary Act's registration requirement on several constitutional grounds, arguing that the white-witness requirement for proving pre-1892 residency and other aspects of the act violated due process. The U.S. Supreme Court rejected these contentions in *Fong Yue Ting v. United States*. For the *Fong* majority, the key was treating deportation decisions like admission decisions; both types of decisions were for the political branches to make, and both types of decisions were therefore unsuitable for court review for constitutional defects.

To reach this conclusion, the *Fong* Court adopted a rationale firmly grounded in immigration as contract. The *Chinese Exclusion Case* and *Nishimura Ekiu* had characterized admission as a conditional, revocable license that the government could withdraw at any time. This contract-based reasoning—that the power to deport is part of the agreement to admit—allowed the Court in *Fong* to conclude that exclusion and deportation are "but parts of one and the same power." The Court thus reasoned that "The right of a nation to expel or deport foreigners . . . rests upon the same grounds, and is as absolute and unqualified as the right to prohibit and prevent their entrance into the country." The Court also invoked this contract-based reasoning in holding that deportation does not trigger the constitutional safeguards, such as the ban on cruel and unusual punishment, that apply to criminal penalties. Thus deportation is not punishment, the Court explained, but merely "a method of enforcing the return to his own country of an alien who has not complied with the *conditions* [on which the host nation] . . . has determined that his continuing to reside here shall depend."[48]

Taken together, the *Chinese Exclusion Case*, *Nishimura Ekiu*, and *Fong Yue Ting* established the plenary power doctrine, which is the keystone of what legal scholar Peter Schuck has dubbed "classical immigration law."[49] According to the plenary power doctrine, noncitizens outside the United States cannot raise constitutional challenges to exclusion grounds or procedures. Noncitizens in the United States cannot raise constitutional challenges to deportation grounds. This is a doctrine founded on strong notions of national sovereignty and clear separation between citizens who can claim protections under the U.S. Constitution and noncitizens who cannot. Though the plenary power doctrine emerged in an era when immigration decisions were premised on Anglo-Saxon superiority, the doctrine also reflects a way of thinking and talking about fairness and justice in immigration and citizenship that reflects viewing immigration as contract.

Contract in Context

The contract-based reasoning in the *Chinese Exclusion Case*, *Nishimura Ekiu*, and *Fong Yue Ting* reflected the view that fair and just treatment of noncitizens in the United States does not require equality between citizens and noncitizens, but rather depends entirely on the terms of the immigration contract. Noncitizens can demand no more than notice of the conditions of their admission. As Peter Schuck has explained, this view of immigration was consistent with the late nineteenth century's consent-based legal culture, in which the idea was pervasive that obligations enforced by law must be based on individual consent.[50]

In the contract law of this period, the guiding principle was the freedom to assume or avoid obligations. Courts were loath to find that a contract was enforceable if it was not based on express consent. If consent was apparent, however, courts readily enforced contracts even if their terms were one-sided. Tort law assigned liability for accidents based on a person's duty not to injure others by acting negligently. As with contract law, the core idea was that liability could be based only on acts and obligations freely undertaken. And in the law governing court jurisdiction, the U.S. Supreme Court established in 1877 that persons obligate themselves to answer to lawsuits in a state only by setting foot or owning property there. Notwithstanding modern objections that there was no true consent or freedom to assume obligations in these three examples, these notions were the rhetorical basis for believing that these rules of law were fair and just.[51]

As applied to immigration, these consent-based ideas likened Americans to property owners with the right to grant, withhold, or set conditions for entry. Lawful immigrants were treated as mere holders of revocable licenses who agreed to abide by the terms of admission. More fundamentally, immigration as contract was rooted in faith in the power of the neutral accuracy of labels and categories like license and contract. Prevailing thought had not yet come to see license and contract as amorphous and subjective, cast a more critical eye on notions of consent and obligation, and reinforce our modern inclination to view these contract-based notions as fictional. Only later did the view emerge that a mere privilege to stay is hard to tell apart from a more robust right to do so, or that an immigrant's ties in America might favor letting him stay regardless of the conditions of admission.[52]

The plenary power doctrine's emphasis on contract is also consistent with other aspects of U.S. history. Earlier ideas of what it meant to be a citizen or a subject, traceable at least as far back as England in the early 1600s, had posited that social and governmental organization reflected subordination and hierarchy, not consent. But by the time of the American Revolution, the prevailing concept of U.S. citizenship drew heavily on the constitutional theory of John Locke, and later of William Blackstone, who argued that society and government were fundamentally based on the voluntary consent of free individuals to join together in communities—and to exclude undesirables. This idea of American citizenship emphasized both the citizen's choice to pledge allegiance to the United States and the national community's consent to accept the citizen.[53]

In this setting, immigration as contract approached equality in immigration and citizenship in ways that were compatible with the era's emphasis on national sovereignty and self-preservation, and with the voluntary basis of binding obligations. Though this may seem narrow or even fictional today, the core rhetoric of immigration as contract—that justice in immigration can be based on promises, notice, and expectations—still strongly influences how issues are framed in both constitutional decisions and legislative policy.

CHAPTER 2

Promises, Promises

★

Peter Harisiades was thirteen when he immigrated to the United States from Greece in 1916. In 1925, Harisiades joined a Communist Party affiliate, where he worked as an organizer, official, and newspaper editor. His wife was a U.S. citizen, as were their two children. Luigi Mascitti came to the United States from Italy in 1920, at the age of sixteen. He was a member of the Communist Party and two affiliated organizations from 1923 to 1929. Mascitti married another immigrant, and they had one child, who was a citizen. Dora Coleman was a thirteen-year-old when she came from Russia in 1914. She belonged to the U.S. Communist Party three separate times: once for a year around 1919, once from 1928 to 1930, and again for a year in the mid-1930s. Coleman married a U.S. citizen, and they had three citizen children. Harisiades, Mascitti, and Coleman were all lawful immigrants. In the 1940s, the federal government tried to deport them.

Immigration, National Security, and Ideology

The story of Peter Harisiades, Luigi Mascitti, and Dora Coleman takes my analysis of immigration as contract beyond its nineteenth-century roots, but it is also an episode in the long—and still ongoing—saga of government efforts to identify, exclude, and deport noncitizens for reasons of national security or ideology. Over time, the focus has shifted from anarchists to subversives, then to communists, and most recently to terrorists. Today, the Immigration and Nationality Act, which is the principal federal immigration statute, makes noncitizens inadmissible or deportable based on terrorism, espionage, sabotage, or the potential for serious adverse foreign policy consequences. These provisions are part of an intricate web of exclusion and deportation statutes that Congress first constructed in the fifty years from 1875 to 1924, and since then has tried to refine.[1]

The origins of laws to exclude or deport noncitizens based on national security or ideology lie in the late 1800s. Economic transformation and the changing composition of the immigrant flow heightened worries about subversive influences, especially with the arrival of more immigrants from eastern Europe and the Mediterranean. The fear was that radical political agitators were coming to America to foment industrial strife. Anarchism, John Higham observed, was the "ism" most feared by nativists. Business interests continued to welcome new, cheap labor, but they were also nervous that immigrant agitators would incite working-class unrest.

An early flash point was the Haymarket Square strike and riot in Chicago on May 5, 1886. Protests around the country were agitating for an eight-hour workday and a nationwide general strike. The police had killed two union members during a strike at the McCormick reaper factory. A few days later, what started as a rally to protest the killings ended with a bomb explosion, a riot, and an exchange of gunfire between the crowd and the 176 policemen dispatched to the scene. Eight policemen and ten protesters were left dead. Eight anarchists—seven of them German immigrants—were convicted for their part in the bombing, and four were hanged.

The Haymarket riot and subsequent trial unleashed a new wave of anti-immigrant public opinion that only heightened when President William McKinley was assassinated in 1901. The assassin, Leon Czolgosz, was an anarchist. He turned out to be a U.S. citizen, but his name sounded alien enough to intensify the xenophobia. "There is no such thing as an American anarchist," declared the journal *Public Opinion*. Congress embraced this public sentiment in 1903 with a statute that barred the admission of "anarchists, or persons who believe in or advocate the overthrow by force or violence of the Government of the United States, or of all government, or of all forms of law, or the assassination of public officials."[2]

This 1903 statute was one of many exclusion laws that Congress had started enacting in 1875. These laws, defining who is *not* admitted rather than who is, were the principal mode of federal immigration regulation until after World War I. Chapter 1 mentioned the 1875 statute that barred convicted criminals and prostitutes, as well as the first Chinese Exclusion Act in 1882. Later federal measures barred a wide variety of undesirables, among them lunatics, idiots, insane persons, contract laborers, polygamists (this clause targeted Mormons), and persons with a loathsome or a dangerous contagious disease.[3]

Along with exclusion laws barring entry, deportation laws provided for the removal of noncitizens already in the United States. The first federal deportation statute in this era was a provision of the 1882 Chinese Exclusion Act that targeted "any Chinese person found unlawfully within the United States." The Geary Act of 1892—the law upheld in *Fong Yue Ting*—was another deportation statute directed against Chinese immigrants. The first federal deportation law that did not target a particular nationality was enacted in 1888. It provided that any immigrant who had entered in violation of the ban on contract laborers could be deported up to one year later. In 1891, Congress broadened this law, so that any alien who had entered "in violation of law" could be deported up to one year later. It served, in effect, as a delayed exclusion statute to correct mistakes or omissions in the inspection process. Successive amendments extended this period to correct mistaken admissions until it reached five years in 1917. In 1924, Congress made noncitizens deportable who had entered unlawfully at any time.[4]

Starting in 1907, Congress expanded the idea of deportation to cover what noncitizens did after arriving in the United States. That year a statute made any aliens deportable who became prostitutes within three years after entry. While both resources and enforcement discretion limited the number of noncitizens who were actually deported before World War I, the deportation statutes marked an important turn in immigration law. A 1917 law introduced deportation for subversive activities and crimes committed in the United States. Deportation statutes soon gained in practical importance, especially with the end of World War I, the Bolshevik Revolution, and the emergence of the Soviet Union.[5]

The period around World War I was one of heightened nationalism. President Theodore Roosevelt was known for his support of the "Swat-the-Hyphen" movement. One sign of the times was the Americanization movement, with its English and civics lessons for immigrants, sometimes motivated by paternalism or philanthropy, but more often accompanied by implied pressure to conform to a white Anglo-Saxon ideal that

submerged other ethnic identifications. The Americanization movement's focus on assimilation of immigrants already in the United States
was soon accompanied by successful efforts in the 1920s to adopt a
racially restrictive scheme for lawful immigrant admissions that later
chapters will discuss. For now, my focus is the climate of the time as a
backdrop for immigration enforcement based on ideology and national security. After the common cause of the Great War ended, any benign or inclusive strands of Americanization soon yielded to anti-immigrant
restrictionism. Matters of ideology turned almost immediately into matters of national security.[6]

A flurry of ideological and national security immigration statutes became law around the end of World War I. In 1918 Congress authorized the
deportation of "aliens who are members of anarchistic and similar classes."
In addition, the government brought criminal charges against some radicals instead of trying to deport them. One much-publicized case involved
the Russian Jewish anarchist Jacob Abrams. He had come from Uman, a
village near Odessa, reaching New York through Ellis Island in 1908, at
the age of twenty-two. He lived in East Harlem and worked as a book-
binder. Abrams was arrested in August 1918 for distributing leaflets in English and Yiddish that criticized President Woodrow Wilson's war
policies and called for a general strike. His conviction under the Espionage Act of 1917 was eventually upheld by the U.S. Supreme Court.
Abrams was sentenced to twenty years, but he was released after serving
two and deported to the Soviet Union.[7]

These leanings turned into intensified efforts to deport subversives
during a period of anti-radical hysteria called the Red Scare. November
1919 brought the first Palmer Raids, named after their instigator, Attorney
General A. Mitchell Palmer. Federal authorities in eleven cities swooped
down on meetings of the Union of Russian Workers and arrested and detained hundreds of noncitizens believed to be radicals and revolutionaries.
A leader of the operation was the young J. Edgar Hoover, head of the Justice Department's General Intelligence Division, who would become FBI
director five years later. The federal government hastily deported hundreds of noncitizens, many on a specially chartered transport ship bound
for Finland. In January 1920, more raids in thirty-three different cities
rounded up about three thousand noncitizens thought to be communists.
Among those who criticized the deportations and represented the deportees in court was Harvard Law School professor and future U.S. Supreme

Court Justice Felix Frankfurter (along with other members of the newly formed American Civil Liberties Union).

In 1920, Congress further broadened exclusion and deportation based on ideology and national security. A deportation ground now covered "aliens who believe in, advise, advocate, or teach, or who are members of or affiliated with any organization, association, society, or group, that believes in, advises, advocates, or teaches . . . the overthrow by force or violence of the Government of the United States or of all forms of law." Eventually, the U.S. Supreme Court held in 1939 that this statute did not authorize deportation for *past* membership in the U.S. Communist Party and other proscribed organizations. When the Communist Party expelled its noncitizen members to shield them from deportation, Congress responded in 1940 with the Alien Registration Act. Part of this law criminalized certain subversive activities, while another part required all aliens to register, be fingerprinted, and notify the government of address changes. The act also made aliens deportable for past membership in subversive organizations "for no matter how short a time or how far in the past."[8]

The number and scope of ideological deportation grounds expanded in the years that followed. The Internal Security Act of 1950 required the Communist Party, party members, and subsidiary organizations to register with the federal government. In 1952, legislation sponsored by the virulent anti-Communists Patrick McCarran and Francis Walter—hence called the McCarran-Walter Act—reorganized the federal immigration statutes, including the 1940 Alien Registration Act's ideological exclusion and deportation grounds, into the Immigration and Nationality Act. Under one provision of this new act, an individual's refusal to testify about subversive activity within ten years of naturalization was a ground for revoking U.S. citizenship.[9]

Contract and the Constitution

It was the 1940 deportation ground for past membership in subversive organizations that the government used to try to deport Peter Harisiades, Luigi Mascitti, and Dora Coleman. The three argued unsuccessfully that the government could not constitutionally deport them for past Communist Party membership. Their first argument was that lawful immigrants have a "vested right" to stay in the United States, so the government could deport them only on "reasonable grounds," which they argued were lacking. Their second was that deportation would violate their First Amendment freedoms of speech, press, and assembly. And their third argument was that deportation for past membership would violate the Constitution's ban on retroactive criminal laws.

In making these constitutional arguments, the three longtime immigrants emphasized their ties in the United States. Chapter 5 will explain how these arguments were based on immigration as affiliation, but my focus here is the Supreme Court's reasoning, which rejected all three arguments. Applying the plenary power doctrine as articulated by the Court in the late 1800s, Justice Robert Jackson wrote for the Court majority that deportation decisions "are so exclusively entrusted to the political branches of government as to be largely immune from judicial inquiry or interference."

Jackson adopted a contract-based skepticism toward any constitutional challenges to the deportation of lawful immigrants. Echoing the *Chinese Exclusion Case, Fong Yue Ting*, and *Nishimura Ekiu*, he explained: "To protract this ambiguous status within the country is not his [the immigrant's] right but is a matter of permission and tolerance. The Government's power to terminate its hospitality has been asserted and sustained by the Court since the question first arose." Once again, the key idea was that immigrants are admitted under certain conditions, and violating them can lead to deportation. It was not for the Court to recognize ties or otherwise invoke values from sources besides the grant of permission at the core of the immigration contract.[10]

Contract-based reasoning played a major role in the U.S. Supreme Court's rejection of a constitutional challenge in *Harisiades*. But just as important, the idea surfaced around the same time as *Harisiades* that immigration as contract might sometimes *support* constitutional protections for lawful immigrants. The first example is a decision from outside the realm of ideology and national security. It is the Supreme Court's 1951 decision in *Jordan v. De George*, which concerned the deportation of Sam De George for two criminal convictions, both for conspiracy to defraud the United States of taxes on distilled spirits. The lower court held that this was a "crime involving moral turpitude," making De George deportable. In the Supreme Court, De George argued that "crime involving moral turpitude" was unconstitutionally vague.

The constitutional doctrine of void-for-vagueness says that laws are void if they are vague about what they require or prohibit. The doctrine usually is applied to hold criminal statutes to minimum standards of clarity. This has three purposes: to make sure that individuals have fair warning that their conduct may lead to criminal prosecution, to restrain law enforcement from applying a vague criminal statute in an arbitrary or discriminatory manner, and to keep uncertainty about a criminal statute's meaning from inhibiting the exercise of constitutional freedoms. At least the first purpose—concerned with proper notice—is grounded in the sort of thinking that underlies immigration as contract.[11]

In *De George*, the Court noted the well-established rule from *Fong Yue Ting* that deportation is not criminal punishment, but said that it would "nevertheless examine the application of the vagueness doctrine to this case . . . in view of the grave nature of deportation." The Court then sustained the statute, noting that a long line of court and agency decisions had made clear that fraud is a crime involving moral turpitude. In spite of this outcome, *De George* established the general principle that noncitizens may challenge immigration statutes as unconstitutionally vague. In this respect, *De George*—unlike the early plenary power cases and *Harisiades*—shows that lawful immigrants can sometimes look to immigration as contract for protection, especially if the government undermines their legitimate expectations or fails to give them fair notice.[12]

Returning to ideology and national security, a much more recent case that adopts immigration as contract as the conceptual foundation for protecting a lawful immigrant is *Rafeedie v. INS*, a 1992 federal district court decision. The case involved Fouad Rafeedie, who became a lawful immigrant in 1975 and lived in Cleveland, Ohio. In 1986, he took a two-week trip to the Middle East. When he came back, the U.S. government alleged that Rafeedie was a member of the Popular Front for the Liberation of Palestine and tried to bar his return under an exclusion ground (later repealed) for "aliens who the consular officer or the Attorney General knows or has reason to believe seek to enter the United States solely, principally, or incidentally to engage in activities which would be prejudicial to the public interest, or endanger the welfare, safety or security of the United States." Invoking a contract-based emphasis on notice, the federal district court held that this statute was unconstitutionally vague because it failed to meet the *De George* requirement that statutes give warning. "The undefined terms of the statute—'activities,' 'prejudicial,' 'endanger'—are so broad and vague as to deny plaintiff a reasonable opportunity to know what he may or may not do," said the court.[13]

Another federal decision that involved ideology and national security and used contract-based reasoning to protect a noncitizen is the 1996 district court decision in *Massieu v. Reno*. The case grew out of the U.S. government's effort to deport Mario Ruiz-Massieu, a former deputy attorney general of Mexico. The Mexican government sought his extradition from the United States to face obstruction of justice charges in connection with investigations into corruption. After several magistrates rejected extradition requests, the secretary of state invoked the deportation ground for any "alien whose presence or activities in the United States the Secretary of State has reasonable ground to believe would have potentially serious adverse foreign policy consequences for the United States." The court found this provision unconstitutionally vague.[14]

The *Massieu* court's concern was notice: "It simply cannot be disputed, and indeed the government does not, that the statute provides absolutely no notice to aliens as to what is required of them under the statute." Any noncitizen lawfully in the United States, "whether here for a day or fifty years and visiting or resident in this country, must live in fear of the Secretary of State informing them, at any time, that our foreign policy requires their deportation to a particular country for reasons unknown to them and beyond their control."[15] Again, the constitutionality of deportation depended on notice, a core value of immigration as contract.

Like the foundation plenary power cases discussed in chapter 1, the court decisions in *Harisiades*, *De George*, *Rafeedie*, and *Massieu* illustrate different ways in which immigration as contract has shaped the constitutional reasoning in immigration cases. Contract-based reasoning has also played a significant role in the making and interpretation of statutes, for example in the areas of welfare eligibility and deportation for crimes.

Contract and Alienage Law

During the Vietnam War, thousands of the Hmong people in highland Laos fought for the United States in a clandestine war against the communist Pathet Lao. After the American withdrawal in 1975, many of these Hmong fled Laos, at first to refugee camps in Thailand. Some eventually made it to the United States. Of these refugees, few had the background or skills to function in the American economy, and many ended up on welfare. Among many of the Hmong, one attitude toward welfare in the United States is closely tied to their war experience and what they call the Promise.

As these Hmong understood it, the Promise was that if they fought for the United States, then the Americans would help the Hmong if, as it happened, American military forces withdrew. In this Hmong telling of the story, the Americans betrayed their comrades-in-arms time and time again after the Pathet Lao proved victorious. The first betrayal was leaving almost all of the Hmong behind in Laos. Then the Americans would not take in all of the Hmong who wanted to come to the United States. Next, those who were let in were denied veterans' benefits, and some Americans criticized the Hmong for going on welfare. The final betrayal came in 1996, when the welfare stopped.[16]

Welfare eligibility is part of what is called "alienage law." This is the law governing the lives of noncitizens inside the United States, as distinguished from "immigration law," which traditionally concerns admission to the United States and deportation. In many contexts, there are no laws that classify by alienage, so citizens and noncitizens are treated equally. Equal treatment is sometimes even taken for granted. Both citizens and noncitizens can call on firefighters to protect them and can file lawsuits in the civil court system. Many regulatory schemes, such as the wage and overtime protections of the Fair Labor Standards Act, protect citizens and noncitizens alike, even if the noncitizens are in the United States unlawfully. Other schemes, like the regulation of union representation and collective bargaining under the National Labor Relations Act, give equal treatment to citizens and lawfully present noncitizens, but limit protection for undocumented workers.[17]

Some laws, varying tremendously in coverage and content, draw a line between citizens and all noncitizens (not just lawful immigrants). Noncitizens may not vote in federal elections. No state allows noncitizens to vote in statewide elections, and noncitizen voting in local elections is rare. Only citizens may serve on federal or state juries. Citizens who live outside the United States can receive Social Security benefits, but noncitizens who live outside the United States cannot, even if they worked and paid into the system for many years. Federal laws restrict property ownership and commercial opportunities for noncitizens. For example, only citizens can get agricultural operating loans, and federal licenses to construct and operate cellular phone systems. State laws addressing an even more diverse set of topics treat citizens and noncitizens differently. A Louisiana statute requires citizenship for hunting, fishing, and fur trading licenses. California requires a minimum of seven U.S. citizens to establish a fraternal organization.[18]

Other alienage laws distinguish citizens and lawful immigrants from noncitizens who are not lawful immigrants. Under federal law, only citizens and lawful immigrants may qualify for agricultural emergency loans, join Americorps, request declassification of certain classified information, recover for injury or death in maritime service cases, or get renewable energy advancement awards. Federal tax law treats citizens and lawful immigrants virtually identically. Citizens and lawful immigrants (but not nonimmigrants) must register for the military draft. Likewise, some state laws distinguish citizens and lawful immigrants from other noncitizens. Arkansas limits certain loan programs to citizens and lawful immigrants. The Colorado youth conservation and service corps is open only to citizens and lawful immigrants. Several states limit financial aid for higher education to citizens and lawful immigrants.[19]

These laws are called alienage laws, or sometimes alienage classifications, because they classify by whether an individual is an alien or not. Because they do not concern the traditional immigration law topics of admission and deportation, alienage laws have historically been regarded as distinct, and the plenary power doctrine does not apply, at least not in full measure. As a matter of common sense, however, it would be a mistake to overlook the strong connections that exist between certain alienage laws and certain immigration laws. This is especially true with welfare eligibility, which has close immigration law counterparts.

The Economy, Immigration Law Enforcement, and Keeping Out the Poor

Alienage laws that limit noncitizen eligibility for welfare are related to state and federal immigration laws that have long tried to keep out the poor. As chapter 1 mentioned, the earliest were state immigration laws. Later, the 1882 federal immigration statute in *Nishimura Ekiu* excluded "any person unable to take care of himself or herself without becoming a public charge." In 1891, a new federal provision added that any alien who became a public charge within one year "after his arrival in the United States from causes existing prior to his landing therein shall be deemed to have come in violation of law" and could be deported.[20]

Federal immigration laws barring the poor are part of a complex story in which public sentiment toward immigrants has typically but imperfectly reflected boom-and-bust economic cycles. When the labor force has expanded in boom periods, immigration has accounted for much of that growth. But recessionary periods, even if short, have consistently heightened concerns about immigration—that poor immigrants burden America by not working or by taking jobs from Americans.

When these first "public charge" exclusion and deportation grounds became law, much of the restrictionist sentiment was rooted in serious economic dislocations that the American working class suffered in the 1890s. Immigrants were willing to work longer hours, at more dangerous jobs, and for lower wages than workers who were already settled in America, though many of these "natives" had not been here for very long themselves. Organized labor recruited immigrants, but these new union members often tried to shut the door behind them, especially when employers began to use even more recent arrivals as strikebreakers.[21]

Though the working class saw immigrant labor as competition for jobs and as a drag on wage levels, American industry and agriculture were ambivalent. They relied on immigrants for cheap essential labor, and immigration restrictions posed a threat to this labor supply. Business interests sought to maintain a free flow of immigrant workers within the law, but some employers began to rely on illegal immigration, especially for farm labor.

Early in the twentieth century, the U.S. government made little or no effort to control its land borders. In 1906, only seventy-five immigration inspectors on horseback patrolled the nineteen hundred-mile U.S.-Mexico border, which was less an international barrier than a string of border cities and towns that were socially and economically paired in spite of the boundary between them. Administration of the immigration laws focused on Ellis Island, on Angel Island in San Francisco Bay, and at other sea ports of entry. Starting a pattern now at the core of today's immigration debates, farmers in the southwestern United States began to rely heavily on Mexican laborers, lawful and unlawful. In 1906, a serious economic depression in Mexico caused the first heavy influx of Mexicans looking for work in the United States. The Mexican Revolution of 1910 only increased the flow, with the number of Mexican-born U.S. residents tripling from an official census of two hundred thousand in 1910 to six hundred thousand in 1930.[22]

Dependence on Mexican labor spread to other industries and regions. Employers knew or soon learned that unlawful workers would be easier to control than lawful ones. Unlawfully present workers had few or no protections against ruthless exploitation by employers. Later, temporary workers would enter lawfully on various programs, as Braceros from 1942 until 1964 and today as H-2A agricultural workers. But the flow of undocumented workers never abated. As illegal immigration increased, many employers acquiesced in restrictions on lawful admission, knowing that workers would come to them no matter what the law said.[23]

Despite the need for cheap labor, starting in the late nineteenth century the tide shifted to favor restrictions on poor immigrants. Industrialization brought urbanization that concentrated immigrants in highly visible and politically volatile ways, producing a prevailing image of urban immigrant squalor. This image was reinforced by the beliefs that the frontier was closing and that new immigrants would aggravate competition for finite national resources and threaten the country's social and political foundations.

This turn against poor immigrants was part of a wider surge in restrictionism that had a strong racial element as well. Much as the Know-Nothings had emerged in the 1850s in response to growing Catholic immigration from Ireland and Germany, restrictionists warned of new waves of eastern European and Mediterranean immigrants. Francis Walker, then superintendent of the U.S. Census, called these new immigrants "beaten men from beaten races." Poverty was seen not just as an economic problem, but also as a sign of racial inferiority. And in the western states, the diminished but continuing flow of Asian immigrants further upset the image of immigrants as Christians from northern and western Europe that had prevailed for much of the 1800s.[24]

Whether the nub of public concern was economics or race or some combination, restrictionists lacked the political strength in these years before World War I to persuade Congress to impose a general cap on the number of immigrants. Enough confidence remained in the overall economy and in the nation's power to absorb and assimilate European immigrants, even if more came from strange places. And as immigrants naturalized and their children came of voting age, they won some influence at the polls. Business and industry shifted their positions on immigration in this period but never came out decidedly for restrictions. A folklore emerged of America as a nation of immigrants passing through the Golden Door, an image celebrated in Emma Lazarus's words now at the foot of the Statue of Liberty: "Give me your tired, your poor, Your huddled masses yearning to breathe free."

In the decade after World War I, however, restrictionist efforts would succeed, mainly in the form of an immigrant admission scheme based on race and nationality. In this sense, the fears about the changing ethnic composition of the immigrant flow proved to be stronger than the fears about poor immigrants or labor competition. But by then, public charge exclusion and deportation had become firmly established in the immigration statutes.

Today, federal law still has a public charge exclusion ground that makes inadmissible any alien who is "likely at any time to become a public charge." Almost all lawful immigrants who qualify based on family ties— over a half-million annually—must present affidavits of support. (There are exceptions for surviving spouses of citizens as well as for battered spouses and children.) In 2002, the government initially denied about forty thousand properly filed immigrant visa applications; about 43 percent of these denials invoked the public charge ground. Though the initial refusal was overcome in a very high percentage of these cases, typically by evidence of financial support, this ground is a major hurdle for many noncitizens wanting to come to the United States.[25]

A corresponding ground makes deportable any alien who "within five years after the date of entry, has become a public charge from causes not affirmatively shown to have arisen since entry." The public charge statute makes it much harder for the government to deport than to exclude. One reason is that deportation requires the government to show that the causes of indigence predated admission. Public charge deportations have been rare: only eight occurred from 1961 through 1970, and only thirty-one from 1971 through 1980, when the government stopped publishing the figures.[26]

Before 1996, nonbinding affidavits of support from a sponsor were not required as a general rule, though federal officials sometimes required them if the sponsored noncitizens could not prove an annual income at or above the federal poverty line. In 1980, the U.S. Senate passed a bill to make affidavits of support legally enforceable, but it failed in the House. Instead, Congress enacted the first of several statutes deeming a sponsor's promised support to be available to a noncitizen who applies for federal welfare. This typically made any noncitizen ineligible for benefits if his admission was based on an affidavit.[27]

Congress imposed the current affidavit requirement in 1996. These affidavits are now legally enforceable against the sponsors, and the obligation is very durable. For example, a sponsor must continue to support a sponsored spouse even if they divorce. The government and the immigrant may collect from the sponsor until the immigrant works for ten years, naturalizes, leaves the United States and is no longer a permanent resident, or dies. A sponsor must be able to support her own household plus all sponsored immigrants at 125 percent of the federal poverty line. In 2004, a family of four in the continental United States required $23,563, or one wage-earner paid $11.78 per hour full-time. Current law still deems a sponsor's resources to be the immigrant's, making the immigrant ineligible for benefits. This practice of deeming generally continues until the immigrant naturalizes or works ten years without receiving federal assistance.[28]

Immigrants, Welfare, and Immigration as Contract

Besides requiring a sponsor's binding affidavit in 1996, Congress also overhauled federal welfare, and here immigration as contract was highly influential. Many changes affected citizens and noncitizens alike, but new eligibility limits hit noncitizens especially hard. Historically, the major federal benefits programs had been open to lawful immigrants, but Congress made many lawful immigrants ineligible for federal food stamps and Supplemental Security Income (SSI). Barred were not just future arrivals, but also noncitizens who were already lawful immigrants on the enactment date, August 22, 1996.[29]

Nearly a million lawful immigrants lost their food stamps, and about a half-million lost SSI. Future lawful immigrants were barred for at least five years from other federal public assistance, except emergency Medicaid, child nutrition programs, and Head Start. As a practical matter, new lawful immigrants would be ineligible even longer, since their sponsor's income would be deemed to be theirs. There were exceptions, notably for anyone who had worked in the United States for ten years, and for veterans and active duty military personnel and their families. Also exempt for their first five years were refugees, asylees, and others fleeing persecution. But the overall effect on immigrant families was severe. The savings from the noncitizen cuts were a substantial part of the total savings from the welfare legislation.

Though Congress later restored benefits to many noncitizens who were lawful immigrants in August 1996, my concern is not the state of the law in 1996 or now, but rather how noncitizen welfare eligibility was debated. Immigration as contract played a prominent role, but the promise was not necessarily the Hmong version. Instead, supporters of the 1996 welfare bars cited the immigration statute in arguing that immigrants promise *not* to go on welfare.

The welfare law's preamble declared: "Self-sufficiency has been a basic principle of United States immigration law since this country's earliest immigration statutes." Along the same lines, President Bill Clinton explained, "when an immigrant comes to America, . . . they have to promise that they won't try to get on welfare and they won't take any public money." The Senate report had similar words: "immigrants make a promise to the American people that they will not become a financial burden," and "It was only on the basis of the assurance of the immigrant and the sponsor that the immigrant would not at any time become a public charge that the immigrant was allowed in this country." And in the debate over the immigration law changes in 1996, proponents of binding affidavits made a contract-based argument that they were needed to enforce each immigrant's promise of financial self-sufficiency.[30]

But the debates about welfare eligibility and affidavits also made clear that contract-based arguments do not always disfavor noncitizens. It all depends on the terms of the contract. As the Hmong story of the welfare Promise suggests, immigration as contract can also be cited *against* the welfare bars and the affidavit requirement. In this way, contract can cut both ways in the welfare arena, just as it did when constitutional challenges to exclusion and deportation used contract-based reasoning both against lawful immigrants in *Harisiades*, and for them in *Rafeedie* and *Massieu*. When supporters of the welfare bars and affidavit invoked contract-based arguments, opponents countered that *taking away* public benefits was the real breach of promise. Congress was changing the rules of the game, disappointing the settled expectations of lawful immigrants who had arrived when they were eligible for the safety net. An objection to the affidavit requirement was similarly contract-based—that it was not needed to enforce any self-sufficiency promise, since deeming a sponsor's resources to be the sponsored immigrant's already made the immigrant ineligible for public benefits.[31]

Immigration as contract also played an important role in shaping litigation that challenged the constitutionality of the 1996 welfare bars. The plaintiffs were only the lawful immigrants with the strongest constitutional claims: those already in the United States and receiving welfare in August 1996. No lawsuit raised the constitutional claims of future lawful immigrants. The plaintiffs' acquiescence in the validity of a cut-off date reflected their acquiescence in casting the controversy in contract terms.[32]

The courts that decided these cases adopted contract-based reasoning in upholding the constitutionality of the distinction between past and future arrivals. One typical decision explained that it was "not wholly irrational for Congress to have decided that it would upset expectations and reliance interests more to cut off lawfully residing aliens who were actually receiving SSI benefits when the reform legislation was enacted than it would to deny those benefits to aliens who had not been receiving them."[33]

After 1996, Congress gradually reversed many of the cutbacks in noncitizen welfare eligibility. Today, almost all noncitizens who were already lawful immigrants in August 1996 have regained eligibility for federal public benefits. And new lawful immigrants and noncitizens granted protection from persecution in their home countries are now eligible for food stamps once they have lived in the United States for five years, or if they are under eighteen years of age. One new law specifically restored food stamp eligibility for Hmong who assisted the U.S. military in the Vietnam era, making good on part of the Promise.[34]

Supporters of these restorations also drew on immigration as contract and the rhetoric of broken promises. Thus Senator Frank Lautenberg: "Congress pulled the rug out from under these people and eliminated their disability benefits." One newspaper editorial argued for restorations: "More and more Republicans are starting to publicly agree that the welfare reform bill goes too far in punishing poor and elderly legal immigrants who had every right to believe American promises that they would not be left homeless and hungry." Opponents of the restorations countered with their own version of promises, as in one editorial: "Noncitizens who reap welfare benefits and their sponsors are breaking their pledge to the American people—the people who granted them the privilege of coming to the U.S. . . . The government did not promise to feed and care for the struggling immigrant; the sponsor did."[35] This, too, shows the strong influence of immigration as contract in alienage law.

Deportation, Retroactivity, and Contract

Contract-based thinking has played a similar role in immigration law, as evident in a recent controversy involving deportation for criminal convictions. For much of early U.S. history, citizens could be banished as punishment for a crime. On rare occasions today, a pardon may be conditioned on leaving the country. In 2004, the U.S. government released Yaser Hamdi, an alleged "enemy combatant" and a dual citizen of the United States and Saudi Arabia, to return to Saudi Arabia on condition that he relinquish his U.S. citizenship. But the basic principle is that citizens cannot be deported unless they lose their citizenship first. This can happen by denaturalization, which means revoking naturalization because of fraud or other defects in the original application. Or someone born or naturalized a citizen may be "expatriated" if she pledges allegiance to a foreign government, accepts certain types of foreign government positions, or commits similar acts while intending to relinquish citizenship.[36]

Noncitizens, including lawful immigrants, have no absolute guarantee that they will be allowed to stay in the United States. Lawful immigrants who leave for an extended period may be deemed to abandon their permanent resident status and may thus lose (even unintentionally) their lawful basis for staying. Even a lawful immigrant who has not abandoned permanent residence may be "removed" (the technical statutory term for deported) under various deportability grounds. For example, noncitizens can be removed on national security grounds or for certain types of criminal convictions. In recent years, the largest category of removals from the interior of the United States has been removals based on criminal convictions.[37]

To understand the pivotal role of contract in this area, the most important piece of background is that deportation grounds are only half of the scheme for removing noncitizens who have been admitted to the United States as either immigrants or nonimmigrants. Even if a noncitizen has become deportable, he may ask the government to waive that ground and let him stay as a matter of administrative discretion. And even if no waiver is forthcoming, an immigration judge may still allow a noncitizen to stay in the United States under a form of discretionary relief called cancellation of removal. A decision on cancellation of removal has two parts. First, the noncitizen must be eligible to apply under requirements that include a minimum residence period in the United States. Then, for a noncitizen who meets the eligibility requirements, an immigration judge may exercise her discretion and decide to grant cancellation. Cancellation of removal allows lawful immigrants to retain their status and stay in the United States even if they are deportable.

Exclusion and deportation grounds for crimes go back to the beginning of state and federal immigration laws. As mentioned earlier, a federal immigration statute in 1875 barred convicted criminals, and a 1917 statute introduced deportation for crimes committed in the United States. In the modern era, the most dramatic developments have taken place since 1988, with Congress making it steadily easier for the government to deport noncitizens convicted of crimes.

For one thing, the crime-related deportation grounds have expanded. For example, an "aggravated felony" conviction makes a noncitizen deportable. When Congress introduced the concept in the Anti-Drug Abuse Act of 1988 as part of the federal government's war on drugs, the only aggravated felonies were murder, firearms trafficking, and drug trafficking. Later, fraud or deceit crimes became aggravated felonies, but only if the loss was $200,000 or more. Since 1996, aggravated felonies have included any fraud or deceit crime with a loss exceeding just $10,000. Today, other crimes that are only misdemeanors under state law can be aggravated felonies for federal immigration purposes.[38]

Not only have deportation grounds broadened, but waivers and cancellation of removal have become much harder to get. Imagine, for example, that Stefan became a lawful immigrant in 1990. Six years later, he committed and was convicted of fraud involving $15,000. The maximum sentence was three years, but he was sentenced to one year. Until 1996, a conviction made a lawful immigrant ineligible for cancellation only if the crime was an aggravated felony and he served a sentence of five years or more. Stefan's fraud was not an aggravated felony because the loss was less than $200,000. It was a crime involving moral turpitude, which would have made Stefan deportable with a sentence of one year or longer, but only if he had committed the crime within five years of admission. Since Stefan's crime was six years after admission, this five-year rule protected him. Even if he had been deportable, he could have applied for the pre-1996 version of cancellation of removal. With strong family or community ties, he had a good chance of being allowed to stay in the United States.[39]

Today, many more crimes are aggravated felonies. Stefan's crime is an aggravated felony because the loss exceeded $10,000. Moreover, an aggravated felony now makes a lawful immigrant ineligible for cancellation no matter how short the sentence. Stefan is not only deportable, but also ineligible for cancellation.[40] All of these changes in the deportation scheme based on criminal convictions raise the question whether the changes apply retroactively, which in turn raises the issues of notice and expectations that lie at the heart of immigration as contract.

Enrico St. Cyr is a Haitian citizen who became a permanent resident of the United States in 1986, when he was about nineteen years old. St. Cyr's brother is also a lawful immigrant; his parents and sister are U.S. citizens. Ten years later, he pled guilty to selling drugs. This conviction made St. Cyr deportable, but he was eligible for the former version of cancellation of removal and hoped to persuade an immigration judge to consider his ties in this country and let him stay. St. Cyr applied for this relief in 1996, right after the eligibility rules tightened. Under the new rules his conviction would make him ineligible, but did the new rules apply to his pre-1996 conviction?[41]

The U.S. Supreme Court answered these questions in 2001 in *INS v. St. Cyr*. This decision strongly reflected immigration as contract, but in ways that protected lawful immigrants by emphasizing their expectations based on prior law. The Court's unstated starting premise was the principle, first articulated in *Fong Yue Ting*, that because deportation is not punishment, the constitutional limits on the retroactivity of criminal laws do not apply. This meant that the Court would decide *St. Cyr* by applying its precedents on the retroactivity of civil statutes in general, not necessarily involving immigration. Key was its 1994 decision in *Landgraf v. USI Film Products*, which established that civil legislation can be retroactive, but only if the statute says so clearly. This presumption against retroactivity, *Landgraf* explained, "finds expression in several provisions in our Constitution," including the Fifth Amendment's due process clause, which "protects the interests in fair notice and repose that may be compromised by retroactive legislation."[42]

Because the Court framed the issue as a matter of expectations, it had to decide exactly what it meant for a change to be retroactive in the context of eligibility for cancellation. In a literal sense it was not retroactive to apply the new rules to cut off St. Cyr's eligibility, since the law had changed before the immigration judge could rule on it. But applying the new rules was arguably retroactive as a practical matter, since the key fact determining eligibility was a conviction entered before the new rules became law.

The Court had to choose between two very different versions of St. Cyr's legitimate expectations under the old rules. One was a contract-based approach reminiscent of the *Fong Yue Ting* characterization of deportation as mere withdrawal of permission to remain. According to this approach, Enrico St. Cyr had no legitimate expectations under the old rules. A Supreme Court decision in 1999 had expressed such an understanding of deportation when it said: "Even when deportation is sought because of some act the alien has committed, in principle the alien is not being punished for that act (criminal charges may be available for that separate purpose), but is merely being held to the *terms under which he was admitted*."[43] Thus it would not be retroactive to bar cancellation eligibility by applying tighter eligibility rules to old convictions.

A very different view of expectations was the basis for the Supreme Court's opinion in *St. Cyr* (and almost all of the federal appeals court decisions that led up to it). The Court reasoned that it was retroactive to apply the new rules to pre-1996 convictions, because St. Cyr and other noncitizens who had been prosecuted for deportable crimes had entered guilty pleas believing that they could apply for discretionary relief if the government tried to deport them. The Court noted that the approval rate for relief was high, about 50 percent. Moreover, immigration judges were required to consider certain factors, so they could not decide on a whim.[44]

Working with this understanding of expectations, the Court made clear that Congress could have made the new eligibility rules retroactive, but that absent anything "unmistakably indicating that Congress considered the question whether to apply its repeal of the old rules retroactively," the new rules would not apply to St. Cyr and other noncitizens who had pleaded guilty to a deportable offense while eligible for relief under the old rules. Applying contract-based reasoning, the Supreme Court in *St. Cyr* held that changing the rules "would surely be contrary to 'familiar considerations of fair notice, reasonable reliance, and settled expectations.'" At least one federal appeals court later applied this reasoning to noncitizen defendants who went to trial instead of pleading guilty.[45]

The Attractions—and Shortcomings—of Contract

With all of the areas that this chapter has examined—ideology and national security, noncitizen welfare eligibility, and deportation, and within these areas both statutes and the Constitution—my main point has not been that one way of looking at notice, promise, or expectations is right and another way is wrong. Rather, what matters is *how* both sides argued immigration-related issues: as a matter of contract. Nor does it matter for my analysis that the meaning of contractual obligation as a legally enforceable promise has changed during the twentieth century, recognizing changes after the terms of an initial agreement and limiting the enforceability of very one-sided arrangements. These changes matter to contract law scholars, but they do not take away from what matters about the areas that I have analyzed in this chapter—that key arguments in each of them were made by invoking the rhetoric of promise, notice, and expectations, which are the core elements of contract-based reasoning.

Immigration as contract has strong, intuitive appeal as an approach to fairness and justice, and to equality in immigration and citizenship. The immigrant has notice of the contract, and the immigrant and the receiving country can rely on its terms. Both sides seem to have their expectations protected.[46] Immigration as contract fully accepts that citizens and noncitizens are not equal. This substitutes for the more complex notions of equality—such as immigration as affiliation and immigration as transition—that would need to emerge if we had to think of the status of noncitizens as something more than the conditions of their admission.

Immigration as contract is a reassuring approach for the many U.S. citizens who want to know who is coming to America and how long they will stay. Many citizens feel that this knowledge is vital to their faith that their country can control immigration, and thus to their faith in U.S. immigration and citizenship policy generally. Immigration as contract is thus the conceptual basis for emphasizing formal legal status and opposing anything that undermines a reliably sharp line between lawfully present noncitizens and illegal aliens. For example, when a temporary worker is initially admitted to the United States, many Americans believe that it is legitimate and even imperative to set a departure deadline that will not be undermined by later developments during his stay. At the same time, immigration as contract is not just an approach for the enforcement-minded. As cases like *St. Cyr* have shown, contract can give noncitizens the rhetoric to demand some certainty and protection against potentially harmful changes.

The attractions of immigration as contract also illuminate its shortcomings. It does not limit *how* noncitizens may be treated, as long as lawmakers give proper notice, which may include changing the terms of contract. The U.S. Supreme Court said in *St. Cyr* that Congress can upset the expectations of lawful immigrants by making retroactive changes to deportation laws, as long as Congress speaks clearly. It has done this many times, for example by making retroactive the greatly expanded definition of aggravated felony.[47]

Because immigration as contract is based on promises, notice, and expectations, it generally protects lawful immigrants against new, harsher rules only if they are already in the United States. For new immigrants, contract-based arguments are inherently unavailing. By coming to the United States, they are presumed to acquiesce in a contract that is less favorable than before, but still attractive enough to accept. Conditions of admission for future immigrants could include heavier tax burdens, or even permanent ineligibility to naturalize. Changes in the terms of the immigration contract could produce multiple classes of lawful immigrants, depending on arrival date. This was the rationale underlying Congress's decision to restore welfare benefits less fully for new arrivals than for lawful immigrants who were already in the United States in August 1996.

The inadequacy of immigration as contract as an exclusive conceptual foundation for immigration law and alienage law is best explained with three related but distinct ideas. The first is that expectations and promises are too easy to manipulate to be analytically useful. This prompts doubt that expectations and promises had much meaning in the first place. In the welfare debates, both sides based their arguments on their own versions of the immigration contract. Precisely because this rhetoric helped both sides, it is impossible to say which version of the contract was the true contract.

The easy manipulation of any "immigration contract" is also evident from the concept of parole. This refers to the practice of letting a noncitizen physically into the United States, but treating her as outside the country for immigration law purposes. This is a very useful fiction, because it denies a noncitizen formal admission to the United States, when admission would entitle a noncitizen to benefits that the government may be reluctant to bestow. If a noncitizen comes to the border without proper papers but is so ill that she needs to be hospitalized before she is sent home, the government can parole her into the United States for medical treatment without admitting her. Or if a noncitizen's lawful admission is uncertain, the government can parole him in, leaving him free to move about while an immigration judge decides his case.

Parole has also served many times as a vehicle for letting in groups of refugees for whom no admission category was readily available.[48]

Parole status can last for years. Many of the Cubans who left for the United States from the port of Mariel in the 1980s—hence known as the Marielitos—were never admitted because of criminal convictions that made them excludable. Instead, they were paroled into the United States, and several thousand remain here in parole status more than twenty years later. Parole is an obvious fiction, because it treats someone as if she never set foot in the United States, when in fact she may have ties nurtured over many years of living here. But parole makes perfect sense from the contract-based perspective that a noncitizen is let onto U.S. soil, but only on condition that her status remain that of someone still outside. Just as deportation is the same as exclusion, by this reasoning parolees are not here.

The second shortcoming of immigration as contract is that it is not necessarily a legally enforceable contract. There are aspects of immigration that make the contract label fit poorly. The contract is a take-it-or-leave-it proposition. The individual immigrant and the U.S. government do not bargain back and forth before she decides to come, so there is no freely negotiated meeting of the minds. At best, it is what lawyers call a "contract of adhesion." This is especially true if the noncitizen has few real alternatives, and if what she gives up under the immigration contract is essential to her individual dignity or is antithetical to other important values. Contract law sometimes does not enforce such one-sided agreements, especially under aspects of contract law that emerged in the twentieth century. For example, the idea of unconscionability sometimes leads courts to not enforce apparent agreements between parties if one side has vastly superior bargaining power and the contract terms are too one-sided. In this sense, immigration as contract is not a real contract at all, but rather an appeal to justice through the rhetoric of contract.

This brings me to the third and most fundamental problem with immigration as contract. Even if the one-sided contract involved in an immigrant's coming to the United States were close enough to mutual consent to be legally enforceable, immigration as contract still would be incomplete as a compass for treatment of lawful immigrants. Even if an agreement is sufficient to legitimize market transactions, it may be quite inadequate for democratic politics.[49]

Digging deeper, the crucial question—which contract terms should be recognized?—will always be answered in the light cast by other values. In the area of federal welfare eligibility, the purposes of public assistance are not better served by tying eligibility to arrival date. If someone needs food or medical care, it serves society very poorly to end discussion of eligibility with a cutoff date. This means, in turn, that contract-based limits on public assistance lack sufficient moral force for their enforcement. This will be especially true as immigrants who arrive after the cutoff date gradually build up ties in America but face hardships that seem especially worthy of public assistance. These concerns about immigration as contract may explain why Congress ultimately abandoned an immigration-as-contract approach to welfare eligibility by restoring food stamps for new lawful immigrants after they have lived in the United States for five years.[50]

More generally, the stark proposition that the government can extinguish rights if it says so with sufficient advance notice is inconsistent with modern understandings of membership in a community or a society. This is what is so unsettling about the U.S. Supreme Court decision in *St. Cyr* and its lesson that Congress can undermine expectations if it does so clearly. Similar second thoughts about heavy reliance on contract justify skepticism of guest-worker programs, if they assume that workers can be held to an agreement to come only temporarily to meet short-term labor needs.[51]

Any mutual consent reflected in immigration as contract loses much of its persuasive and moral force as time passes and many of these workers build lives in America. Many will gradually lose their ties with their country of origin and no longer call it home. Their children born in the United States will be citizens and know life nowhere else. It seems unjust to deport these workers, whether or not they once promised to leave at harvest's end. As the Swiss author Max Frisch once wrote about labor migration to northern Europe during the 1950s and 1960s, "we called for workers, but people came."[52]

Even more fundamentally, the reasons for these shortcomings of immigration as contract become clearer by thinking about the basic functions of immigration law and alienage law. Both are part of the large project of national self-definition—of deciding who belongs to America. I am not suggesting that those who make immigration law and alienage law necessarily act consciously or purposefully with this national self-definition project in mind. A legislator may want only to improve the

American economy by admitting professionals in industries in which few U.S. citizens have comparable training and experience. But even if each decision in isolation reflects narrower motivations, national self-definition is at stake.

This project of defining America is necessarily and properly influenced by values beyond the notions of promises, notice, and expectations that lie at the core of immigration as contract. Contract has considerable rhetorical and analytical power, but the terms of agreements with immigrants should be outweighed by broader values. In the context of national self-definition, focusing only on promises, notice, and expectations is too narrowly utilitarian and cavalier in its dismissal of equality, even where, as in immigration and citizenship, some inequality is assumed. An exclusive reliance on immigration as contract amounts to the misguided conviction that what is fair and just in immigration can be achieved without trying to think more seriously about a version of equality for lawful immigrants. So it should not be surprising that other views of immigration that are counterweights to contract and give fuller meaning to equality have emerged.

CHAPTER 3

All Persons Within the Territorial Jurisdiction

Yick Wo came from China to Gold Mountain in 1861. Like many Chinese immigrants, he opened a laundry, which was inexpensive to set up and did not require him to know much English. The near absence of women in Chinese immigrant communities created an opening for men to make a living in a traditionally female occupation. The laundry business was also one of the options left after the enactment of various laws that forced Chinese immigrants out of factory work and other wage labor, and into self-employment. Chinese commercial laundries soon dominated the market. An estimated twenty-six hundred Chinese worked in laundries in California, thirteen hundred of them in San Francisco, where they represented 12 percent of the Chinese in the city.[1]

Yick Wo's laundry would become the centerpiece of a celebrated U.S. Supreme Court decision that contrasts sharply with the *Chinese Exclusion Case*, *Nishimura Ekiu*, *Fong Yue Ting*, and other Court decisions of the same period. The basis for the contrast is the Supreme Court's recognition of Yick Wo's constitutional rights as a lawful immigrant by adopting a rationale that I will call territorial personhood.

Territorial Personhood and the Rights of Immigrants

Among the most prominent anti-Chinese crusaders in California during the 1870s and 1880s was Dennis Kearney, an Irish immigrant. This was a period when Irish immigrants were a group that was racially uncertain, not yet regarded as white but able to assert their racial superiority over Asian immigrants and other immigrants who were less white than the

Irish. Kearney's Workingmen's Party unified labor unions around the issue of expelling Chinese immigrant laborers to keep them from working for lower wages and sometimes as strikebreakers.[2]

The anti-Chinese agitators succeeded in having discriminatory laws enacted, for example a San Francisco municipal ordinance that required 500 cubic feet of air for each tenant and thus effectively banned living in the close quarters typical of Chinatown. Another San Francisco ordinance imposed much higher taxes on laundries that did not use horses to deliver; this included almost all laundries run by Chinese immigrants. Yet another San Francisco ordinance directed against Chinese required the sheriff to cut the hair of all prisoners in the local jail to a length of one inch. The Workingmen's Party won one-third of the seats in California's 1878 constitutional convention, which produced a new state constitution that provided "no native of China" would ever be allowed to vote. It also prohibited the employment of Chinese in private and public sectors, and it authorized localities to confine Chinese to ghettos or even expel them. Lower federal courts struck down some of these provisions as discrimination that violated the equal protection clause of the U.S. Constitution, but similar state and local laws kept coming.[3]

By 1884, Yick Wo had run his laundry in San Francisco for twenty-two years. One of the most prominent anti-Chinese local laws had been enacted in 1880 to regulate laundries. It was phrased innocuously as a fire-protection measure that required laundry structures to be made of brick. It did not name any racial or ethnic group, but city officials used it to shut down laundries operated by Chinese immigrants. At the time, there were approximately 320 commercial laundries in the city, about 240 of them Chinese-owned and -operated. The city health officer and Board of Fire Wardens had inspected Yick Wo's laundry and found that it was properly maintained and posed no fire hazards or danger to public health, but Yick Wo was jailed for violating the ordinance by operating a laundry in a wooden building without special permission.[4]

Was the San Francisco ordinance constitutional? The U.S. Supreme Court answered this question in its 1886 decision in *Yick Wo v. Hopkins*. The key issue was the scope of the equal protection clause of the Fourteenth Amendment to the U.S. Constitution. By providing that no state shall "deny to *any person* within its jurisdiction the equal protection of the laws," did the clause protect noncitizens in the United States? This question had great practical importance, since the political forces that had just led to the Chinese Exclusion Act and other immigration laws were also pushing for more discriminatory alienage laws as well.

Yick Wo's case reached a Supreme Court whose decision three years later in the *Chinese Exclusion Case* would reject a constitutional challenge to an immigration law. What about other laws affecting noncitizens in the United States? Would Chinese immigrants be allowed to work or attend public schools? Would a court hear a claim that it was unconstitutional to discriminate against Chinese by keeping them out of the laundry business? Perhaps not; the Supreme Court had suggested in an earlier case that the Fourteenth Amendment protected only persons of African ancestry.[5]

Yick Wo interpreted "any person" more broadly and adopted the general rule that the equal protection clause bars discrimination at state hands against noncitizens in the United States: "The fourteenth amendment to the constitution is not confined to the protection of citizens." Striking down the ordinance because city officials were enforcing it in a discriminatory way, the Court reasoned that Chinese immigrants had "fundamental rights to life, liberty, and the pursuit of happiness," based on "their harmless and useful occupation, on which they depend for a livelihood." Most important, the Court defined the scope of equal protection: "These provisions are universal in their application, to *all persons within the territorial jurisdiction*, without regard to any differences of race, of color, or of nationality."[6] With this statement, *Yick Wo* became the source of a long line of court decisions recognizing that noncitizens in the United States enjoy some protections under the Constitution.

Why didn't the plenary power rationale that would control the *Chinese Exclusion Case* and the other plenary power decisions also lead the Court to a hands-off attitude in *Yick Wo*? One possible answer is that *Yick Wo* involved local, not federal law. Even if the federal government could exclude Chae Chan Ping, deport Fong Yue Ting, and shut down Yick Wo's laundry, perhaps states and localities could not. This explanation draws support from U.S. Supreme Court decisions like *Chy Lung* and *Henderson*, which invalidated state laws that directly regulated immigration. But a decision ten years after *Yick Wo* makes clear that the federal-state line does not explain why the *Chinese Exclusion Case* and *Yick Wo* came out differently.

In 1896, the Supreme Court struck down a federal statute in *Wong Wing v. United States*, decided the same day as the Court's landmark endorsement of racial segregation in *Plessy v. Ferguson*. *Wong Wing* concerned the same 1892 Geary Act with the white-witness deportation provisions challenged in *Fong Yue Ting*. A different section of the Geary Act imposed criminal penalties by providing that any Chinese person in the United States in violation of the certificate and white-witness requirements "shall be imprisoned at hard labor." *Wong Wing* found this provision unconstitutional. The Court held that noncitizen criminal defendants, like citizen defendants, are guaranteed a Sixth Amendment right to a trial in court rather than the administrative proceeding called for in the statute. The Constitution requires "a judicial trial to establish the guilt of the accused" before such "infamous punishment" may be imposed. The Court echoed the territorial personhood idea from *Yick Wo*: "all persons within the territory of the United States are entitled to the protection" of the fifth and sixth amendments.[7]

Because *Wong Wing* struck down a federal statute, it casts doubt on any explanation for *Yick Wo* as a decision that limits only discrimination by state and local governments. Instead, what mattered was that neither *Wong Wing* nor *Yick Wo* involved admission or deportation—the core immigration law issues involved in the *Chinese Exclusion Case* and *Fong Yue Ting*. Though *Wong Wing* concerned criminal penalties for unlawful presence in violation of immigration laws, like *Yick Wo* it did not directly address admission or deportation. The Court's decision upholding deportation in *Fong Yue Ting* confirmed this conceptual difference when it distinguished *Yick Wo* as concerning "the power of a State over aliens continuing to reside within its jurisdiction, not of the power of the United States to put an end to their residence in the country."[8]

In *Yick Wo*, the Court could have invoked the conditions of admission and the contract-based rationale that would later be central to the *Chinese Exclusion Case*, *Fong Yue Ting*, *Nishimura Ekiu*, and other plenary power decisions. Instead, *Yick Wo* found room under the constitutional umbrella for these immigrant laundrymen. As legal scholar Thomas Joo has explained, this outcome may not have reflected solicitude for Chinese immigrants. *Yick Wo* may have instead represented the Court's recognition that the U.S. Constitution protects economic rights of the sort jeopardized by government regulation of business.[9] This may be an accurate appraisal of the decision at its inception, but courts in later decades would come to cite *Yick Wo* for the idea that they will seriously examine the constitutionality of laws that discriminate against noncitizens.

The modern legacy of *Yick Wo* as applied to alienage laws is not necessarily to require *equal* treatment of citizens and noncitizens. Laws that treat citizens and noncitizens differently may well pass constitutional muster in the end. Yet, the *Yick Wo* tradition in alienage law—to take constitutional challenges seriously in recognition of noncitizens' right to constitutional protection—has always contrasted with the plenary power doctrine's requirement that courts defer to Congress and the executive branch if noncitizens challenge the constitutionality of the government's immigration law decisions. By featuring territorial personhood as a counterweight to the contract-based thinking that would permeate immigration law, *Yick Wo* is an early landmark in the evolution of limited constitutional protection for noncitizens in the United States.

Territorial Personhood in Immigration Law and Alienage Law

The *Yick Wo* tradition has been centered in alienage law, but the decision and its conceptual basis in territorial personhood have also influenced immigration law. This is most evident in cases challenging the constitutionality of deportation procedures. When *Fong Yue Ting* upheld the requirement of residency certificates based on "at least one credible white witness," three justices dissented. They seemed to agree with the *Fong* majority that Congress could treat Chinese immigrants differently. But the dissenters thought it was unconstitutional to arrest and deport on the basis of procedures that left the final decision to the discretion of immigration officials without review in the courts. Citing *Yick Wo* and adopting reasoning similar to *Yick Wo* and *Wong Wing*, the *Fong* dissenters emphasized the Chinese immigrants' lawful presence in U.S. territory.[10]

Just ten years later, the Supreme Court held for the first time that deportation procedures must satisfy requirements of fairness under the Constitution. Kaoru Yamataya was a sixteen-year-old Japanese immigrant. Just four days after landing in Seattle, she was arrested and found to be deportable on the ground that she was likely to become a public charge. Yamataya challenged this finding, arguing that the government's procedures were constitutionally inadequate. She did not understand English, she had not received notice of the charges against her, and she had not been allowed to consult friends or a lawyer. The Court duly noted Congress's plenary power to establish admission and deportation categories, but this case involved procedures. For admission procedures, the Court continued, "the decisions of executive or administrative officers, acting within powers expressly conferred by Congress, are due process of law." For *deportation* procedures, however, the Court held that the government must meet a constitutional minimum standard of due process.[11]

Yamataya established two principles. First, courts reviewing deportation should examine procedures more closely than what is sometimes called the "substance" of immigration law—the categories for admission and deportation. Second, noncitizens in the United States have more constitutional protections than noncitizens seeking admission. Relying on the idea of territorial personhood, the Court held that with regard to immigration procedures the Constitution protects any alien "who has entered the country, and has become subject in all respects to its jurisdiction."[12] Combining these principles, *Yamataya* and the idea of territorial personhood at its center launched the gradual erosion of the plenary power doctrine, largely through courts deciding that procedures applied to noncitizens in the United States are constitutionally inadequate.

But this would take time. In *Yamataya* itself, the Court found no violation. It is hard to believe that a court faced with the same facts today would uphold the procedure, but the U.S. Supreme Court did so in 1903. For fifty years after *Yamataya*, courts seemed willing to examine deportation procedures, but the typical outcome was deference to the government.[13] The *Yamataya* Court's acceptance of territorial personhood in the immigration law context seemed to do little to weaken plenary power's stranglehold on immigration law. *Yamataya* would eventually emerge as a key influence in the expansion of constitutional protections for noncitizens in immigration law, but only much later.

In alienage law, the influence of *Yick Wo* evolved in two distinct branches. One evolved into modern versions of territorial personhood. The significance of this branch of *Yick Wo* was not at all evident in the treatment of noncitizens in the early 1900s. Consistent with Thomas Joo's reading of *Yick Wo* in its time as a decision about economic rights and not racial equality, courts consistently upheld the constitutionality of the many laws that expressly disadvantaged noncitizens. These decisions often limited *Yick Wo*'s holding that persons within the meaning of equal protection included noncitizens in the United States.[14]

Prominent in these decisions was the idea that a state could constitutionally treat citizens and noncitizens differently to protect a "special public interest" in its property or resources. This idea emerged in a 1915 U.S. Supreme Court decision, *Truax v. Raich*. Under an Arizona statute, if any employer had more than five employees, at least 80 percent had to be U.S. citizens (or eligible voters, at a time when some noncitizens could vote). Mike Raich, an Austrian lawfully in the United States, worked as a cook in Truax's restaurant in Bisbee, Arizona. The restaurant had nine employees, but only two counted toward the 80 percent. When Raich learned he would be fired, he sued. Citing *Yick Wo*, the Supreme Court held that the statute unconstitutionally discriminated against noncitizens, because a state could not reasonably "deny to lawful inhabitants, because of their race or nationality, the ordinary means of earning a livelihood." Harkening back to the Court's decisions invalidating state immigration laws, the Court said that putting Raich out of work because he was not a citizen would infringe on exclusive federal immigration authority.[15]

Although *Truax* struck down the Arizona statute, the Court may have focused, as in *Yick Wo*, as much on economic rights as on noncitizens' rights. The Court left open the possibility that states could treat citizens and noncitizens differently to protect a "special public interest." Other decisions of this era relied on this idea to uphold state alienage laws. The U.S. Supreme Court rejected an equal protection challenge to a Pennsylvania law that forbade noncitizens from owning shotguns or rifles and from killing wild birds or animals except in defense of person or property. Justice Oliver Wendell Holmes, Jr., explained that noncitizen gun ownership was banned to protect wildlife, "which the state may preserve for its own citizens if it pleases." Similarly, the Court sustained a New York state law that limited public works employment to U.S. and New York citizens, by noting the law regulated "property which it holds for its own citizens."[16]

Much closer in intent to the discriminatory practices struck down in *Yick Wo* were restrictions on land ownership. Like the enforcement of the San Francisco laundry ordinance, these laws targeted certain noncitizens for discrimination by nationality or race. Starting in 1907, the California legislature began to consider laws prohibiting Japanese immigrants from owning land. They made little headway at first, because of President Roosevelt's opposition based on concerns about U.S.-Japan diplomatic relations, but in 1913 California enacted its Alien Land Law. It was intended to stop farming by Japanese immigrants, though its effectiveness was limited by loopholes and the growing number of native-born Japanese American sons and daughters who as citizens could hold legal title for their parents. The Alien Land Law did not name any nationality, but applied apparently neutrally to aliens "ineligible to citizenship." The significance of this phrase is evident only from the history of racial bars to citizenship.

Belonging, Citizenship, and Race

From the nation's founding, attitudes toward immigrants concerned not only migration into an area of land, but the more fundamental issue of who belonged to America. Today, immigration debates assume that the United States is a fixed geographical location, with borders that are defined if porous. But the United States that immigrants settled during much of the 1800s was more of an aspirational concept than a defined physical reality. The sheer size of the country and the rudimentary nature of communication and transportation precluded serious immigration and customs control at the national border.

Questions of belonging were also complicated by conquest and settlement, and by the absorption or displacement of the peoples captured by the expanding frontier. Territorial expansion continued as white settlers, many of them recent immigrants from Europe, struggled to win and maintain control of new lands in the West and Southwest. In 1821, Mexico granted land to Stephen Austin in what is now Texas, and other Anglo settlers followed. Even before then, tensions had begun to emerge between the Spanish-speaking and native populations and the newcomers from the north—many of them the illegal aliens of their time. In 1829, the Mexican government abolished slavery, a move directed against Anglos in Texas, and then announced the end of legal immigration into the territory. This had even less effect than U.S. government efforts today to control immigration in the other direction.[17]

General Antonio López de Santa Anna then suspended the Mexican Constitution in 1835, ending what rights Texans had enjoyed within Mexico. In 1836, Texas declared its independence from Mexico, and the Mexican-American War followed. When it was over, Mexico and the United States signed the Treaty of Guadalupe-Hidalgo on February 2, 1848. For a sum of $15 million paid by the United States, Mexico ceded what are now California, Nevada, Texas, Utah, and parts of Arizona, Colorado, Kansas, New Mexico, Oklahoma, and Wyoming. The treaty made

Mexican Americans strangers in their own land. According to the treaty, everyone living in the ceded territory had one year to either leave or announce their intent to remain Mexican citizens. The estimated sixty thousand who did neither of these things automatically became U.S. citizens. These new Americans did not come to the United States; the United States came to them.[18]

In California, the politically and economically dominant social group in the mid-1800s was the Californios, the Spanish-speaking settler families who traced their ancestry back to Spain or Mexico. The Spanish conquest had been based on a network of missions founded to convert the native population to Christianity. The conquerors imposed military control through a system of forts, while working the land through farming and ranching. Spanish control ended with Mexican independence in 1821. The Mexican government took control of the mission lands in 1834 and soon gave vast land grants to this small number of favored families, who in turn created great ranching empires with enormous herds of cattle.

The Californios maintained their political and economic influence for a few years after the Treaty of Guadalupe-Hidalgo handed California to the United States, but waves of Anglo immigrants soon arrived to follow gold rush dreams. It took these new arrivals less than a generation to cast themselves as the natives entitled to exclude those who dared to join them. Over time, especially as their daughters married Anglo men, the Californios lost the land holdings that had been the source of their power and wealth.[19]

One legacy of Guadalupe-Hidalgo was to bring into the United States large populations whose race and ethnicity continued to set them apart even if the expansion of the frontier gave them citizenship. But an even larger question was which of the immigrants who came to America would be regarded as belonging. Chapter 1 explained how concerns about immigrants in the mid-1800s led to state and then federal laws on admission. But just as important, especially with elusive physical borders, were legal issues concerning the acquisition of U.S. citizenship.

Here, as in immigration law, race played a huge role. As historian Matthew Jacobson has commented, "what a citizen really was, at bottom, was someone who could help put down a slave rebellion or participate in Indian wars." Racial restrictions were part of U.S. citizenship from the first years of the Republic and persisted until 1952. The first naturalization statute in 1790 applied only to "free white persons."[20] Early in the nation's

history, however, the most contentious questions concerned not naturalization, but citizenship by birth, especially for African Americans.

Countries around the world have adopted blends of two approaches to
the acquisition of citizenship by birth. One is called *jus sanguinis*, a Latin
phrase that literally means law of blood. *Jus sanguinis* ties citizenship to descent; the children of citizens generally become citizens at birth no matter
where they are born. *Jus sanguinis* plays a role in U.S. citizenship law, in that
persons born outside the United States may be citizens at birth, if one or
both of their parents are citizens. But the core principle of U.S. citizenship
by birth is *jus soli*, or literally law of land or ground, which makes citizenship depend on place of birth, no matter who the child's parents are. *Jus
soli* is embodied in the first sentence of the Fourteenth Amendment to the
Constitution: "All persons born or naturalized in the United States, and
subject to the jurisdiction thereof, are citizens of the United States and of
the State wherein they reside."[21]

Almost everyone born in the United States today is a citizen, even if his
parents are here unlawfully, but it was not always so. In the first half of the
nineteenth century, Northern states recognized free blacks born in the
United States as citizens, while Southern states did not. This changed
with the U.S. Supreme Court's 1857 decision in *Dred Scott v. Sandford*,
which held that blacks born in the United States were not citizens. It com-
presses volumes into a half-sentence to say that the *Dred Scott* decision
triggered events that led to the Civil War. After the war, the 1866 Civil
Rights Act and then the Fourteenth Amendment in 1868 effectively over-
ruled *Dred Scott*, confirming the citizenship of African Americans and
making clear for the first time that the citizenship mentioned in the U.S.
Constitution is national citizenship.[22]

Central to the *Dred Scott* controversy, and then to the Civil War, were
questions of citizenship. But the Fourteenth Amendment seemed to leave
one big topic unaddressed: the citizenship of persons who were born in
the United States but viewed as neither white nor black. In 1884, the U.S.
Supreme Court found that Native Americans were not citizens under the
Fourteenth Amendment, though over the next fifty years they would
gradually acquire citizenship through various treaties and statutes. The
question then remained whether the children born in the United States to
Asian parents acquired citizenship at birth.[23]

The Supreme Court decision that answered this question involved Wong
Kim Ark, born in San Francisco in 1873, the son of a Chinese merchant. After

a trip to China, he returned to the United States in 1895 and sought readmission as a citizen. In 1898, the Court held in *United States v. Wong Kim Ark* that persons born in the United States to Chinese parents are native-born citizens under the common law of the United States, the Fourteenth Amendment, and the Civil Rights Act of 1866. In reasoning that cited *Yick Wo* and reflected territorial personhood—albeit in the context of citizenship, not equal protection—the Court explained that Congress clearly intended in 1866 to extend birthright citizenship to children born on U.S. soil to resident noncitizen parents, including Chinese.[24]

Naturalization, in contrast to citizenship by birth, remained limited by uniform federal law to free white persons from the first naturalization statute in 1790 until 1870, when eligibility was extended to "aliens of African nativity and to persons of African descent." Though the original limitation to free white persons seems remarkably exclusionary today, for much of the 1800s it was just as likely seen as inclusive, perhaps excessively so, because it permitted the naturalization of many white immigrants—Irish Catholics, for example—who seemed threateningly different from the Anglo-Saxon, Protestant immigrants who had dominated the flow before midcentury.[25]

After the Civil War, the broadening of citizenship by birth to African Americans reopened debate on racial qualifications for naturalization as well. On July 28, 1868, the same day that the Fourteenth Amendment was ratified, the United States and China signed the Burlingame Treaty. As chapter 1 described, the treaty officially acknowledged Chinese immigration to the United States, but it also said: "nothing herein contained shall be held to confer naturalization upon . . . subjects of China in the United States."[26]

In 1870, when Congress allowed blacks to naturalize, it considered but rejected proposals to open naturalization to all regardless of race or nationality. At the heart of the debate was naturalization of Chinese immigrants. Paralleling the campaign against Chinese immigration, the campaign against Chinese naturalization played heavily on racial bias. Its leaders stirred up fear of invasion by Asian hordes and attacked Chinese labor as another form of slavery. President Ulysses S. Grant told Congress: "I advise such legislation as will forever preclude the enslavement of the Chinese upon our soil under the name of coolies." In this sense, Chinese exclusion began not with the Page Act's prohibition on prostitutes in 1875 or the first Chinese Exclusion Act in 1882, but with this 1870 naturalization statute, the 1868 Burlingame Treaty, and the 1862 ban on Chinese "coolie" labor.[27]

From 1870 until after World War II, a key open question was the meaning of "free white persons." In 1878, a federal appeals court denied naturalization petitions by several Chinese immigrants, rejecting their arguments that they were eligible. Any hope of Chinese naturalization ended with the part of the Chinese Exclusion Act of 1882 that said: "hereafter no State Court or Court of the United States shall admit Chinese to citizenship." In *Fong Yue Ting,* the Supreme Court declared: "Chinese persons not born in this country have never been recognized as citizens of the United States, nor authorized to become such under the naturalization laws." The affirmation of birthright citizenship in *Wong Kim Ark* did nothing to lift this naturalization bar.[28]

In spite of the apparent bar to Asians, a few Chinese, Japanese, and Indian immigrants naturalized up through the early 1920s. In 1922, the U.S. Supreme Court unanimously put a stop to this in *Ozawa v. United States.* Takao Ozawa was born in Kanazawa Prefecture, Japan, in 1875 and came to San Francisco in 1894, when he was in his late teens. He graduated from Berkeley High School and attended the University of California for three years. In 1906, he moved to Honolulu, where he worked for an American company. He was married with two children. Ozawa met all naturalization requirements except race, and he was "the paragon of an assimilated Japanese immigrant," in historian Yuji Ichioka's words. Like others who sued to naturalize, he argued that he was "white" but did not challenge the racial bar itself. The Supreme Court rejected Ozawa's petition. Adopting a reasoning that mixed popular and scientific notions of race, the Court held that a "person of the Japanese race" was not white. Japanese continued to be barred from naturalization until 1952.[29]

A year after *Ozawa,* the Supreme Court heard the case of Bhagat Singh Thind, "a high-caste Hindu of full Indian blood" who was serving in the U.S. Army at Fort Lewis, Washington. Again, the Court held that this Asian immigrant was not white. The Court echoed the popular notions of race in *Ozawa,* but this time its reasoning repudiated any reliance on scientific definitions. "White" was to be interpreted "in accordance with the understanding of the common man," whether or not "certain scientific authorities" would classify someone as "Caucasian." In contrast to these rejections of applicants from Japan and India, numerous lower courts in this period held that immigrants from the Middle East were white and eligible to naturalize.[30]

Eligibility began to expand with the Nationality Act of 1940, which included "races indigenous to the Western hemisphere," including Native Americans and persons of Mexican ancestry. Congress extended eligibility to immigrants from China in 1943 and India in 1946. The situation was more complex for the Philippines, a U.S. possession ceded by Spain after the Spanish-American War of 1898. Filipinos became noncitizen U.S. nationals, a status between citizen and alien. They were able to travel freely to the United States, but they could not naturalize because they were neither white nor black. In 1946, just two days before the United States granted the Philippines independence, which made Filipinos noncitizens, federal legislation repealed the bars to Filipino naturalization. Only in 1952, in a Cold War arena in which the United States could ill afford the taint of a racist citizenship law, did citizenship open up to all. Section 311 of the Immigration and Nationality Act now provides: "The right of a person to become a naturalized citizen of the United States shall not be denied or abridged because of race or sex or because such person is married."[31]

The link between citizenship and race should make clear that the phrase "ineligible to citizenship" in various alienage laws up through and even beyond World War II was a thinly veiled reference to Asian immigrants. The phrase allowed legislators to leverage racial naturalization bars into other laws that discriminated by race. For example, a proposed amendment in 1920 to the U.S. Constitution would have denied birthright citizenship to any child born in the United States to parents who were "ineligible to citizenship." The amendment's principal sponsor was U.S. Senator James Phelan of California, who had been mayor of San Francisco from 1897 to 1903 and was an outspoken antagonist of Asian immigrants—having proposed, for example, that San Francisco's Chinatown be moved outside the city limits after the 1906 earthquake.[32]

This role for the concept of "ineligible to citizenship" was most clear in the alien land laws, which barred noncitizen acquisition of property by deed or inheritance, and conveyance of property by will. Laws limiting property ownership by noncitizens had historical roots in the common law of property, with its feudal notions of fealty to the landowner. But California Attorney General Ulysses S. Webb, the author of his state's 1913

Alien Land Law, explained: "The fundamental basis of all legislation upon this subject, State and Federal, has been, and is, race undesirability." In 1920, California closed a loophole in its 1913 law that had allowed leasing land or holding title in the name of a native-born minor. By World War II, statutes that barred land ownership by aliens ineligible to citizenship were on the books in nine states: Arizona, California, Idaho, Kansas, Louisiana, Montana, New Mexico, Oregon, and Washington.[33]

A few decisions in this period invalidated other types of alienage laws. Besides *Truax*, decided by the Supreme Court in 1915, its 1931 decision in *Russian Volunteer Fleet v. United States* held that the Fifth Amendment prohibits the government from taking the property of non-enemy noncitizens in the United States without just compensation. But these decisions did not invalidate race or nationality discrimination as *Yick Wo* had done. In a series of decisions starting in 1923, the U.S. Supreme Court upheld the constitutionality of the alien land laws, citing the need to monitor the quality and allegiance of landowners and rejecting arguments that these provisions violated treaties and the Fourteenth Amendment. The Court relied on the formal distinction between noncitizens who could become citizens and those who could not, without ever examining its racial foundation.[34] These decisions sustaining the alien land laws show how little effect *Yick Wo* and its idea of territorial personhood had during this period. Constitutional protections for noncitizens seemed very limited not only in immigration law but in alienage law as well. A broader recognition of noncitizens' rights would emerge, but only with time.

Territorial Personhood Today

A 1943 amendment to California's Fish and Game Code barred the issuance of commercial fishing licenses to "alien Japanese." In 1945, the legislature changed this to bar any "person ineligible to citizenship," which still included Japanese, Koreans, and non-Chinese from Southeast Asia. In 1948, the U.S. Supreme Court struck down this statute in *Takahashi v. Fish and Game Commission*. The Court rejected California's argument, based on *Truax*, that the state was an owner-trustee of all fish in its coastal waters, reserved for citizens as a special public interest. Relying on territorial personhood and citing *Yick Wo* and *Truax*, the Court held that the Constitution protects "all persons lawfully in this country" from state discrimination that curtails opportunities for individuals to make a living.

Takahashi did not completely outlaw distinctions between citizens and noncitizens, and it merely distinguished (without overruling) prior decisions upholding alien land laws as involving the traditional state power to control ownership of land, peculiar to real property. But the *Takahashi* Court's attitude toward noncitizens, especially its adoption of territorial personhood by extending protections to "all persons lawfully in this country," was much more in keeping with *Yick Wo* than with the earlier Court decisions upholding race-based alienage laws.[35]

In 1952, the California Supreme Court, relying largely on this reading of *Takahashi*, finally struck down its alien land laws as race discrimination that violated the Fourteenth Amendment to the U.S. Constitution.[36] And yet, *Takahashi* left open many questions about the constitutionality of other alienage classifications that were not race-based, and these questions would take time to resolve. But first I should discuss the leading recent example of territorial personhood in a U.S. Supreme Court decision.

The thinking based on the idea of territorial personhood articulated in *Yick Wo* reached its modern zenith more than thirty years after *Takahashi*, in *Plyler v. Doe*, a 1982 U.S. Supreme Court decision. In 1975, Texas enacted a statute that effectively barred undocumented children from attending public schools. The *Plyler* case started in the city of Tyler in eastern Texas. The local school board, which had at first ignored the state law, decided in July 1977 to charge undocumented children $1,000 to attend public schools. A lawsuit in Tyler, and then other suits elsewhere in Texas, challenged the statute's constitutionality. In hearing this challenge, the U.S. Supreme Court required the state of Texas to show only that the statute furthered "some substantial goal of the State," as opposed to the more demanding requirement of a compelling state interest. But the Court found that the statute served no such substantial goal and that it was therefore unconstitutional.

Plyler is an important example of a modern constitutional decision that emphasized territorial personhood even when the noncitizens were unlawfully in the United States. Relying heavily on *Yick Wo* and *Wong Wing*, the *Plyler* Court established that even some undocumented noncitizens are entitled to some protections under the U.S. Constitution. Justice Brennan wrote for the Court that the basis for this protection is their presence on U.S. territory: "Aliens, even aliens whose presence in this country is unlawful, have long been recognized as 'persons' guaranteed due process of law by the Fifth and Fourteenth Amendments."[37]

This rationale contrasts with the contract-based approaches that the Court might have adopted. It could have but did not cite a contract-based rationale to support its decision to grant relief. For example, the Court might have emphasized that undocumented workers (and their children) have been invited to come to the United States through the historical pattern of recruiting Mexican workers for jobs in Texas, and that this invitation implied certain promises. Justice Brennan did hint at this view of unlawful presence, but he did not rely on contract in his core analysis. Or, instead of granting relief, the Court might have denied it on the ground that undocumented noncitizens had violated the terms of the immigration contract in the most basic way—by being illegally present. Although, as legal scholar Linda Bosniak has observed, it mattered a great to deal to the Court that the *Plyler* plaintiffs were children whose presence in the United States was involuntary, the Court could have concluded that it was the families that had violated the immigration contract. But *Plyler* says nothing of this sort.[38]

The *Plyler* Court briefly mentioned ties in the United States and cited an attorney general's report that called the undocumented population "productive and law-abiding members" of the community who had a "permanent attachment" to the United States. This language hints at immigration as affiliation, but it appeared only in a fleeting footnote, and it did not seem to matter to the Court if individual noncitizens had been in the United States for any length of time or had any actual ties. *Plyler* extended constitutional protections to the undocumented not based on immigration as contract or affiliation, but rather on presence on U.S. territory. In this key sense, *Plyler* is a decision very much in the territorial personhood branch of the *Yick Wo* tradition.

Crucial to the development of territorial personhood from *Yick Wo* to *Plyler* was the parallel emergence of international human rights as a strong influence on prevailing thought about immigration and immigrants. The inclusion of international law—and with it, international human rights law—in talk about immigration completes a full circle that began more than a century ago in the formative years of the plenary power doctrine. Legislators and judges of that era talked about immigration law as a part of international law as traditionally conceived—as governing relations among sovereign states, or as a law of nations, as international law was often called. It was not a concept of international law that recognized individuals as having rights and responsibilities, or as having much of a role at all.[39]

In a fundamental shift, this traditional version of international law yielded gradually to the idea that sovereign states owe international law obligations to individuals, both citizens and noncitizens. The recognition of international human rights goes back at least as far as the Treaty of Westphalia in 1648, which required religious toleration by the signatory princes and monarchs. But the most obvious sign of the modern phase of international human rights has been the dramatic proliferation since World War II of conventions that address the relationship between sovereign states and individuals. Some of these obligations toward noncitizens concern immigration law, including human rights–based limits on a country's power to deport or exclude noncitizens. A key example is the principle that a country may not send noncitizens to a country where they would face certain forms of persecution. Exponential growth in international trade and travel has also heightened awareness of the status of individuals in international law. International human rights also draws support from transnational and postnational scholarship that questions the very legitimacy of national boundaries. All of these changes make it natural to think about noncitizens in the United States as a matter not only of U.S. law, but also of international human rights.[40]

The emergence of an international human rights emphasis brings international law into immigration law in ways that often help noncitizens—a contrast to the early plenary power cases, in which international law arguments generally went against noncitizens. For example, the international law foundation of the *Chinese Exclusion Case* led the Supreme Court to conclude that if exclusion of Chinese immigrants was wrongful, the Chinese government would have to seek any available remedy from the U.S. government. Today, international human rights serve as the foundation of arguments that international migration should be unregulated, that national borders should not exist, or that distinctions between citizens and noncitizens are inherently illegitimate. More modest versions of arguments based on international human rights link human rights protections to presence within a country's borders, and in this sense these arguments come close to the idea of territorial personhood that started in *Yick Wo* and continued through *Plyler* and beyond.[41]

CHAPTER 4

Alienage and the Ties That Bind

★

Elsie Mary Jane Leger was born in Scotland in 1937 and came to the United States as a lawful immigrant in 1965, at the age of twenty-eight. She worked for two years for a family in Havertown, Pennsylvania, then left in 1967 for a better paying job in Philadelphia, ten miles to the east. In 1969, illness forced both her and her husband to stop working. They applied for public assistance, but neither was eligible for federal programs. Her husband qualified for the Pennsylvania state program, but Elsie Leger was denied state coverage because she was not a citizen. She challenged Pennsylvania's citizenship requirement in a class-action lawsuit.

The U.S. Supreme Court heard her case together with a challenge to an Arizona law that said noncitizens were eligible for welfare only if they had lived in the United States for fifteen years. In 1971, the Court struck down both state laws in *Graham v. Richardson*, holding that they violated equal protection by treating citizens and noncitizens differently without adequate justification. The Court also held that these laws exceeded state power to distinguish citizens from noncitizens.[1]

Territorial personhood was not the only legacy of *Yick Wo*. Far more significant than the territorial personhood branch of *Yick Wo* has been the branch that became immigration as affiliation. The Supreme Court's reasoning in *Graham v. Richardson*, while clearly part of *Yick Wo*'s modern legacy, went beyond the territorial personhood that was key to *Yick Wo* and *Wong Wing*, and later to *Plyler*. Over the second half of the twentieth century, immigration as affiliation emerged to compete with immigration as contract as the two dominant ways of thinking and talking about lawful immigrants.

Equal Protection and Alienage

The U.S. Constitution sometimes forbids the government from treating two groups of persons differently. Of course, not all differences in treatment violate the Constitution. For example, laws treat persons differently if they have been convicted of crimes. Whether any difference is permissible depends heavily on what test the court applies to decide its constitutionality. At one end of the spectrum, courts are highly deferential and simply ask if the difference in treatment has a "rational basis." In some situations, courts apply an intermediate level of scrutiny, for example by requiring a substantial state goal, as the Supreme Court did in *Plyler v. Doe*. At the other end of the spectrum, courts intervene much more assertively and apply "strict scrutiny." The government then can justify the different treatment only by showing that it is the least onerous way to serve a compelling government interest. Strict scrutiny applies, for example, to discrimination against racial minorities.

Graham is sometimes cited for the idea that noncitizens enjoy a degree of judicial protection against discrimination that approaches strict scrutiny. The source of this idea in *Graham* is the Court's statements that laws that distinguish by alienage are "inherently suspect" and that noncitizens are a " 'discrete and insular' minority" for whom "heightened judicial solicitude is appropriate."[2] The apparent rationale is that noncitizens, unable to vote, have little or no political power, so they need the courts to protect them. This suggestion of strict scrutiny by courts is the part of *Graham* that has attracted the most attention, but how the Court thought more generally about immigrants is at least as significant.

In asking when citizens and noncitizens may be treated differently in alienage law, *Graham* did not view immigration as contract. The Court did not characterize the position of noncitizens as a matter of the terms of their admission, or as a matter of any promise by them to be self-sufficient. And though the Court cited *Yick Wo*, *Truax*, and *Takahashi*, its rationale was not limited to the territorial personhood that had been central to the outcomes in those cases. Instead, the *Graham* Court stressed that these lawful immigrants had meaningful ties in the United States: "Aliens like citizens pay taxes and may be called into the armed forces . . . [A]liens may live within a state for many years, work in the state and contribute to the economic growth of the state."[3]

The Court also emphasized these immigrants' ties when it rejected the argument that these state alienage laws were justified by a special public interest that states could reserve for their own citizens. According to *Graham*, "There can be no 'special public interest' in tax revenues to which aliens have contributed on an equal basis with the residents of the States."[4] Adopting a view of immigration that went beyond immigration as contract and territorial personhood, the *Graham* Court in this passage recognized immigration as affiliation as a central basis for explaining the place of noncitizens in America.

After *Graham*, immigration as affiliation became more influential as courts invalidated a number of alienage laws as unconstitutional. In 1973, the Supreme Court struck down a New York requirement that state employees be U.S. citizens. The Court again relied on a lawful immigrant's ties: "A resident alien may reside lawfully in New York for a long period of time. He must pay taxes. And he is subject to service in this country's Armed Forces." Another Supreme Court decision adopted the same rationale to find that states may not require attorneys to be citizens.[5]

Though immigration as affiliation is grounded in the territorial personhood recognized in *Yick Wo*, affiliation implies more robust protections for noncitizens based not just on their presence in the United States, but also on the ties that they acquire. The differences between noncitizens and citizens should diminish as noncitizens' ties to American society become more meaningful. This is true for all noncitizens in the United States, but especially for lawful immigrants. With the emergence of immigration as affiliation, thinking about lawful immigrants moved away from exclusive reliance on the terms of their initial admission or physical presence in the United States. Instead, lawful immigrants derive the position in law from their role in society's everyday functioning, especially in the home and workplace—or as Peter Schuck has put it, "from the nature of their social interactions and commitments."[6]

Alienage Law, Federalism, and Affiliation

Graham involved state law, not federal. Because many of the laws that treat citizens and noncitizens differently have historically been state or local laws, *Graham* effectively reduced differential treatment of citizens and lawful immigrants. But it left open the question of how much power the *federal* government has to treat citizens and noncitizens differently. The backdrop for this question is the shift from state to federal immigration law in the mid- to late 1800s described in chapter 1. That shift involved the power to address the core immigration areas of admission and deportation, and not necessarily to enact alienage laws. But the federal preemption of state authority over immigration law at least raised the question whether the federal government would similarly have greater, if not exclusive, power to enact alienage laws as well.

The plaintiffs in the class-action lawsuit that would largely answer this question were three Cuban refugees. Santiago Diaz and Jose Clara were old enough for federal Medicare, but they did not meet the requirement that noncitizens be permanent residents who have lived in the United States for five years.[7] Diaz and Clara were lawfully in the United States but were not permanent residents. At the time, it was common practice for the U.S. government to parole Cubans into the country. Parole allowed them to live and work here, and eventually almost all of them became permanent residents under special legislation. Another plaintiff, Victor Carlos Espinosa, was a permanent resident, but not for the required five years. Diaz, Clara, and Espinosa challenged the five-year and permanent residence requirements as unconstitutional discrimination.

In 1976, the U.S. Supreme Court rejected this challenge in *Mathews v. Diaz*. The Court started by listing a number of federal constitutional provisions and statutes that treat citizens and noncitizens differently. Distinguishing *Graham*, the Court relied heavily on the greater power of the federal government to classify by alienage as compared to states and localities. But the Court did not just apply the simple preemption-based idea that the federal government can treat noncitizens differently while the states cannot. Justice Stevens's analysis for the unanimous Court was more textured: "equal protection analysis . . . involves significantly different considerations because it concerns the relationship between aliens and the States rather than between aliens and the Federal Government."[8] Therefore a federal law that treats citizens and noncitizens differently needs only a rational basis to be constitutional. In contrast, state alienage laws like the welfare statutes in *Graham* must meet the much more demanding (and usually fatal) requirement that it be the least onerous way to meet a compelling state interest.

In *Graham*, the states of Arizona and Pennsylvania could not point to needs based on national interest or national citizenship to justify their welfare laws. Nor could Arizona or Pennsylvania claim that they were trying to control immigration by means of welfare-based disincentives to settle there, given exclusive federal authority to regulate immigration. In contrast to the state laws in *Graham*, federal alienage laws typically withstand constitutional challenges, because the federal government can classify by citizenship in ways that states cannot. As the *Diaz* Court put it, "it is the business of the political branches of the Federal Government, rather than that of either the States or the Federal Judiciary, to regulate the conditions of entry and residence of aliens."[9]

As with *Graham*, most of the attention that courts and commentators have paid to *Diaz* has focused on the outcome. The noncitizens won in *Graham*; they lost in *Diaz*. Lower courts have relied on *Diaz* in upholding various rules requiring federal citizenship. They typically quote this sentence from Justice Stevens's opinion: "In the exercise of its broad power over naturalization and immigration, Congress regularly makes rules that would be unacceptable if applied to citizens." This language from *Diaz* seems to suggest that the courts' reluctance under the plenary power doctrine to examine immigration laws for constitutionality should apply to alienage laws as well. If this is true, then the federal government's power to treat citizens and lawful immigrants differently may be practically unrestrained by the Constitution.[10]

I doubt that *Diaz* goes so far. As legal scholar Alex Aleinikoff has observed, Justice Stevens's statement referred to admission and deportation decisions, not alienage law distinctions between citizens and noncitizens. Moreover, *Diaz* took a constitutional challenge to an alienage law seriously, in contrast to immigration law decisions that rely on plenary power. *Diaz* carefully examined the rule that barred some permanent residents from Medicare, rather than rejecting out of hand the argument that the rule was unconstitutional. *Diaz* contrasts with a Supreme Court decision just one year later—*Fiallo v. Bell*, discussed later in this chapter—that was much more deferential to the federal government in upholding an immigration admission statute that treated certain fathers and mothers differently.[11] Nothing in *Diaz* suggests that the Court was exercising the sort of blanket judicial deference that would have upheld a Medicare eligibility rule that treated fathers and mothers differently.

The most significant aspect of the U.S. Supreme Court's constitutional scrutiny in *Diaz* is how the Court's approach closely resembled the affiliation-based reasoning in *Graham*, even if the outcome was different. *Diaz*, like *Graham*, started with the territorial personhood that was central to *Yick Wo* and *Wong Wing*, and which later figured prominently in *Plyler*. *Diaz* thus first looked beyond citizenship or immigration status: "The Fifth Amendment, as well as the Fourteenth Amendment, protects every one of these persons from deprivation of life, liberty, or property without due process of law." The Court cited *Wong Wing* for the principle that the Constitution protects noncitizens from deprivations of life, liberty, or property without due process, even if their presence in the country is unlawful, involuntary, or transitory.[12]

Then, however, *Diaz* went beyond territorial personhood and embraced affiliation as essential to understanding the constitutional rights of noncitizens. The real question, Justice Stevens wrote, "is not whether discrimination between citizens and aliens is permissible; rather it is whether the statutory discrimination within the class of aliens—allowing benefits to some aliens but not to others—is permissible." Some noncitizens can share in the nation's resources, but others cannot. "Neither the overnight visitor, the unfriendly agent of a hostile foreign power, the resident diplomat, nor the illegal entrant, can advance even a colorable constitutional claim to a share in the bounty that a conscientious sovereign makes available to its own citizens and some of its guests."[13]

What matters are a noncitizen's ties. "The decision to share that bounty with our guests may take into account the character of the relationship between the alien and this country: Congress may decide that as the alien's tie grows stronger, so does the strength of his claim to an equal share of that munificence." Stevens continued: "it is unquestionably reasonable for Congress to make an alien's eligibility depend on both the character and the duration of his residence." And finally: "In short, citizens and those who are most like citizens qualify. Those who are less like citizens do not." All of this reflects immigration as affiliation.[14]

Affiliation and Welfare Reform

Part of chapter 2 analyzed the significant role of immigration as contract in both legislation and litigation in the 1990s concerning welfare eligibility for noncitizens. But immigration as affiliation played just as large a role, which should not be surprising since both *Graham* and *Diaz* were cases involving public assistance. Affiliation shaped Congress's decision first to enact the 1996 bars, then the legal challenges, and later the laws restoring eligibility for some noncitizens. Like contract, affiliation was crucial to arguments on both sides. In the original legislation, for example, noncitizen eligibility depended partly on ties; the bars never applied to noncitizens who had worked ten years in the United States without receiving federal welfare.[15]

Affiliation next became the conceptual basis for the many court decisions that sustained the bars as constitutional. Typical is the 1999 federal appeals court decision in *City of Chicago v. Shalala*. The individual plaintiffs were lawful immigrants who had been in the United States and who had received or were eligible to receive federal Supplemental Security Income (SSI) and food stamps in August 1996. Their co-plaintiff, the city of Chicago, claimed that the restrictions imposed substantial financial burdens on it. The plaintiffs together alleged that it was unconstitutional to bar lawful immigrants from these federal benefits.[16]

Both *Graham* and *Diaz* were central to the reasoning in *City of Chicago*. The appeals court easily distinguished *Graham* as involving state laws. The harder question was whether the government's victory in *Diaz*, upholding a federal law, controlled so as to compel the same result. That a federal citizenship requirement *could* be invalid was clear from *Hampton v. Mow Sun Wong*, decided the same day as *Diaz*. In *Mow Sun Wong*, the Court struck down a Civil Service Commission citizenship requirement for federal employment, because the commission had not acted pursuant to the federal immigration and naturalization power. The Court suggested, however, that both Congress and the president could bar noncitizens from federal jobs. The citizenship requirement for federal employment was invalid because the wrong federal agency had adopted it. Lower courts later upheld an executive order from President Gerald Ford that imposed a requirement almost identical to the original version.[17]

In contrast to *Mow Sun Wong*, the 1996 welfare bars came directly from a Congress fully aware of the immigration and naturalization implications. Accordingly, the federal appeals court in *City of Chicago* found little room for second-guessing Congress. The court framed the issue as whether there was a rational basis for barring these lawful immigrants from food stamps and SSI. The court then found that the welfare bars had at least four rational purposes: encouraging noncitizens' financial self-sufficiency, discouraging immigration that might be motivated by availability of welfare benefits, reducing the costs of federal benefits programs, and encouraging naturalization.[18]

Like the Supreme Court in *Diaz*, the appeals court in *City of Chicago* saw the issue not as a line between citizens and noncitizens, but between two groups of noncitizens. Then, to explain the constitutionality of the line that Congress had drawn, *City of Chicago* relied heavily on ties and immigration as affiliation. Congress could rationally extend benefits to noncitizens who had made "special contributions to this country," either to "reward such service or to encourage other aliens to make similar contributions in the future." Other federal court decisions that rejected similar constitutional challenges also emphasized ties to distinguish some noncitizens from others. And in Congress, many of the critics of the 1996 cutbacks made affiliation-based arguments that Congress had not recognized ties adequately. These arguments led to the restoration of many of the benefits taken away in 1996.[19]

To be sure, the outcomes in *Graham*, *Diaz*, and *City of Chicago* can be explained in ways that do not involve immigration as affiliation. One could argue, for example, that these decisions follow *Yick Wo* and *Plyler* in reflecting territorial personhood. The Court *could* have reached the outcomes in *Graham* and *Diaz* with a rationale based on territorial personhood or something else, perhaps even based on immigration as contract or immigration as a transition to citizenship. But my focus is the rhetoric and rationale that actually have surfaced in alienage law to allow lawful immigrants and citizens to be treated alike in many situations. Here the key has been an emphasis on the ties that noncitizens develop in the United States—or in other words, immigration as affiliation.

Affiliation in Context

Affiliation's emergence as a basis for recognizing lawful immigrants makes sense—as Peter Schuck has analyzed—against the backdrop of trends in the American legal tradition and a sea change toward a more complex and interdependent society. In the generation following the Depression and New Deal, the United States evolved into a modern welfare state. This transformation fundamentally changed the relationship between the government and the economy. Government programs expanded dramatically during the 1930s to include the white middle class, city dwellers and farmers, citizens and noncitizens alike. The idea emerged that legal obligation should not and perhaps could not be defined, explained, or justified exclusively by express agreement and consent freely undertaken between private parties or a private party and the government, but rather by less concrete and more elusive notions of justice that were not necessarily based on express and voluntary consent or other elements of contract.[20]

In tort law, accident liability expanded to include the modern idea that liability for harm caused by defective products would be strict liability. If a defective automobile hurt someone using it, the manufacturer would be liable, even without the user having to prove that he had bought the automobile directly from the manufacturer, or that the manufacturer was negligent. Liability did not require the defendant's actual fault. Similarly, contract law shifted emphasis away from obligation defined principally by freedom of contract based on express consent and toward greater reliance on concepts beyond consent and agreement. Courts used the idea of unconscionability to decline to enforce apparent agreements between parties if one side had vastly superior bargaining power and the contract terms were so one-sided that they seemed unfair. Courts more readily enforced contracts that had not formed under the traditional rules requiring offer, acceptance, and an exchange of value. Absolute property rights based on the physical possession of land gave way to broader societal controls like zoning.[21]

Under prior law, a court in one state could hear a lawsuit and render judgment against a defendant who did not live in that state, but only if the defendant or his property could be found physically within state boundaries. Such physical presence was taken as a sign of voluntary submission to court jurisdiction. This sort of jurisdiction over nonresident defendants came to depend not on physical presence, but on an overall assessment of direct and indirect contacts with that state, and on an unstructured inquiry into whether jurisdiction would be consistent with "fair play and substantial justice." These changes in contract, tort, and property law, as well as in court jurisdiction, were all consistent with a greater emphasis on the everyday effects of government decisions, especially how those decisions would affect noncitizens' ties in America.[22]

Understanding Immigration as Affiliation

Understanding immigration as affiliation begins with comparing it to immigration as contract, which reflects a belief that fair and just decisions can be reached without equality for lawful immigrants. As I explained at the end of chapter 2, this is a model of justice, but it is justice without equality, or what might be called unequal justice. Its rationale is that the need for equality presumes belonging, and that this presumption is misplaced in immigration and citizenship, where it is fundamental that noncitizens do not belong.

By comparison, immigration as affiliation responds to the question of who may claim equality with an answer that is much more inclusive of lawful immigrants. However, immigration as affiliation does not say that equality is inherent in lawful immigrant status. Rather, lawful immigrants can earn an imperfect approximation of equality as they establish ties in the United States over time. They do not earn complete equality while they are still noncitizens, for doing so would mean attaining citizenship itself. But based on ties, some lawful immigrants earn something closer to equality with citizens than other noncitizens acquire. Immigration as affiliation produces not a bright citizen-noncitizen line, but rather a spectrum that arrays lawful immigrants depending on whether they are more like citizens or less like citizens.

This affiliation-based approach reflects two strong intuitions, which combine to explain why immigration as affiliation has persuasive power. One of these intuitions is that coming to America is not a stark moment of choice on the immigrant's part or a sudden acceptance on her new country's part. Instead, it is a gradual decline in a newcomer's attachment to her former country as part of an incremental process in which her life's center of gravity shifts to the United States. Immigration as affiliation recognizes this change in an immigrant's life.[23]

Immigration as affiliation also reflects the intuition that in this world of nation-states, it is an essential part of personal identity to belong to one of them, and that belonging is principally a matter of social connections. Even if this belonging is something less than citizenship itself, it seems unjust to disregard a lawful immigrant's life in America. To do so would leave her recognized as belonging only in another country, typically where she is a citizen but lacks real connections. This sense of injustice may be keen if she did not come to America as a choice freely made, but due to flight under economic or political duress. This is also why it is troubling to deny birthright citizenship to the children of the undocumented; they may end up with citizenship nowhere.[24]

Beyond these two intuitions, immigration as affiliation is also appealing because it is conveniently neutral on the very difficult question of whether the integration of immigrants into American society should be a goal of government policy. Immigration as affiliation regards noncitizens' ties as natural phenomena, with no government position to foster or not foster those ties. If ties emerge, immigration as affiliation recognizes them. In contrast, immigration as contract and immigration as transition raise contentious questions that immigration as affiliation does not. Contract implies that a noncitizen's terms of belonging are predetermined at the time of his arrival, but it is hard to determine what those terms are. And as later chapters discuss, immigration as transition implies affirmative government support for integration of lawful immigrants, but it is hard to decide what support should look like. Affiliation avoids these hard choices by letting official policy be minimalist or nonexistent. It may be bad policy to avoid hard choices, but the opportunity to do so may further explain why immigration as affiliation is attractive for some decision makers.

Another persuasive feature of immigration as affiliation is that it rightly acknowledges—though indirectly—that immigration law and alienage law affect noncitizens and citizens. The question is one of perspective for evaluating a statute or government decision that excludes or deports a group or an individual. One option is to ask only how the decision affects the noncitizens who are excluded or deported. Or the inquiry might broaden to ask how the government decision affects U.S. citizens who are the immigrants' relatives or employers, or who belong in some sense to the same community, or who otherwise have an interest in having the noncitizen lawfully in the United States.

Two U.S. Supreme Court cases from the 1970s raised the issue. The first is the Court's 1972 decision in *Kleindienst v. Mandel*. Ernst Mandel was a well-known Belgian author who described himself as a revolutionary Marxist but said that he was not a member of any Communist party. In 1969, professors and student groups at Stanford, Princeton, Amherst, Columbia, and Vassar invited him to give lectures. Mandel also had speaking invitations from groups in New York City and Cambridge, Massachusetts.

As chapter 2 sketched, federal immigration law has long excluded noncitizens for a variety of ideological and national security grounds. When Mandel applied for a temporary visitor's visa, the statute barred aliens who advocated "the economic, international, and governmental doctrines of world communism."[25] On Mandel's two prior visits to the United States, the government had—unknown to Mandel—waived this exclusion ground, granted the visa, and admitted him. This time, the government denied a waiver on the ground that he had violated the terms of his earlier admissions by straying from the stated purposes of those visits. Mandel and several of his host professors sued to challenge the denial of the visa. They claimed that applying this exclusion ground to Mandel and denying a waiver violated their First Amendment freedoms of speech and association.

The Supreme Court decided *Mandel* by first dismissing the argument that Mandel had any constitutional right to entry into the United States. It then addressed what the Court apparently saw as the central question in the case: whether U.S. citizens had a right to meet with Mandel and hear him speak in the United States. The Court's response was dismissive; the citizen professors' "First Amendment argument would prove too much. In almost every instance of an alien excludable under [the statute], there are probably those who would wish to meet and speak with him." Citing the plenary power doctrine, the Court found that the visa denial was constitutional because the government had satisfied the undemanding standard of a "facially legitimate and bona fide reason" for the decision.[26] The nominal issue was the rights of U.S. citizens, but the Court saw citizens' rights in immigration law matters as very weak and as adding very little to whatever weak rights Mandel could assert.

This citizens' perspective issue resurfaced five years later in the Supreme Court's 1977 decision in *Fiallo v. Bell*. This case combined the efforts of several families to be reunited in the United States. One situation involved Cleophus Warner, who had immigrated from the French West Indies. His son, Serge, was born there out of wedlock in 1960. Cleophus acknowledged paternity and provided financial support from birth, and his name was on Serge's birth certificate. Cleophus naturalized as a U.S. citizen and tried to sponsor Serge to immigrate. In another family, the brothers Trevor and Earl Wilson were born out of wedlock in Jamaica in the late 1950s. They lived there with their father, Arthur Wilson, until 1968, when Trevor was eleven and Earl nine years old. That year, the boys moved to New York City with their mother as lawful immigrants. Arthur kept in touch with his sons through letters and occasional visits, and he supported them financially. When their mother died in 1974, the boys asked their father to join them in New York.

Though admission as a lawful immigrant can be based on a parent-child relationship, the statute at that time defined the parent-child relationship to include unwed mothers but generally not unwed fathers.[27] One exception was through legitimation under the law of the child or father's residence or domicile. But Serge's mother had remarried, which made it impossible for Cleophus to legitimate Serge under French West Indies law. Cleophus, though a U.S. citizen, thus could not petition for Serge to immigrate. Similarly, the lawful immigrants Trevor and Earl had never been legitimated under Jamaican law, so they could not petition for their father. The Warners, the Wilsons, and a third family—the Fiallos—argued that this statute unconstitutionally discriminated by gender and legitimacy.

The Supreme Court rejected the families' argument that treating unwed fathers differently "infringed upon the due process rights of citizens and legal permanent residents, or implicated 'the fundamental constitutional interests of U.S. citizens and permanent residents in a familial relationship.'" But there was precious little analysis of the statute's effects on citizens and their constitutional rights. Instead, the Court simply cited the plenary power doctrine for deference to Congress, and *Mandel* for having rejected "the suggestion that more searching judicial inquiry is required" when effects on U.S. citizens are at stake.[28]

In both *Mandel* and *Fiallo*, the U.S. Supreme Court refused to take seriously the argument that denying admission to noncitizens can hurt citizens. A few other challenges to government immigration decisions have proceeded as citizens' rights claims, but they have generally been just as unsuccessful. An example from the early 1990s, very similar in reasoning to *Mandel*, is the federal appeals court decision in *Haitian Refugee Center v. Baker*. The government had restricted access by Haitian asylum seekers to volunteer legal counsel. The plaintiffs were not the asylum seekers, who might have asserted a right to counsel under the Fifth Amendment's due process clause. Instead, the plaintiffs were U.S. citizens who asserted a right to *provide* counsel as part of their First Amendment freedoms of association and speech. The court rejected this argument, reasoning that because the asylum seekers had no rights, it would be "nonsensical" to find that the plaintiffs had a right to advise the asylum seekers of their rights.[29]

An example of somewhat more successful citizens' rights argument involved the closure of some immigration proceedings for national security reasons soon after the terrorist attacks of September 11, 2001. Chief Immigration Judge Michael Creppy, acting on orders from Attorney General John Ashcroft, issued a directive that closed immigration proceedings in more than one thousand "special interest" cases to all observers, including family members and the press. The directive did not define this category of cases, but most involved removal of noncitizens who are from predominantly Arab or Muslim countries. Several lawsuits challenged the constitutionality of this directive. The plaintiffs were not the noncitizens who were being threatened with removal, but rather newspapers and other media that asserted their right of access as part of freedom of the press under the First Amendment. In one lawsuit, a federal appeals court in Michigan ordered that an immigration court hearing be opened. In another lawsuit, a federal appeals court in New Jersey kept an immigration hearing closed. The U.S. Supreme Court declined to address the issue.[30]

The Creppy directive cases resembled *Mandel* and *Fiallo*, but were crucially different. When the appeals court in Michigan opened the immigration court hearing, it vindicated the access rights of the media as distinct, non-immigration rights that were grounded in First Amendment freedom of the press, and which were therefore unlike the rights of the professors in *Mandel* or the citizen-sponsors in *Fiallo*. The appeals court did not act to protect the interests of citizens who wanted to prevent the removal of the noncitizens whose cases were in immigration court.

By avoiding a serious analysis of the rights of affected citizens in immigration cases, *Mandel* and *Fiallo* have had the practical effect of disregarding a noncitizen's ties in the United States. This is because citizens who are affected by a government immigration decision often *are* the ties that a noncitizen, especially a lawful immigrant, has in the United States. In this sense, *Mandel* and *Fiallo* run counter to immigration as affiliation. But the fact that these decisions do not seriously analyze the rights of affected citizens is precisely one of the reasons that it is attractive to view immigration as affiliation. If courts will not take a serious look at the rights of affected citizens, it makes sense as an alternative to capture the effects of government decisions on U.S. citizens indirectly, by evaluating noncitizens' ties in the United States.

This is exactly what immigration as affiliation does. By definition, it generates laws and policies that protect noncitizens with stronger ties to this country. In alienage law, for example, if affiliation-based rules grant welfare to lawful immigrants who have been in the United States for a long time, then those eligible will be those most likely to have citizen spouses and children. And as chapter 5 will explain, affiliation-based rules limit the deportation of noncitizens who have close relatives who are citizens or lawful immigrants. Immigration as affiliation thus minimizes the adverse effects on citizens of the government's decisions. This compensates for the tendency of courts to assess the rights of noncitizens who want to come to the United States or stay here but to disregard the rights of citizens who want them here.

Though these attractions of affiliation help account for its emergence over the past half-century as a counterweight to immigration as contract, immigration as affiliation remains an incomplete view of immigration. Affiliation cannot substitute for contract-based ideas in providing some sense of control over immigration and what it means to have immigrants in the United States. Immigration as contract responds to this need for apparent control by suggesting, for example, that the costs associated with welfare eligibility can be predetermined as a matter of what is promised and what is not. It may sometimes seem as if official recognition of a longtime lawful immigrant's ties has displaced the idea of an agreement implicit in coming to America, but the appeal of contract-based ideas remains powerful.

A second problem with immigration as affiliation comes from its core idea that lawful immigrants should be treated more like citizens with the passage of time. This means that immigration as affiliation reduces or eliminates incentives to naturalize after the qualifying period, normally five years. Take, for example, the Medicare eligibility rule upheld in *Diaz*, which treats lawful immigrants like citizens after five years. At precisely the time that they would generally become eligible to naturalize, this type of affiliation-based law eliminates one reason they might want to do so.

This dynamic is complex. Consider three potential incentives to naturalize: Medicare eligibility, public employment, and voting. Affiliation-based laws and policies may or may not reduce these incentives, depending on the individual. If Stella, an imaginary lawful immigrant, is keen on a government job open only to citizens, she has a strong incentive to naturalize. But if the job is open to citizens and lawful immigrants alike, and Stella has no other reasons to naturalize, her interest in doing so will drop to zero. Recent increases in naturalization applications suggest that a great many lawful immigrants are like Stella and do respond to tangible or intangible incentives. But some lawful immigrants will not. The same citizenship requirements that prompt Stella to naturalize may draw a very different reaction from Makoto, another lawful immigrant who thinks that limiting Medicare, voting, or government jobs to citizens reflects a deep reluctance to accept immigrants.[31]

The figures suggest that the Stellas outnumber the Makotos. Naturalization applications jumped after Congress limited noncitizen access to federal welfare in 1996. The number of applications also rose more modestly after the September 11 terrorist attacks, perhaps ascribable to a heightened identification with America or to a greater sense of vulnerability among noncitizens reacting to racial or ethnic profiling by the government.[32] This means that naturalization—even if it is easy—loses some of its attraction as longtime permanent residence becomes more like citizenship.

One way to understand this problem with disincentives to naturalize is to say that immigration as affiliation makes citizenship less meaningful. But that is only part of the problem with a large non-naturalizing population. To be sure, a large portion of longtime lawful immigrants may be generally content in the social and civil sphere, or else they would naturalize. Yet, as noncitizens they will remain less than full participants, especially in the political sphere, where unequal treatment of lawful immigrants is typically most persistent. This means that reducing naturalization incentives undermines the potential of citizenship as an important vehicle for inclusion and integration of immigrants.[33]

CHAPTER 5

The Most Tender Connections

★

A few blocks off Interstate 70 in Aurora, Colorado, just outside the Denver city limits, a sprawling, low, pink cinder-and-concrete building hides behind a row of gas stations, tire stores, and fast-food restaurants. This is the immigration detention center that the GEO Group operates under contract with the Department of Homeland Security. It is a private prison. On the north side of the building, the detainees are brought into the building and taken out. Some of them were stopped at the border when they tried to enter the country; others are longtime residents of the United States whose lawful status is now in question, perhaps because a criminal conviction has made them deportable. At the Aurora City Council's insistence, these comings and goings are kept from public view by a chain-link fence covered with the same sort of green fabric windbreak that shields tennis courts. Most days, government officers escort a group of detainees to a waiting bus. If they are Mexican nationals, as most of them are, the bus will take them to nearby Denver International Airport to board a chartered plane to take them south of the border.

Deportation and Affiliation

Chapter 1 showed that the U.S. Supreme Court's early plenary power decisions characterized deportation as part of an agreement with newcomers, who were admitted on condition that permission to stay could be revoked. In this spirit, *Fong Yue Ting* called the power to deport a mere extension of the power to admit or exclude. *Nishimura Ekiu* held—in language later quoted prominently in the legislative history of the 1952

Immigration and Nationality Act—that every sovereign nation may "forbid entrance of foreigners within its dominions, or . . . admit them only in such cases and upon such conditions as it may see fit to prescribe."[1] And as chapter 2 explained, immigration as contract has strongly influenced thinking about deportation up through the present.

That said, immigration as affiliation also has played a key role ever since the first deportation statutes. For example, some deportation grounds have exempted noncitizens after a period of time in the United States. One early statute made any alien deportable for engaging in prostitution, but only within three years after entry. These safe harbors are affiliation-based, in that they make it harder to deport noncitizens who are more settled here. Over the years, such affiliation-based safe harbors have also been part of many legislative proposals to reform deportation laws. For example, in 1953 President Harry Truman's Commission on Immigration and Naturalization recommended that no lawful immigrant be deportable after twenty years in the United States.[2]

Today, the most important affiliation-based safe harbor is in the deportation ground for a "crime involving moral turpitude." This ground covers many types of crimes against persons and property. An alien is deportable for a single crime involving moral turpitude if the sentence of one year or longer may be imposed, but only if the crime is "committed within five years . . . of the date of admission." The same five-year safe harbor appears in the deportation grounds for alien smuggling and for becoming a public charge.[3]

But most other deportation grounds have no such affiliation-based safe harbors, so they give no special consideration to noncitizens who are longtime lawful immigrants. For example, noncitizen drug offenders are deportable whether they are new lawful immigrants, longtime lawful immigrants, or nonimmigrants. And even safe harbors are not always safe, for the time period starts with "admission." This may include returning from a short trip outside the United States, though some affiliation-based exceptions protect longtime lawful immigrants in this situation.[4]

The strong influence of immigration as affiliation is more clearly evident not in the categories of deportable aliens, but rather in the rules that allow noncitizens to stay in the United States even if they fall into a deportable category. Recall that deportation raises legal questions in two stages. First, deportation grounds define categories of noncitizens who have been admitted to the United States but now may be forced to leave. Second, even noncitizens who are deportable may be allowed to stay on a case-by-case basis, through waivers, cancellation of removal, and other forms of discretionary relief. All such case-by-case relief relies heavily on affiliation.

Immigration as affiliation thus counters the contract-based notion that noncitizens should be deported if they have violated the conditions of admission by staying longer than authorized, or by committing certain crimes. For example, only noncitizens who have been lawful immigrants for seven years are eligible to apply for a waiver of some criminal deportation grounds. And once eligibility to apply for a waiver is established, whether the government will grant it depends heavily on the noncitizen's ties in the United States, especially the hardships that the noncitizen's deportation will cause for close relatives who are citizens or lawful immigrants.[5]

If the government declines to waive a deportation ground or if no waiver for that ground is available, lawful immigrants who become deportable may still be allowed to stay in the United States as permanent residents through cancellation of removal. Chapter 2 showed how immigration as contract played a key role in deciding the retroactivity of the 1996 eligibility rules for cancellation. At the same time, the actual application of the rules for cancellation has always relied heavily on immigration as affiliation.

The first precursor of cancellation came into use in the 1930s, when advocates for case-by-case leniency cited the human cost of deportation in terms of broken families and economic hardship. These advocates argued that many deportable noncitizens were part of American society and had committed only minor or technical immigration law violations, or that these noncitizens were deportable only for minor crimes for which they had already served a prison term and thus paid their debt to society. Immigration officials responded to these affiliation-based arguments by providing relief from deportation under a previously obscure statute. This form of relief assumed several legislative incarnations, eventually becoming what is now called cancellation of removal.[6]

Today, cancellation still strongly reflects affiliation by recognizing the roots that noncitizens put down in America. Assuming no aggravated felony convictions, a lawful immigrant is eligible for one type of cancellation of removal if he has lived in the United States for five years as a permanent resident and for seven years after having been lawfully admitted in any status. If eligible, a lawful immigrant can ask the immigration judge to exercise his discretion to cancel removal based on family ties, community ties, work history, and a clean criminal record. Similar affiliation-based thinking is the basis for arguments to expand eligibility for cancellation and for arguments against removal of lawful immigrants who came to the United States as children. Though some of these arguments invoke the rhetoric of international human rights, their strong emphasis on ties—especially family ties—shows that they are essentially affiliation-based.[7]

A closely related argument, also based on affiliation, is that because longtime lawful immigrants have strong ties in the United States, deportation for crimes is an issue for the criminal justice system, not for immigration law. This thinking was the basis for an important example of affiliation-based relief that no longer exists. Until 1990, federal and state judges in criminal cases could issue a "judicial recommendation against deportation," or JRAD. Although it was a called a recommendation, a JRAD precluded deportation based on the conviction. Judges granted or denied JRADs based heavily on a noncitizen's ties in the United States.[8]

An affiliation-based emphasis on ties also drives arguments that because deportation amounts to criminal punishment, deportable noncitizens should have the same constitutional protections as criminal defendants, including appointed counsel and the prohibition against retroactive criminal laws. In *Fong Yue Ting*, for example, Justices Brewer and Field dissented that deportation was criminal punishment for constitutional purposes. Both quoted James Madison, whose critique of the 1798 Alien Friends Act portrayed deportation as punishment because it banished a noncitizen from "a country where he may have formed the most tender connections." Brewer stressed that a deported immigrant would be "punished by removal from home, friends, family, property."[9]

Immigration as affiliation is evident in other forms of relief from deportation. There is another type of affiliation-based cancellation that is available even to unlawfully present noncitizens if they can show exceptional and extremely unusual hardship to a close relative who is a citizen or lawful immigrant. In addition, noncitizens who have been in the United States since January 1, 1972—whether lawfully or not—may become lawful immigrants at the government's discretion. And in 1986, Congress enacted two legalization programs for most noncitizens who had been in the United States unlawfully since 1982. Both programs, as well as more recent proposals for amnesty or earned legalization for the undocumented, recognize a noncitizen's ties in the United States.[10]

Plenary Power in Spite of Ties

Immigration as affiliation has also played a central role in the constitutional aspects of immigration law. Here I resume the story of ideological and national security exclusion and deportation, which chapter 2 took from the 1886 Haymarket riot up through the Supreme Court's *Harisiades* decision in 1952. In the 1950s, the government's use of immigration laws against the perceived Communist threat prompted a steady stream of court challenges. But several constitutional decisions from the U.S. Supreme Court reinvigorated the plenary power doctrine's core teaching that courts should be very reluctant to hear constitutional challenges to the government's immigration law decisions. Two key Court cases rejected affiliation-based arguments.

The first involved Ellen Knauff, who fled her native Germany after the Nazi seizure of power and served in Great Britain's Royal Air Force during World War II. She later worked for the Allied occupation forces in Germany and in 1948 married Kurt Knauff, a U.S. citizen. Later that year, she tried to come to the United States under the War Brides Act, which eased immigration by noncitizen spouses and children of U.S. citizens who had served in the U.S. military. Without ever granting Knauff a hearing or access to the evidence against her, the government ordered her permanently excluded. The attorney general acted under a regulation that allowed him to deny a hearing "on the basis of information of a confidential nature, the disclosure of which would be prejudicial to the public interest." Knauff challenged this order in court.[11]

In *United States ex rel. Knauff v. Shaughnessy*, the Supreme Court held that security concerns "during a time of national emergency" were sufficient to justify exclusion without a hearing. In language much like the nineteenth-century plenary power cases, the Court characterized admission as a privilege granted on whatever terms and conditions the government may prescribe. Courts will not enforce any constitutional limits on that power, which includes the power to set not only admission and exclusion categories but also immigration procedures. *Knauff* declared with a chilling brutality: "Whatever the procedure authorized by Congress is, it is due process as far as an alien denied entry is concerned."[12]

The government later revealed the adverse information at a full hearing and tried to show that Knauff had engaged in espionage for the government of Czechoslovakia. The Board of Immigration Appeals—the federal administrative body that reviews immigration judge decisions—eventually held that there was no substantial evidence supporting this contention. The board ordered Ellen Knauff admitted, but only after the Supreme Court had established the plenary power landmark.[13]

Just three years later, the Court said that the same national security regulation could be applied to bar the readmission of a lawful immigrant, Ignatz Mezei, who had lived in Buffalo, New York, for twenty-five years. In 1948, leaving his wife at home, he traveled to eastern Europe to visit his dying mother. While there, he had trouble obtaining the necessary exit papers to embark on his journey back home. Twenty-one months later, when he finally arrived in New York with a visa issued by the American consul in Budapest, the U.S. government excluded him without a hearing. No other country would take Mezei, so the government ordered him confined indefinitely on Ellis Island.[14]

Mezei's case raised this question: Can the federal government, citing national security, constitutionally exclude a returning lawful immigrant without a hearing, using the same procedure that would apply to a noncitizen seeking first-time admission, as in Ellen Knauff's case? Mezei argued that as a returning resident he was entitled to more procedural protection than a first-time entrant. Mezei also argued that the government was not only excluding him but also imprisoning him indefinitely.

Relying on plenary power and national security, the Court rejected both arguments. It acknowledged the main holding in *Yamataya*, that deportation procedures must meet a constitutional minimum standard even if exclusion procedures do not. But the Court rejected Mezei's affiliation-based argument that his twenty-five years in Buffalo should make a constitutional difference. According to the Court, the Constitution protects a returning lawful immigrant no more than a first-time entrant, for both are resisting exclusion. And on indefinite detention, the Court reasoned: "Neither [Mezei's] harborage on Ellis Island nor his prior residence here transforms this into something other than an exclusion proceeding." His incarceration was a "temporary harborage, an act of legislative grace." Only after four years in detention was Mezei later paroled into the United States under a special clemency measure.[15] *Mezei* thus rejected the argument that the Constitution guarantees some minimum of due process for lawful immigrants who leave the United States. But there were already signs that such affiliation-based arguments would ultimately prevail.

Affiliation and the Due Process Exception to Plenary Power

Immigration as affiliation began to exert influence in immigration law in a case decided shortly before *Mezei*. Kwong Hai Chew was a lawful immigrant who served as a seaman aboard a U.S. merchant ship a few years after World War II. In 1950, he filed a naturalization application to become a U.S. citizen. While the application was still pending, Chew shipped out on a five-month voyage. On his return, the government excluded and detained him without a hearing, invoking the same regulation as in *Knauff* and *Mezei*. In a decision issued just five weeks before *Mezei*, the U.S. Supreme Court found that Chew was entitled to a hearing because the regulation did not apply to him. As it turned out, the hearing that Chew received was just the start of his battle against deportation, which dragged on even after his naturalization application was approved seventeen years later, in 1967. But in his 1953 Supreme Court case, Chew won his hearing.[16]

Chew is significant because its invocation of immigration as affiliation began the slow but steady recognition that the plenary power doctrine does not apply to constitutional challenges to immigration *procedures*. In other words, courts will require a minimum of due process even if they are highly deferential to the admission and deportation categories set by Congress and the executive branch. *Yamataya* had announced this procedural exception to plenary power but gave it little content, leaving it for cases like *Chew* to develop a half-century later.[17]

Chew applied this exception by first avoiding the question that *Knauff* and *Mezei* answered: Was it constitutional for the government to use the national security regulation to deny a hearing? Though *Knauff* and *Mezei* said yes, *Chew* avoided this constitutional question by holding—based on immigration as affiliation—that the regulation did not apply in the first place. To explain why the regulation did not apply to Chew, the Court emphasized his ties to the United States, noting that he had "married a native American and bought the home in which they reside in New York." In *Mezei*, the Court contrasted Mezei's trip "behind the Iron Curtain" with Chew's service aboard a U.S. flag ship, observing that such service counts toward the five years of residency required for naturalization.[18]

Affiliation is also evident in *Chew*'s reliance on the 1950 U.S. Supreme Court decision in *Johnson v. Eisentrager*, which held that German soldiers convicted overseas of war crimes by a military tribunal could not ask a U.S. civilian court to release them. *Chew* adopted the *Eisentrager* Court's affiliation-based approach to the constitutional status of noncitizens, especially in this passage: "The alien, to whom the United States has been traditionally hospitable, has been accorded a generous and ascending scale of rights as he increases his identity with our society."[19]

Chew also relied heavily on Justice Murphy's concurring opinion in *Bridges v. Wixon*, a 1945 Supreme Court case arising from the government's efforts to deport the union activist Harry Bridges, who had emigrated from Australia in 1920. In *Bridges*, the Court interpreted the statute not to authorize deportation, so it did not have to decide if the statute violated Bridges's First Amendment rights. The Court thus avoided the constitutional question, as it had in *Chew*. But the Court noted, "we are dealing here with deportation of aliens whose roots may have become, as they are in the present case, deeply fixed in this land." Justice Murphy, writing separately, addressed the constitutional rights of noncitizens in more detail, also focusing on ties in the United States: "Freedom of speech and press is accorded aliens residing in this country." He continued: "The Bill of Rights is a futile authority for the alien seeking admission for the first time to these shores. But once an alien lawfully enters and resides in this country he becomes invested with the rights guaranteed by the Constitution to all people within our borders."[20]

Besides *Chew*, the other major U.S. Supreme Court decision in the 1950s and 1960s that insisted on some procedural protections for noncitizens was *Woodby v. INS*, decided in 1966. *Woodby* held that in a deportation case the government must show the relevant facts by "clear, unequivocal, and convincing evidence," not just a "preponderance of the evidence." Much as in *Chew*, the reasoning in *Woodby* was affiliation-based. Justice Stewart wrote for the Court: "This Court has not closed its eyes to the drastic deprivations that may follow when a resident of this country is compelled by our Government to forsake all the bonds formed here and go to a foreign land where he often has no contemporary identification." Stewart continued: "many resident aliens have lived in this country longer and established stronger family, social, and economic ties here than some who have become naturalized citizens."[21]

In spite of what *Chew*, *Eisentrager*, *Bridges*, and *Woodby* seem to suggest, immigration as affiliation had only limited influence on the constitutional aspects of immigration law in the 1950s and 1960s. As in *Yamataya* in 1903, the Supreme Court said in several other cases that deportation procedures had to meet a minimum constitutional standard, but then found that the procedures in question were sufficient.[22] Because exclusion and deportation were regarded as civil matters, they required significantly less due process than criminal cases. Moreover, neither *Chew* nor *Woodby* actually found that the government failed to meet the minimum procedural standards required by the U.S. Constitution. In both decisions, the Court only interpreted a statute or regulation as giving the noncitizens more procedural protections than the government had been willing to provide. Neither case reached the constitutional issues presented.

A quarter-century after *Mezei*, two landmark U.S. Supreme Court decisions combined to let immigration as affiliation apply full force to assess the constitutionality of procedures in immigration law. As a result, challenges to immigration law procedures emerged as a significant exception to plenary power. The first landmark was *Mathews v. Eldridge* in 1976, which had nothing directly to do with immigration or immigrants; it concerned welfare benefits for citizens. *Eldridge* combined with other Court decisions from the early 1970s to change the accepted understanding of what the Constitution requires by way of fair procedures. Most important, *Eldridge* set out a three-factor balancing test for deciding when procedures in civil cases before administrative agencies meet minimum standards of notice, a right to a hearing, and other aspects of "procedural due process." The first factor is the person's interest that will be affected by government action. The second factor is the risk of a mistake because of inadequate procedures, and whether more extensive procedures will reduce that risk. And the third is the government's interest, including the cost and administrative savings if more extensive procedures are *not* employed. After *Eldridge*, it would mean something that deportation must meet minimum due process standards.[23]

The second landmark was the Supreme Court's 1982 decision in *Landon v. Plasencia*. Maria Plasencia was a lawful immigrant who took a short trip to Tijuana, Mexico, and then tried to reenter the United States. When she and her husband attempted to cross the international border on the evening of June 29, 1975, an immigration inspector at the port of entry found six Mexican and Salvadoran nationals in their car. The government arrested and attempted to exclude her, alleging that she tried to help the six cross the border illegally. Plasencia argued that the government had violated her constitutional right to procedural due process by inadequately informing her of the charges against her and the consequences of waiving legal representation.

The crucial question was whether Maria Plasencia, as a lawful immigrant seeking readmission, could claim procedural due process. *Mezei*, having rejected the affiliation-based argument that courts should recognize a returning lawful immigrant's ties, strongly suggested that she could not. And *Yamataya*, the source of the procedural due process exception to plenary power, was a deportation case involving a noncitizen inside the United States. In *Plasencia*, however, the Court relied on returning lawful immigrants' ties to hold that they can claim procedural due process even if they are outside the country seeking admission. As in *Chew*, the Court in *Plasencia* cited the affiliation-based reasoning in *Eisentrager* to explain: "Once an alien gains admission to our country and begins to develop the ties that go with permanent residence, his constitutional status changes accordingly."[24]

Plasencia adopted immigration as affiliation in another way. The first *Eldridge* factor for deciding whether a given procedure is constitutional is the interest of the individual affected by a government decision. For a lawful immigrant who faces the threat of deportation, the magnitude of this interest depends on the strength of her ties. A longtime lawful immigrant will have a stronger interest in full procedures before the government can order her deported. When *Plasencia* used the *Eldridge* balancing test to decide whether the procedures in Maria Plasencia's case were adequate, the Court was also saying that the minimum due process standard for a lawful immigrant depends heavily on her ties in the United States.

Affiliation and the First Amendment

The affiliation-based erosion of plenary power in immigration law has taken place mainly in challenges to immigration procedures in such cases as *Chew*, *Woodby*, and *Plasencia*. Challenges to the substance of immigration law—the categories for admission and deportation—have been much less successful. Most courts remain reluctant to intervene and decide that admission and deportation categories are unconstitutional. For example, among the arguments that the U.S. Supreme Court rejected in *Harisiades* was that deporting Harisiades, Mascitti, and Coleman because of their

Communist Party affiliations violated the First Amendment. The Court rejected this argument by adopting contract-based reasoning and declining to consider affiliation. Critics of *Harisiades* have typically responded with affiliation-based arguments that emphasize noncitizens' ties.[25]

Notwithstanding this background, *Harisiades* has become the source of an affiliation-based argument that the First Amendment protects noncitizens with ties in the United States. This is clearest in the *American-Arab Anti-Discrimination Committee* (*AADC*) litigation, which started in January 1987 when the federal government arrested and tried to deport seven native Palestinians and one native Kenyan. All lived in Southern California, and all were affiliated with the Popular Front for the Liberation of Palestine (PFLP), which according to the government is an international terrorist and communist organization. Six of the eight—Aiad Khaled Barakat, Naim Nadim Sharif, Julie Nuangugi Mungai, Ayman Mustafa Obeid, Amjad Mustafa Obeid, and Bashar Amer—were in the United States as nonimmigrants, either as students or visitors. The remaining two—Khader Musa Hamide and Michael Ibrahim Shehadeh—were lawful immigrants.[26]

The government initially invoked the deportation grounds against aliens "who advocate the economic, international, and governmental doctrines of world communism." Against the six nonimmigrants, the government also cited violations of the terms of admission, including staying in the United States longer than authorized and failing to maintain student status. The government acknowledged that it was trying to deport all eight for activity that the First Amendment would protect if they were citizens. Director of the FBI William Webster testified before Congress that "if these individuals had been United States citizens, there would not have been a basis for their arrest."[27]

The eight asked a federal district court to stop the proceedings because the ideological deportation grounds violated the First Amendment. Against the six nonimmigrants, the government dropped the ideological grounds but continued to charge visa violations. Against the lawful immigrants Hamide and Shehadeh, the government invoked a different ideological ground, one against aliens who were members of organizations advocating "the duty, necessity, or propriety of the unlawful assaulting or killing of any [government] officer or officers" and the "unlawful damage, injury, or destruction of property." Although the formal charges changed, William Odencrantz, regional counsel for the

Immigration and Naturalization Service, said at a press conference "that the change in charges was for tactical purposes and that the INS intends to deport all eight plaintiffs because they are members of the PFLP."[28]

The eight plaintiffs further charged that the government was selectively prosecuting them in violation of their First Amendment rights. In 1990, with the case still pending, Congress repealed the ideological deportation grounds that the government had been using, but the government persisted. It kept after the six nonimmigrants for visa violations, and the two lawful immigrants under a newly enacted deportation ground against "any alien who has engaged, is engaged, or at any time after admission engages in terrorist activity."[29]

In 1995, a federal appeals court ruled that the government could not deport the eight for their alleged PFLP ties. More generally, the court also held that the First Amendment protects noncitizens living in the United States against deportation. The appeals court rejected the government's argument that "Congress' plenary power over immigration" meant less First Amendment protection for noncitizens in the deportation setting. Rather, the court held that the same First Amendment protections apply to citizens and noncitizens alike.[30]

This perhaps surprising turn in *AADC* can be traced back to the Supreme Court's silence in *Harisiades* as to *why* the deportations of Harisiades, Mascitti, and Coleman did not violate the First Amendment. *Harisiades* offered no detailed explanation but apparently relied on *Dennis v. United States*, a 1951 U.S. Supreme Court decision involving U.S. citizens who were Communist Party organizers. *Dennis* had upheld their criminal convictions under the Smith Act, which—as a rider to the same 1940 statute used in *Harisiades*—prohibited knowingly or willfully advocating the overthrow of the U.S. government.[31] Because *Dennis* had taken a narrow view of First Amendment protections for *citizens*, the *Harisiades* Court could easily conclude that the First Amendment did not shield Harisiades, Mascitti, and Coleman from deportation.

First Amendment protection against the government expanded with the Supreme Court's 1969 decision in *Brandenburg v. Ohio*, which invalidated a statute that was like the Smith Act upheld in *Dennis*. Clarence Brandenburg was a Ku Klux Klan leader. He gave a speech at a Klan rally that included such statements as: "We're not a revengent organization, but if our President, our Congress, our Supreme Court, continues to suppress the white, Caucasian race, it's possible that there might have to be some revengeance taken." After local and national television aired a film of the speech, Brandenburg was convicted under Ohio's criminal syndicalism statute.

When Brandenburg argued that the statute was unconstitutional, the Supreme Court agreed by reinterpreting the First Amendment to impose stricter limits on the government's power to regulate speech and activity. According to the Court, the government may not "proscribe advocacy of the use of force or of law violation except where such advocacy is directed to inciting or producing imminent lawless action and is likely to incite or produce such action."[32]

With *Brandenburg* having superseded *Dennis* and enhanced *citizens'* First Amendment protections, the question in immigration law was whether this enhanced version of the First Amendment now shielded noncitizens from deportation. The appeals court in *AADC* said that *Harisiades* rejected a First Amendment defense to deportation only because *Dennis* had narrowly viewed the First Amendment as a general matter for all persons. But because *Harisiades* assumed that the First Amendment applies equally to citizens and noncitizens alike, *AADC* held that noncitizens could use the broader *Brandenburg* shield against deportation.[33]

To reach this conclusion, *AADC* relied heavily on immigration as affiliation. This is clear from the court's rejection of the government's main argument, which relied on the Supreme Court's 1972 decision in *Kleindienst v. Mandel*. *AADC* rejected *Mandel* as precedent because Ernst Mandel was outside the United States and seeking admission for his speaking tour. In other words, he had insufficient ties. For noncitizens already here—apparently including noncitizens who are not lawful immigrants—what mattered to the *AADC* court was being part of "our community." Referring to the First Amendment, the *AADC* court said: "Because we are a nation founded by immigrants, this underlying principle is especially relevant to our attitude toward current immigrants who are a part of our community." *AADC* then adopted an affiliation-based definition: "aliens with substantial ties through family and work form part of our 'national community.' "[34]

Procedural Surrogates and Phantom Norms

It is time to assess the relationship between contract and affiliation in broader perspective. Chapter 1 started by showing how courts used the rhetoric of immigration as contract to justify the plenary power doctrine.

This is understandable, for as chapter 2 explained, immigration as contract reflects the intuition that sound immigration policy requires some advance understanding of who is coming to America and how long they will stay. Yet immigration as contract does not always favor the government and hurt noncitizens. Chapter 2 showed how immigration as contract has influenced the treatment of lawful immigrants, not only historically but also in recent years, not only in constitutional law but also in legislative debates, and not only to diminish but also to enhance protections for lawful immigrants.

As chapter 3 explained, the alienage law decision in *Yick Wo* laid the conceptual foundation for territorial personhood, which became a competing approach that gives noncitizens more protection than they could derive solely from immigration as contract. Territorial personhood remains important, as the role it played in *Plyler v. Doe*, the most prominent recent example, makes clear. However, a real counterweight to immigration as contract did not mature until immigration as affiliation became more influential in the middle part of the twentieth century. Chapter 4 discussed landmark alienage law decisions that went beyond territorial personhood and embraced immigration as affiliation as a constitutional rationale, most prominently in *Graham v. Richardson* and *Mathews v. Diaz*. Chapter 4 also discussed immigration as affiliation in the statutory aspects of federal public benefits.

Immigration as affiliation has been influential not only in alienage law, but also in immigration law. This chapter has analyzed how affiliation-based thinking has shaped the statutory scheme for deporting noncitizens for criminal convictions. And in the constitutional aspects of immigration law, immigration as affiliation has eroded the plenary power doctrine. Courts have developed a significant, affiliation-based exception to the plenary power doctrine for procedural due process.

This procedural due process exception deserves a closer look because it sheds further light on the interaction between immigration as contract and immigration as affiliation. Procedural due process has become a vehicle for the courts to hear constitutional claims that the plenary power doctrine would seem to bar. This has been especially important when noncitizens have wanted to challenge the constitutionality of government decisions in the gray area between immigration procedure and substantive admission and deportation categories. Here noncitizens have been able to avoid the plenary power by casting their constitutional claims as procedural.

A good example is a group of court challenges to section 5 of the Immigration Marriage Fraud Amendments in 1986, which Congress enacted out of concern that many marriages between noncitizens and U.S. citizens are sham marriages intended only to confer immigration benefits on the noncitizen spouse. Section 5 required any noncitizen who was in deportation or exclusion proceedings when he married a citizen to spend two years outside the United States before his citizen-spouse could sponsor him to become a lawful immigrant. Section 5 was arguably an admission category that excluded noncitizens who got married in these situations from immediate eligibility for admission. Under this characterization, the plenary power doctrine would immunize it from constitutional challenge. Some courts struck down section 5 in spite of the plenary power doctrine, however, reasoning that section 5 was a procedural rule that delayed a hearing on the noncitizen's immigration eligibility for two years.[35]

At least as far back as the Supreme Court's 1953 decision in *Chew*, and certainly by its 1982 decision in *Plasencia*, immigration as affiliation had become the driving force behind the procedural due process exception— and, in turn, the erosion of plenary power. This role for affiliation makes sense. In contrast to immigration as contract, immigration as affiliation reflects the intuition that immigration control is imperfect and that the terms of admission are not enough to determine whether immigration decisions are fair and just. Instead, concepts of fairness and justice are only persuasive if they capture the circumstances of a noncitizen's life in America in a more textured way. Since alienage law addresses the everyday aspects of a noncitizen's life in the United States, it is only natural that such decisions as *Graham* and *Diaz* would make affiliation central to constitutional thinking in alienage law. It is not surprising, then, that immigration as affiliation would also be the basis for erosion of plenary power in immigration law.

The same attractions of immigration as affiliation that have driven the procedural due process exception also explain a different type of affiliation-based erosion of plenary power. This erosion has taken place because judges who may be reluctant to strike down an immigration decision as unconstitutional have sometimes interpreted statutes or regulations in a manner that reaches the same result. Here the key notion is that constitutional law not only determines if statutes and other government decisions are consistent with the U.S. Constitution, but also influences the interpretation of statutes. A judge can use a constitutional idea to decide what a statute means, even if she stops short of striking down that statute as unconstitutional.

To explain how this works, take an example from outside immigration law and alienage law. In its 1983 decision in *Bob Jones University v. United States*, the U.S. Supreme Court found that a nonprofit private university with racially discriminatory admissions did not qualify for the federal income tax exemption for institutions "organized and operated exclusively for religious, charitable, . . . or educational purposes." The Court did not decide that an exemption for a school that discriminated by race was unconstitutional. Rather, it held that the statute did not allow the exemption.[36]

According to the Court, the statute's text was silent on the issue, but the exemption assumed that any qualifying organization would provide public services of value to society. The Court read the statute to deny the exemption to any organization whose activities were "contrary to a fundamental public policy." Citing *Brown v. Board of Education*, the Court noted that "racial discrimination in education violates a most fundamental national public policy, as well as rights of individuals." This reasoning was consistent with the established canon that courts should interpret ambiguous statutes to avoid deciding serious constitutional issues. Therefore, no exemption for Bob Jones University.[37]

To show how similar reasoning has eroded the plenary power doctrine in immigration law, consider the 2001 U.S. Supreme Court decision in *Zadvydas v. Davis*. This case involved two noncitizens. Kestutis Zadvydas was born soon after World War II to Lithuanian parents in a refugee camp in Germany. He was eight years old when he and his family came to the United States, but he never naturalized and remained stateless. He was not a citizen of Germany, Lithuania, Russia, or the Dominican Republic (where his wife was a citizen). Zadvydas's case was eventually consolidated with the case of Kim Ho Ma, who had come as a small child with his family to the United States as a refugee from Cambodia. He grew up in the Seattle area, but like Zadvydas he never became a U.S. citizen.

Both Zadvydas and Ma were convicted of crimes that made them deportable, and after a series of hearings each was ordered removed. Those orders formally ended their permanent resident status. No country would take the stateless Zadvydas, and until 2002 Cambodia refused to accept its own citizens as deportees from the United States.[38] Unable to deport

Zadvydas and Ma, the government detained both on the ground that they posed a danger to society if released. The two argued that their detention was unlawful because it was indefinite, possibly for life.

A federal statute authorizes the government to detain noncitizens until they can be sent to another country. The Supreme Court did not strike down this statute as unconstitutional, but instead held that the statute did not authorize the government to hold Zadvydas or Ma indefinitely if they could not be sent elsewhere. Though the Court's holding was statutory, its thinking was constitutional. The Court found that the statute was ambiguous and then invoked—as it had in *Bob Jones University*—the canon that courts should interpret ambiguous statutes to avoid deciding serious constitutional issues. Just as allowing a tax exemption to Bob Jones University might have conflicted with the constitutional value of freedom from racial discrimination, *Zadvydas* found that interpreting the immigration statute to authorize indefinite detention might result in unconstitutionally indefinite incarceration.

To find this potential conflict with the Constitution, the Supreme Court reasoned that the Constitution may protect Zadvydas and Ma. The Court rejected the argument by the government—and by Justice Scalia in dissent—that a lawful immigrant who has been ordered removed is constitutionally just like someone who has never been in the United States. This was essentially a contract-based argument that a final removal order, by revoking the terms of admission, erases any presence or ties that a permanent resident has ever had. Similar reasoning in *Fong Yue Ting* said that deportation and exclusion were constitutionally the same thing. In rejecting this contract-based argument, the Court relied principally on a mixture of territorial personhood and immigration as affiliation by citing Zadvydas's and Ma's presence and their ties in the United States.

Zadvydas adopted what I have called "phantom" constitutional norms—constitutional standards and principles that the plenary power doctrine keeps courts from recognizing openly, but which nonetheless prompt courts to read statutes in favor of noncitizens. *Zadvydas* is only the latest in the string of such phantom norm decisions going back to the mid-1900s. A prime example is *Chew*, which did not hold that the national security regulation denying a hearing was unconstitutional, but rather that it did not apply to Chew when he tried to return to the United States. Another example is *Woodby*, which interpreted a statute to require that the government prove deportability by "clear, unequivocal, and convincing evidence." In *Chew*,

Woodby, and other phantom norm decisions that have eroded contract-based plenary power, immigration as affiliation played a pivotal conceptual role. The noncitizen's significant ties in the United States led the Court to find a constitutional question serious enough to interpret the statute in the noncitizen's favor.[39]

Immigration Law and Alienage Law, Promises and Ties

In spite of the erosion of the plenary power doctrine, courts still adhere to it and remain reluctant to invalidate admission and deportation categories. In this regard the federal court of appeals decision in *AADC* remains unusual. And yet, immigration as affiliation and its conceptual foundation of earned equality have gradually emerged alongside a previously dominant view of immigration as contract. Though immigration as affiliation will never completely displace immigration as contract, affiliation-based thinking about immigration has come to be taken seriously.

One reason that immigration as affiliation has permeated not just alienage law but also immigration law is that the line between alienage law and immigration law is elusive. Immigration rules and alienage rules can substitute for each other, and they overlap functionally and conceptually. Many alienage rules knowingly affect immigration, and immigration rules may substitute for alienage rules. For example, First Amendment protection in alienage law against criminal prosecution for membership in a subversive organization means little to a noncitizen if immigration law can deport him.[40]

In November 1994, California voters approved Proposition 187, which would have barred access by the undocumented to most state public services, including nonemergency health care and public education. It also would have required certain state and local government employees to verify the immigration status of persons whom they encountered in their duties, and to report all suspected undocumented noncitizens to federal immigration officials. In addition, Proposition 187 introduced substantial new criminal penalties for manufacturing, selling, and using false documents.

Lawsuits immediately challenged Proposition 187 as a state immigration law that conflicted with exclusive federal immigration power. A federal court agreed and blocked implementation except for the criminal penalties. Though Proposition 187 did not directly regulate admission, it was meant to deter undocumented immigration to California and to encourage undocumented noncitizens already there to leave. Governor Pete Wilson expressed his hope that they would "self-deport."[41] Proposition 187 shows not only how immigration law and alienage law overlap, but also how both are needed to understand what it means to be or not to be a citizen. This suggests that when immigration as affiliation emerged alongside immigration as contract in immigration law, affiliation would emerge alongside contract in alienage law as well.

This two-dimensional story of immigration as contract and immigration as affiliation elucidates key themes in immigration and citizenship law in the United States. Consider one final example: the occasional debate over *jus soli* citizenship in the United States. In recent years, Congress has considered and rejected several proposals to amend the Constitution so that children born on U.S. soil are citizens only if their parents are here lawfully. The argument against *jus soli* citizenship for the children of the undocumented is largely based on immigration as contract—that the Constitution adopts a consent-based approach to citizenship, and that this consent is absent when a child is born to undocumented parents. The standard defense of *jus soli* citizenship is based on immigration as affiliation. Especially important is the idea that a noncitizen's ties to this country should be recognized by conferring citizenship on her children who are born in the United States and then typically grow up here, regardless of the parent's immigration status.[42]

This example shows yet again that the emergence of immigration as affiliation alongside immigration as contract helpfully explains many choices in matters of immigration and citizenship in general, and in the treatment of lawful immigrants in particular. Today, the treatment of lawful immigrants under the U.S. Constitution and under the statutes and regulations that comprise immigration law and alienage law reflects various blends of contract-based and affiliation-based influences. But contract and affiliation do not pose the full range of choices, and for this reason the two-dimensional contract-affiliation framework is incomplete without examining immigration as transition and the idea of Americans in waiting.

CHAPTER 6

The Lost Story of Americans in Waiting

★

The phrase "to naturalize" is a bit odd, at least in its literal meaning, "to make natural." It refers to becoming a citizen, as opposed to being born one. The word's origins lie in a time when divine will and natural law were thought to explain why someone was born a subject of one worldly ruler or another. Anyone who was not born to that status of subject, but later became one, was naturalized.[1] The drafters of the U.S. Constitution gave Congress the power to enact a uniform rule of naturalization, rather than leave this making of new citizens to the states in an era when frontiers were vast, fluid, and unpatrolled.

Citizenship laws—especially naturalization laws—drew more federal attention than direct control over admission itself. In the Republic's early years, naturalization required only a short period of residence. Signaling the new nation's willingness to admit newcomers—or at least certain newcomers—the first naturalization statute in 1790 allowed "free white persons" to become citizens in "any common law court of record in any of the States" if they had resided in the United States for two years, were of "good character," and took an oath to support the U.S. Constitution.[2]

In 1795, Congress increased the qualifying residency period from two to five years, and adopted a requirement of special interest here. Three years before applying for naturalization, every applicant had to file "first papers." This term referred to a declaration of intent to become a citizen, which could be filed at any time after arrival. The declaration served an administrative function by allowing an early review of eligibility in the form of an examination under oath before a court clerk. The declaration entailed no obligation to naturalize, though many immigrants did take that next step and became citizens.[3]

The 1798 Naturalization Act increased the qualifying residency period to fourteen years and required a declaration of intent five years before naturalization. That year, the Alien and Sedition Acts authorized the President to order the deportation of enemy nationals and "dangerous" aliens. Those acts and the stiffer naturalization rules in 1795 and 1798 reflected the fears of the Federalists, who suspected that their political opponents, the Jeffersonians, drew key support from Irish and French immigrants. The Jeffersonians soon regained power, and in 1802 Congress generally restored the more lenient 1795 scheme, including five-year qualifying residency with a declaration three years in advance. Starting in 1824, the declaration had to be filed only two years in advance, and Congress began to relax the requirement with exceptions.[4]

A declaration of intent in advance was a prerequisite for naturalization from 1795 until 1952, when it became optional. During this period, the noncitizens who filed one—whom I will call "intending citizens"—enjoyed a favored status, something close to citizenship itself. Even for the most recent arrivals, a declaration by a newcomer who was eligible to naturalize embodied the expectation of citizenship. Of course, the prerequisite that the intending citizen had to be eligible for citizenship was an enormously significant barrier as long as naturalization was racially restricted. For white immigrants, however—and after 1870 for the few immigrants who were black—the declaration conveyed a special status that showed how the idea of Americans in waiting was central to thinking about immigration and citizenship.[5]

Intending Citizens as Voters and Near-Citizens

One prominent sign of the idea of Americans in waiting was the practice of allowing intending citizens to vote. Today only a few scattered localities in the United States allow any noncitizen voting, but it was commonplace until the early 1900s. Noncitizen voting began in the late 1700s, when giving some male immigrants the right to vote was consistent with the young nation's desire to attract European newcomers. As attitudes toward immigrants changed, noncitizen voting waxed and waned. It fell into disfavor during the War of 1812 amid fears of foreign influences.[6]

As the nation expanded westward with new territories and states, a

pattern emerged of compromise between extending voting to all noncitizens or to none of them. Starting with the Wisconsin Constitution of
1848, only noncitizens who filed declarations of intent could vote in
many states and territories. The 1850 Michigan Constitution and the
1851 Indiana Constitution also allowed intending citizens to vote. Congress then let intending citizens vote in the Dakota, Kansas, Minnesota,
Nebraska, Nevada, Oklahoma, Oregon, Washington, and Wyoming Territories. Voting by intending citizens—who sometimes were expressly
required to be white males—survived in most of these territories
when they attained statehood, and a number of other states adopted
the practice.[7]

In much of the period when noncitizen voting was unremarkable, the
connection between voting and citizenship was a loose one. During the
Civil War, noncitizen voting in some states served Northern interests by
expanding the political influence of immigrants, especially on the slavery
issue. The practice of noncitizen voting also helped to justify the drafting
of noncitizens into the Union Army, which was almost a quarter foreign-
born. And after Appomattox, expanding noncitizen voting was a way to
recognize noncitizens who had served.[8]

When Congress debated the first naturalization statute in 1790, the
main rights associated with citizenship were not voting but property
ownership and eligibility to hold public office. For voting, citizenship
generally mattered less than race, gender, and owning property. The U.S.
Supreme Court's 1874 decision in *Minor v. Happersett* rejected suffragist
Virginia Minor's efforts to register to vote in St. Louis, Missouri. According to the Court, barring women who were citizens from voting did not
violate the Constitution, since citizenship did not necessarily include the
right to vote. Not all voters were citizens, and not all citizens were voters.
Today, the connection between voting and citizenship is much closer, although some adult citizens, notably convicted felons, still may not vote
even after serving their sentences.[9]

But voting and citizenship were not completely uncoupled, and here the
idea of Americans in waiting was pivotal. When *Minor* explained that voting and citizenship were not always linked, it cited voting by noncitizens.
But the Court did not say that *all* noncitizens could vote, for that was not
true. Instead, the Court cited the widespread acceptance of voting by "persons of foreign birth, who have *declared their intention* to become citizens of
the United States." The Court cited Alabama, Arkansas, Florida, Georgia,

Indiana, Kansas, Minnesota, Missouri, and Texas in an incomplete list of states that allowed voting by intending citizens.[10]

When a declaration of intent was a prerequisite for naturalization, it was clear that intending citizens were not actually citizens, but they were treated like citizens for many purposes. Many laws drew a line that put citizens and intending citizens on one side, and all other noncitizens on the other side. The laws that treated intending citizens like citizens addressed a wide array of topics, but underlying all of them was a view of immigrants as Americans in waiting and immigration as a transition to citizenship. For example, an 1804 federal statute automatically conferred citizenship on the widow and children of any intending citizen who died before he naturalized. The Homestead Act of 1862 made noncitizens eligible for homesteads once they filed their declarations. During the Civil War and World War I, intending citizens but not other noncitizens were obligated to military service. At one time, intending citizens could get U.S. passports if they had lived in the United States for three years and filed a declaration of intent to naturalize. Under a 1918 federal statute, noncitizen seamen who were intending citizens were deemed to be U.S. citizens for the purpose of serving on any U.S. merchant or fishing vessel.[11]

In one celebrated—though ultimately atypical—episode, the United States extended diplomatic protection to an intending citizen. Martin Koszta was an émigré of Hungarian descent who left Austria as a political refugee around 1850. He first fled to Turkey, where the Austrian authorities unsuccessfully tried to bring him back to Austria to face charges. Koszta soon left Turkey and came to the United States, where he filed a declaration of intent to become a U.S. citizen in July 1852. The next year, Koszta returned temporarily to Turkey, where Austrian agents found and kidnapped him, and held him in irons aboard the warship *Huszar*. When the commander of a nearby U.S. naval vessel demanded Koszta's release, the *Huszar*'s crew delivered him to the French consul general until his fate could be resolved. In September 1853, U.S. Secretary of State Robert Marcy adopted the position, as U.S. government policy, that intending citizens like Koszta were sufficiently "clothed with an American nationality" to warrant U.S. diplomatic protection.[12]

Other examples show that the status of intending citizen mattered. States and localities hired intending citizens for public works projects and some other public employment on the same basis as citizens in an era when other noncitizens typically were excluded. The Revenue Act of 1918 imposed on nonresident noncitizens an income tax rate twice that for citizens, prompting thousands of noncitizens to file declarations to avoid the nonresident rate. The idea of immigrants as Americans in waiting also mattered in the private sector. In the assimilationist fervor that swept the country after World War I, many employers promoted only citizens or noncitizens in the process of naturalizing.[13]

A perceived problem with this treatment of intending citizens, as discussed at the end of chapter 4, was that they could enjoy many of the benefits of citizenship without ever naturalizing. A few states allowed intending citizens to vote only until they had been in the United States long enough to naturalize and vote as citizens. A 1906 federal statute responded more generally by forcing an intending citizen who did not petition for naturalization within seven years of filing a declaration to restart the process by filing a new declaration and again waiting the required two years before applying for naturalization. The same statute also made declarations of intent "invalid for all purposes" after seven years.[14]

Fundamental to the declaration of intent was the idea of immigration as a transition to citizenship. This contrasts sharply with immigration as contract, which reflects an idea of justice without equality for lawful immigrants, as long as promise, notice, and expectations are respected. Transition also contrasts with immigration as affiliation, which reflects an idea of earned equality for lawful immigrants based on ties acquired over time in the United States. In contrast to both contract and affiliation, immigration as transition reflects an idea of presumed equality for lawful immigrants, historically triggered by the declaration of intent to naturalize.

A New Look at Some Old Constitutional Cases

The idea of Americans in waiting influenced not only the drafting of statutes, but also how courts understood the constitutional rights of lawful immigrants. Chapter 3 focused on the racial aspects of state laws that barred land ownership by "aliens ineligible to citizenship," but the Supreme Court decisions that upheld the constitutionality of those laws is worth revisiting for the way they treated intending citizens unlike other noncitizens.

In *Terrace v. Thompson*, the Supreme Court upheld the state of Washington's alien land law by explaining: "The rights, privileges and duties of aliens differ widely from those of citizens; and those of alien declarants differ substantially from those of nondeclarants." The Court noted that declarants were obligated to military service while nondeclarants were not. The Court further reasoned: "Formerly in many of the states the right to vote and hold office was extended to declarants, and many important offices have been held by them. But these rights have not been granted to nondeclarants."[15]

Though this was a highly racialized line in the context of the alien land laws, the idea of Americans in waiting resurfaced strongly in settings where race played less of a role. An example is *Eisentrager*, in which the Supreme Court's analysis of the rights of noncitizens included this recognition of the constitutional significance of being an intending citizen: "Mere lawful presence in the country creates an implied assurance of safe conduct and gives him certain rights; they become more extensive and secure when he makes preliminary declaration of intention to become a citizen, and they expand to those of full citizenship upon naturalization."[16]

At the same time, the idea of Americans in waiting in constitutional analysis assumed that lawful immigrants were headed toward citizenship. The filing of a declaration of intent was the most obvious basis for that assumption, especially when declarations were required. After declarations became optional in 1952, courts seemed to assume that a lawful immigrant who did not yet meet the residency requirement would naturalize as soon as she did meet the requirement. But just as some state laws allowed intending citizens to vote only until they could naturalize, courts sometimes withdrew favorable treatment from lawful immigrants who did not naturalize. Until 1952, this meant that favorable treatment was withdrawn for failure to file a declaration, and after 1952, for failure to apply for naturalization when the immigrant became eligible.

For example, the Supreme Court decision in *Harisiades* relied partly on the idea of Americans in waiting. Justice Jackson seemed to assume that Harisiades, Mascitti, and Coleman could have naturalized but did not. Perhaps relying on the fact that they all had been in the United States for more than twenty years, Jackson wrote about the three deportees: "Each was admitted to the United States, upon passing formidable exclusionary hurdles, in the hope that, after what may be called a probationary period, he would desire and be found desirable for citizenship." Openly skeptical of constitutional claims by lawful immigrants who decline to become citizens, Jackson continued: "Each has been offered naturalization, with all of the rights and privileges of citizenship, conditioned only upon open and honest assumption of undivided allegiance to our Government. But acceptance was and is not compulsory. Each has been permitted to prolong his original nationality indefinitely."[17]

The Supreme Court adopted similar reasoning in *Carlson v. Landon*, decided the same day as *Harisiades*. *Carlson* arose when the federal government arrested and detained five lawful immigrants who were Communist Party members. The five sued to be released pending deportation hearings, arguing that denying release on bond violated the Fifth Amendment due process clause and the Eighth Amendment right to reasonable bail. The Court rejected these arguments, finding that the attorney general had discretion to hold the five "as a menace to the public interest." The Court's reasoning emphasized their failure to naturalize: "So long . . . as aliens fail to obtain and maintain citizenship by naturalization, they remain subject to the plenary power of Congress to expel them under the sovereign right to determine what noncitizens shall be permitted to remain within our borders."[18]

Another example of this approach to the constitutional rights of non-naturalizing lawful immigrants goes back much further, to the Supreme Court's 1893 decision in *Fong Yue Ting*. The Court reasoned that Fong Yue Ting, Wong Quan, and Lee Joe could not avail themselves of the Constitution to fight deportation, "having taken no steps towards becoming citizens, and incapable of becoming such under the naturalization laws."[19] Not naturalizing because of racial ineligibility was one reason to deny recognition of constitutional rights in *Fong Yue Ting*. The situation in *Harisiades* was somewhat but not entirely different. No racial bar kept Harisiades, Mascitti, and Coleman from naturalizing. However, their Communist Party membership was not only the basis for the government's efforts to deport them but also a serious obstacle to their naturalization. Justice Jackson seemed not to take this naturalization bar into account, perhaps because he thought they had squandered their chance to naturalize by joining a prohibited organization. In spite of these differences between *Fong Yue Ting* and *Harisiades*, both cases reflect the same principle: lawful immigrants who are not on their way to citizenship are treated less well than those who are.

Other cases reflecting the same rationale involved lawful immigrants who apparently would have had no trouble naturalizing but still declined to do so. A 1979 case involved two lawful immigrants who lived in the state of New York and applied for teaching certificates. Susan Norwick was from the United Kingdom, Tarja Dachinger from Finland. Both were married to U.S. citizens, and both were eligible to naturalize but chose not to. A state statute barred noncitizens from public school teaching unless they "make due application to become a citizen and thereafter within the time prescribed by law become a citizen." The apparent assumption was that lawful immigrants would apply for naturalization when they became eligible. What mattered under the New York statute was applying for naturalization, not filing a declaration of intent, which by then was no longer required for naturalization itself. The Supreme Court upheld this statute as constitutional in *Ambach v. Norwick*. The Court did not cite *Harisiades* or *Carlson*, but similarly reasoned that Norwick and Dachinger had "rejected the open invitation" of citizenship. The statute, said the Court, "bars from teaching only those aliens who have demonstrated their unwillingness to obtain United States citizenship."[20]

Noncitizen voting and court decisions like *Harisiades, Carlson,* and *Ambach* all reflect the same idea of Americans in waiting, but they involve different periods in a lawful immigrant's life in America. The core idea is that the declaration of intent created a form of precitizenship that conferred significant benefits on a lawful immigrant who could not yet naturalize. This idea can help or hurt immigrants. It was the foundation for the *Eisentrager* passage about "more extensive and secure" rights upon the filing of a declaration of intention, and for the New York statute that allowed lawful immigrants to teach *until* they became eligible to naturalize. In contrast, *Harisiades, Carlson,* and *Ambach* treated lawful immigrants less well *after* they had been in the United States long enough to naturalize but had not done so.

One caveat: the outcomes in these cases reflected a complex combination of factors. Even if Harisiades, Mascitti, Coleman, and Carlson had been intending citizens, or even if they had not been lawful immigrants long enough to naturalize, the Supreme Court probably would have ruled against them anyway. The same might be true for Norwick and Dachinger as well. The plenary power doctrine strongly influenced the Court in *Harisiades* and *Carlson*. And *Ambach* relied heavily on the concept that states and localities can require citizenship for jobs closely related to political functions. The Court had first clearly articulated this idea in 1973, when *Sugarman v. Dougall* invalidated the state of New York's requirement that *all* of its civil service employees be U.S. citizens. *Sugarman* created this important exception: "We recognize a State's interest in establishing its own form of government, and in limiting participation in that government to those who are within 'the basic conception of a political community.' "[21] *Ambach* applied this exception.

Even with these other factors in *Harisiades, Carlson,* and *Ambach,* the Supreme Court's reasoning in these decisions shows that immigration as transition has played a significant role in deciding the constitutionality of distinctions between citizens and noncitizens.[22] In doing so, the Court did not just lay down a principle of constitutional law. It also articulated an important public value: lawful immigrants, at least while en route to citizenship, are treated like citizens because they are Americans in waiting.

Race and Americans in Waiting

But not all immigrants could be Americans in waiting. Another part of the lost story is that it paralleled the story of racial restrictions on immigration and citizenship. As chapter 3 explained, naturalization—and therefore the declaration of intent and the status of intending citizen—was open only to whites from 1790 to 1870, and only to whites and blacks from 1870 until the 1940s, when "races indigenous to the Western hemisphere" were allowed to naturalize, including Native Americans and persons of Mexican ancestry, and then some Asians. Only in 1952 were all racial barriers finally repealed. During the entire period from 1795 to 1952 when declarations of intent were required—and more fundamentally when the underlying ideas of Americans in waiting and immigration as transition were most influential—racial barriers severely limited who could take advantage of these ideas and the sort of welcome that they implied.

This racial backdrop greatly complicates the lost story of Americans in waiting. America treated lawful immigrants most generously when laws doubly limited access to the status of intending citizen by race, not only by limiting who could naturalize as a citizen, but also who could become a lawful immigrant in the first place. To explain, I now resume the account of racially restrictive immigration laws started in chapter 1. It turns out that the Chinese Exclusion Acts and the Gentlemen's Agreement of 1907 that severely curtailed Japanese immigration were just the first of many racial restrictions on immigration that persisted in some form at least until 1965.

Growing nativist concerns about the influx of immigrants around the turn of the twentieth century were largely a response to the shift in the ethnic origins of the immigrant flow. Part of the shift was within the European immigrant pool, away from northern and western European countries of origin and toward southern and eastern Europe. The percentage of European immigrants from southern and eastern Europe rose from 13.1 percent in 1882 to 81 percent in 1907.[23] Another part of the demographic shift was an increasing number of immigrants from Asian countries. With the Chinese exclusion laws in effect, the largest group of Asian immigrants came from Japan.

Closely related to the racial and ethnic focus of restrictionist efforts was the increased role of eugenics in the making of immigration policy. The "science" of eugenics reflected the belief that there was an objective, measurable, and scientific basis for racial differences, and that public policy choices should reflect this body of knowledge. Therefore, sound immigration policy would choose those immigrants whose racial genetic makeup would best contribute to American society, and would keep out immigrants whose genes would degrade the population. Earlier race-based aspects of immigration and citizenship law—for example the Chinese exclusion laws and the foundation plenary power decisions that upheld those laws—had assumed Anglo-Saxon racial superiority, but eugenics lent these sentiments the patina of science.

Race as understood during this period—and indeed at least until the 1930s—did not imagine a single "white" race, but rather thought of Europeans as belonging to multiple races, all with different degrees of suitability as immigrants in the United States. The most influential nativist work of the period, Madison Grant's *The Passing of the Great Race*, published in 1916, separated Europeans into three races: the superior Nordics, the lowly Mediterraneans, and between them the Alpines. Voluminous scientific data—ranging from measurements of inferior races' limited cranial capacity and shares of the population of insane asylums—purported to support fine distinctions and comparisons among the genetic virtues of different races. This same body of work became part of the bedrock of racial attitudes and laws in Nazi Germany.[24]

Eugenics became the dominant approach to immigration policy in the United States in this crucial period through the work of the Dillingham Commission, established by Congress in 1907. The commission's report, forty-two volumes issued in 1911, distinguished new immigrants from the old immigrants and concluded that the new immigrants from southern and eastern Europe were of intellectually inferior, unassimilable races. From 1911 through the 1920s, debates over immigration centered on the expressed fear that America was in jeopardy if it continued to take in more newcomers of inferior racial pedigree and with shortcomings rang- ing from low intelligence and mental illness to various moral failings in- cluding propensity for crime.[25]

The fear of racially inferior immigrants led to a push for literacy tests, which proponents hoped would curtail the flow of southern and eastern European immigrants. These efforts persisted for more than twenty years before achieving success in 1917. Congress adopted one in 1897, but Presi- dent Grover Cleveland vetoed it. The literacy test stayed on the legisla- tive docket and passed again in 1913, only to be vetoed by President William Howard Taft, with the override effort succeeding in the Senate but falling five votes short in the House. When President Wilson vetoed a literacy test in 1915, Congress failed to override by four votes in the House. As World War I dragged on, however, the immigration debate took on a more nationalist tone that popularized restrictionist beliefs. Fi- nally, in 1917, the year that the United States entered the war, President Wilson again vetoed a literacy test, but this time Congress easily over- rode the veto. To administer the test, the law provided that "immigration inspectors shall be furnished with slips of uniform size, . . . each contain- ing not less than thirty nor more than forty words in ordinary use, printed in plainly legible type in some one of the various languages or di- alects of immigrants."[26]

Though the movement for a literacy test was directed against immi- grants from southern and eastern Europe, Congress also added restric- tions on Asian immigration. In the same 1917 law that introduced the literacy test, Congress broadened Asian exclusion beyond Chinese immi- grants by prohibiting immigration from what came to be called the Asiatic barred zone. Excepting U.S. possessions—most significantly the Philippines—this barred zone included everywhere from Saudi Arabia to Southeast Asia, and India, Sri Lanka, and Indonesia up through Afghanistan and the Asian parts of what soon would become the Soviet Union. The 1917 law also barred anyone who traced his or her ancestry to these countries. The barred zone did not include Japan, partly because the Gentlemen's Agreement made a new ban seem unnecessary, and partly out of hesita- tion to offend the Japanese government any further.

The National Origins System

With the major exception of Asian exclusion, federal immigration law up to this time did not limit the number of immigrants allowed into the United States, but rather just defined exclusion and deportation categories. Then, in 1921, Congress enacted the first numerical limits on immigration. Part of the backdrop was fear of new waves of immigrants, but also important were growing isolationism in global affairs, continuing fear of radical foreigners, and an economic depression that had raised the U.S. unemployment rate to 12 percent. The 1921 law did not apply to immigration from the Asiatic barred zone, nor to immigration from the Western Hemisphere. Annual immigration from other countries was limited to 3 percent of "the number of foreign-born persons of such nationality resident in the United States as determined by the United States census of 1910." The commissioner general of immigration was charged with issuing annual calculations. Since most immigrants from southern and eastern Europe arrived after 1910, this scheme not only limited the total number of new immigrants but also ensured that most would come from western and northern Europe.[27]

The 1921 law turned out to be an interim step toward the 1924 National Origins Act—sometimes called the Johnson-Reed Act—which was the first comprehensive permanent federal statute regulating the number of immigrants admitted to the United States. Cosponsor Albert Johnson called the Dillingham Commission report the "great impetus" for the National Origins Act. It maintained the basic idea behind the 1921 system—the maintenance of a white, Anglo-Saxon America, its superiority established by scientific research. Toward this end, the National Origins Act capped immigrant admissions with limits on nationality groups that were intended to reflect the existing U.S. population. These limits were called "quotas," although the term may mislead, since nothing required that immigrants be admitted up to the limit. Also, certain immigrants—most important, spouses and unmarried children under eighteen of U.S. citizens—were not counted against the quota, so it would be a mistake to think that the quota set an absolute cap on immigration.[28]

The National Origins Act adopted an interim quota system to be in effect until 1927, and it set out a permanent system to take its place. The interim system lowered the 1921 quota for each qualifying nationality group from 3 percent to 2 percent of the foreign-born population of that nationality. The interim system also moved the baseline year from the 1910 census back to 1890, which favored immigrants from northern and western Europe even more than the 1910 baseline. The 1921 law had already increased the proportion of northern and western European immigration substantially over pre-1921 levels to 55 percent of the available European slots, leaving 45 percent for southern and eastern Europe. The 1924 law boosted that northern and western European share even more, to 84 percent.[29]

The National Origins Act also set up a permanent system with a 1927 effective date, which would later be deferred to July 1, 1929. The permanent system capped total annual quota admissions at 150,000, less than half of what the 1921 figures had yielded. A committee administered jointly by the Departments of Labor, Commerce, and State was charged with setting ceilings for each eligible nationality, based on its proportional share of the annual cap. The permanent system also changed the method of apportioning quotas. What counted now was not the foreign-born population of each nationality, but rather the number of "inhabitants in [the] continental United States" in 1920 who could trace their ancestry to that country. Because the new method reached back further in U.S. history, it almost doubled the United Kingdom quota, while almost halving them for Germany, Ireland, and the Scandinavian countries.

For all that the National Origins Act did to limit the number of "inferior" immigrants from southern and eastern Europe in favor of increased immigration from northern and western Europe, especially from the United Kingdom, it is at least as significant for the stark distinction that it drew between all European immigrants and all other immigrants. As historian Mae Ngai has observed, "the law constructed a white American race, in which persons of European descent shared a common whiteness distinct from those deemed to be not white." Of course, the naturalization laws, the Chinese exclusion laws, and the 1917 law creating the Asiatic barred zone were also major elements in this construction of whiteness. But only in 1924 did Congress set up a comprehensive scheme of immigrant quotas for Europeans, with all Asian nationalities expressly barred from lawful admission under that scheme.

The National Origins Act accomplished the exclusion of Asian immigrants by granting quotas only to nationalities included within the term "inhabitants in continental United States," which was defined to exclude "aliens ineligible to citizenship and their descendants." This clearly meant Asian immigrants after the *Ozawa* and *Thind* Supreme Court decisions in 1922 and 1923 had confirmed that Asian immigrants could not be white. Thus the exclusion of "aliens ineligible to citizenship and their descendants" barred anyone of Asian ancestry from immigrating under the quota system. Asian spouses and children of U.S. citizens were also barred from admission as non-quota immigrants. The only quotas allotted to Asian countries were quotas to allow their white inhabitants to immigrate to the United States.

Because the Asiatic barred zone created in 1917 had already shut out all other East Asian and South Asian immigrants countries except those from U.S. possessions like the Philippines, the practical effect of this part of the National Origins Act was to broaden the ban on Asian immigration to bar immigration from Japan, shutting off what Japanese immigration continued after the 1907 Gentlemen's Agreement. The only Asian immigration that continued in significant numbers after 1924 was from the Philippines because it was a U.S. possession, and for this reason Filipino workers became especially attractive to employers looking for cheap labor.[30]

Immigration to the Western Hemisphere from independent countries was exempt from the National Origins Act's system for immigrant admissions and so remained uncapped, but this exemption did not cover blacks from dependencies in the Caribbean. Reflecting the views of some legislators that black immigrants would not respect segregation and antimiscegenation statutes, the act's permanent quota system defined "inhabitants in continental United States" to exclude "the descendants of slave immigrants," thus stopping practically all black immigration to the United States.[31]

The absence of a cap on Western Hemisphere immigration in the National Origins Act was a setback for restrictionists. In theory, Mexican and other Western Hemisphere immigrants could work lawfully in the United States if they met qualitative requirements, such as the public charge exclusion ground and the literacy test. But even without a numerical cap or the sort of direct statutory exclusion that operated against Asian immigrants, discriminatory administrative and enforcement practices made much of the Mexican immigrant flow illegal. In the late 1920s and 1930s, the federal government enforced the public charge exclusion ground with particular severity against Mexicans. This, along with the

1885 ban on contract labor and the 1917 literacy test, reduced lawful immigration from Mexico to about one-fifth of prior levels, though surely the Great Depression of the 1930s also played a complex role in both stimulating and retarding Mexican immigration. At the start of this period, border control was almost nonexistent, but in 1924 Congress established the Border Patrol, and over time the federal government steadily increased the resources devoted to border enforcement.[32]

In addition to these restrictions on lawful immigration from the Western Hemisphere, the avenues of discretionary relief created after the National Origins Act to allow deportable noncitizens to stay in the United States lawfully were practically (and sometimes formally) unavailable to Mexicans, as Mae Ngai has shown. For example, the precursor to what is now cancellation of removal was used principally by Europeans and Canadians, whose immigration law violations were often regarded as merely technical or outweighed by the strength of their ties in the United States.[33]

As the Asian labor supply shrank with each new restriction on Asian immigration—the Chinese exclusion laws, the 1907 Gentlemen's Agreement, the 1917 Asiatic barred zone, and then the 1924 National Origins Act—the need for Mexican farmworkers became more acute. The irrigation of new croplands and the invention of the refrigerated railroad car had enabled the growth of large-scale commercial farming around the turn of the twentieth century. These developments spurred the search for armies of low-wage workers to tend and harvest the fields. Farmers in the southwestern United States began to rely heavily on Mexican laborers. Of the Mexicans who were able to enter legally, many did so not as lawful immigrants, but as commuters or temporary farmworkers. In this setting, southwestern agricultural interests benefited from the absence of a rigid Western Hemisphere cap in the National Origins Act, which combined with the discriminatory but flexible administrative practices to ensure a supply of immigrant labor, both lawful and unlawful.

Unlawful workers from Mexico offered the advantage that employers could exploit them when they were in the United States and send them back to Mexico when they were no longer needed. During the joblessness of the Great Depression, state and local authorities encouraged and promoted repatriation of Mexicans as well as some U.S. citizens of Mexican ancestry. The result was a 41 percent reduction in the Mexican population in the United States. This economically driven fluctuation in patterns of immigration law enforcement against Mexican immigrants, especially in the American Southwest, started a pattern of partial tolerance of unlawful immigration that continues to the present day.

The McCarran-Walter Act and the Persistence of National Origins

Chinese exclusion and the bar on Chinese naturalization were repealed in 1943 as part of America's wartime diplomacy at a time when China was an ally against Japan. Immigrants of Chinese descent were still severely limited to only 105 per year, but with an important exception: spouses were exempt from this cap. After World War II, Congress lifted the formal bars to immigration from India and the newly independent Philippines, but the flow from these countries remained a tightly regulated trickle, with annual caps of only 100 immigrants per country. These were small steps, but they started the process of dismantling the discriminatory framework of Asian exclusion and the National Origins Act.[34]

In 1952, the McCarran-Walter Act reworked the federal immigration laws into the Immigration and Nationality Act, which remains its current statutory framework. Though Congress removed the remaining racial bars to naturalization, the price of achieving this consensus on naturalization was preserving the discriminatory national origins system for immigrant admissions. Outright Japanese and Korean exclusion ended, but total annual quota immigration from a so-called Asia-Pacific triangle was limited to two thousand, with individual country allotments of only one hundred. This limit was based on race rather than country of origin. It applied only to an immigrant "attributable by as much as one-half of his ancestry to a people or peoples indigenous" to the region. The McCarran-Walter Act also established separate subquotas for colonial dependencies in the Western Hemisphere, a move designed to continue stifling black Caribbean immigration. Overall, the level of annual immigrant admissions under the quota system was the 150,000 allowed by the 1924 National Origins Act, plus several thousand immigrant admissions for small quotas assigned to newly eligible countries.[35]

At the same time, the McCarran-Walter Act significantly ameliorated the national origins system by no longer counting spouses and children of U.S. citizens against the nationality quotas. For the Chinese-American community, this non-quota immigration helped to begin redressing the severe gender imbalance and stunted family formation that had resulted from several generations of Chinese exclusion and from laws that took U.S. citizenship away from citizen women who married noncitizens. In fact, after 1952, non-quota immigrant admissions ran as high as quota-based immigrant admissions in the same time period.[36]

The McCarran-Walter Act became law over President Truman's veto. His veto message charged that the "greatest vice" of the national origins system was "that it discriminate[d], deliberately and intentionally, against many of the peoples of the world," and that it violated "the great political doctrine of the Declaration of Independence that 'all men are created equal.'" The view that prevailed, however, was set out in a Senate Judiciary Committee report, which explained that the national origins system served to "preserve the sociological and cultural balance in the United States," and to allow the admission of immigrants "more readily assimilable because of the similarity of their cultural background." Congress overrode Truman's veto with only two votes to spare in the Senate. Although a 1961 statute repealed the annual limit of two thousand Asia-Pacific Triangle admissions, the national origins system remained intact as the foundation of immigrant admissions.[37]

The 1965 amendments to the Immigration and Nationality Act abolished the national origins system in favor of a new selection system that took effect on July 1, 1968. Immigrant admissions from countries outside the Western Hemisphere were capped at 170,000 annually and divided into seven "preferences" for various close relatives of citizens and permanent residents, for workers of various education and skill levels, and for refugees. Annual immigration from any single country outside the Western Hemisphere was limited to 20,000.

For the Western Hemisphere, the annual limit was 120,000, which was subject neither to limits on immigration from any single country, nor to the system of immigration preferences. The apparent overall annual limit was thus 290,000, but because a citizen's spouse, minor children, and parents of adult citizens did not count toward the limit, this figure drastically understates lawful immigrant admissions. Subsequent legislation adjusted this scheme. For example, Congress in 1976 applied the per-country limit of 20,000 to all countries, in 1980 lowered the overall limit to 270,000, and in 1990 redefined some of the preferences. Overall, however, the 1965 amendments set up the basic outline of today's immigrant admissions system.[38]

The 1965 amendments were a sea change in U.S. immigration law, marking the first time that it adopted a basic nondiscrimination principle. In sharp contrast to pre-1952 naturalization statutes and the 1924 national origins system, the immigration system after 1965 was apparently race-neutral. The 1965 immigration amendments crystallized the sentiments that had already led to the repeal of restrictions on Asian immigration and naturalization. And in broader perspective, the amendments were part of a basic movement toward civil rights in American public law that included the Civil Rights Act of 1964 and the Voting Rights Act of 1965.[39]

In the spirit of President Truman's unsuccessful veto of the McCarran-Walter Act in 1952, then-Senator John F. Kennedy called for an end to the national origins system in his book, *A Nation of Immigrants*, published in 1958.[40] During the early 1960s, many in Congress expressed the view that the end of the national origins system was, like the repeal of racial bars to naturalization in 1952, an essential part of an emerging civil rights program. Many of these legislators were from the very southern and eastern European immigrant groups targeted by the National Origins Act—among them Congressmen Peter Rodino of New Jersey and Dan Rostenkowski of Illinois.

These calls for an end to national origins were especially persuasive against the backdrop of the Cold War with the Soviet Union, and even more so given the widespread view that the United States had failed miserably by not taking in more refugees before World War II. Texas Congressman Kika de la Garza argued: "At a time when the true spirit and philosophy of the United States must be made evident to the world, we can no longer afford to have on our statute books any reference to the fact that people are welcome to this country depending upon their race or ethnic origin." Signing the 1965 amendments into law at the base of the Statue of Liberty, President Lyndon Johnson declared that they "repair a deep and painful flaw in the fabric of American justice . . . . The days of unlimited immigration are past. But those who do come will come because of what they are, not because of the land from which they sprung."[41]

Immigration After 1965

The profound shifts in immigration to the United States that took place after 1965 are important because they round out the story of race in immigration that parallels the lost story of Americans in waiting. To start, the statistics on the immigrant flow are arresting. The increase in the sheer volume of immigration has raised the foreign-born percentage of the U.S. population from around 5 percent in 1970 to about 11.7 percent in 2003. At least as significant is the fact that the ethnic composition of the immigrant flow changed. From 1951 through 1960, 53 percent of new lawful immigrants came from Europe, and of those European immigrants, more than half came from two countries: Germany and the United Kingdom. In 2003, only 14.3 percent of new lawful immigrants came from Europe; more than 76 percent came from Asia and Latin America. The combined Asian and Latin American share of total immigration today is even greater if the undocumented are included.[42]

Why the dramatic increase in Latin American and Asian immigration? The links between causes and effects are complex. The 1965 amendments created a more open framework in which demographic and economic pressures in Asia and Latin America found a new outlet in immigration to the United States, but the trends that became very visible after 1965 were already under way when Congress acted. Asian immigration had already risen, especially through non-quota immigration by the spouses and children of U.S. citizens of Asian ancestry. For example, the Korean population in the United States, very small when the Korean War started in 1950, grew dramatically between the end of the war in 1953 and 1965. In the same period, relative prosperity in western Europe and the Soviet-imposed exit controls in eastern Europe kept the European quotas partly unused. If it seems high that 53 percent of all immigrants from 1951 to 1960 came from Europe, this percentage would have been higher if more Europeans had wanted to come. As historian Roger Daniels has noted, the majority of lawful immigrants came from Europe in only two of the thirteen years between the 1952 McCarran-Walter Act and the 1965 amendments.[43]

Before 1965, the shift in the ethnic composition of the immigrant flow toward immigration from Asia was limited because the quotas were still extremely restricted. But once Congress abolished the national origins system, the foothold immigrant communities that had established themselves by 1965 were able to expand dramatically. Also important were several new immigration categories that emphasized family reunification. Citizens could petition for their siblings, new lawful immigrants could petition for their spouses and children, and in turn these newcomers could later petition for qualifying relatives. In addition, a large number of Asian immigrants took advantage of the occupational preferences, and they, too, could then include their immediate family and later petition for siblings.[44]

For Latin America, the effects of the 1965 amendments were even more complex. Western Hemisphere immigrants generally had been able to immigrate lawfully without regard to numerical caps, but the 1965 amendments introduced a limit that took effect on July 1, 1968. Many in Congress feared a dramatic increase in Latin American immigration and were able to insist on limiting Western Hemisphere immigration in exchange for the end of national origins. The reformers who were intent on abolishing national origins were unable to refute the logic that if the law would henceforth treat all countries equally, the sort of overall numerical cap on immigration that had applied to the Eastern Hemisphere since the 1920s should apply to the Western Hemisphere as well.[45]

Although the new cap might logically have meant that Western Hemisphere immigration to the United States would drop, it actually increased, which is largely attributable to immigrant flow from Mexico. There were several causes. First, Western Hemisphere immigrants faced more obstacles before 1965 than the absence of a numerical cap would suggest. They had to meet the labor certification requirement, which meant that unless they were admitted based on family ties, they could be barred if the secretary of labor found that they would take jobs away from willing, able, and qualified U.S. workers. However, this seldom happened before 1965, when the presumption flipped. From then on, immigrants were excluded unless *they* showed that they would *not* be taking jobs from U.S. workers. More important, other exclusion grounds applied, such as the public charge ground and failure on the literacy test. This mattered because U.S. government agencies continued to enforce exclusion and deportation grounds vigorously against Mexicans—by far the largest Latin American immigrant group.[46]

Against this pre-1965 enforcement backdrop, and with the fees charged for an official crossing, many Mexicans who wanted to come to the United States found two alternatives more attractive than coming as lawful immigrants. Some came as temporary farmworkers under the Bracero program, which admitted around four hundred thousand Mexican workers annually from 1942 to 1964, the year it ended. Many chose the other alternative: to cross the border without immigration formalities at all, especially when economically driven fluctuations in enforcement patterns made it easy to do so.[47]

Latin American and especially Mexican immigration to the United States increased after 1965 for several reasons. First, generations of lawful and unlawful Mexican immigration—of which the Bracero program had been only the most recent lawful phase—had created and institutionalized expectations on the part of sending communities, employers in the United States, and the migrants themselves. The end of the Bracero program blocked one lawful avenue for satisfying those expectations, but it would have been naïve to think that the flow would simply stop. Sociologist Douglas Massey has documented that many Mexicans who could no longer come as Braceros became lawful immigrants before the new Western Hemisphere cap took effect in 1968.[48]

Mexican immigration also increased because of a steady downturn in the Mexican economy combined with an explosion in the Mexican population. Moreover, Mexican government development funds were directed toward Mexico-U.S. border cities. This drew migrants northward, and many continued across the border. Soon the number of Mexican immigrants hit the new Western Hemisphere cap, and later the even stricter per-country limit of twenty thousand immigrant visas that took effect in 1976. But by then, foothold communities had established themselves in the United States, and the new system of family and employment-based immigration categories allowed their compatriots to follow. Many who did not qualify under these categories came to the United States by means outside the law.

This chapter started by telling the lost story of Americans in waiting—intending citizens who were met generously with the expectation that they would become citizens. They could vote, homestead, and otherwise be treated like citizens from arrival. The idea of the intending citizen was part of what it meant to be an immigrant, and immigration was a transition to citizenship. But this chapter then explained how from 1795 to 1952, when the declaration of intent was required for naturalization and established lawful immigrants as Americans in waiting, both immigration and citizenship were formally restricted by race. Immigration as transition was for *some* immigrants only. The next question is what happened to the idea of Americans in waiting once immigration became more open.

CHAPTER 7

Transition at a Crossroads

★

The end of racial barriers to naturalization in 1952 and the discriminatory national origins system in 1965 were triumphs for the idea that national citizenship can be inclusive and treat all persons alike regardless of race or ethnicity. But this victory was more hollow than it seemed, for as immigration and naturalization opened up by race and ethnicity, immigration as transition and the idea of immigrants as Americans in waiting lost much of its influence. As immigration became more open to all, being an immigrant meant less.

The same 1952 McCarran-Walter Act that ended racial bars to naturalization also made the declaration of intent optional. The Senate report seemed to characterize the change as a concession to reality. The report explained only that "at the present time only 30 percent of those receiving naturalization have first filed a declaration of intention." This decline reflected the result of a growing list of groups exempted from the requirement, including spouses of citizens and honorably discharged members of the U.S. armed forces.[1]

Today, the declaration remains optional and may be filed by any permanent resident more than eighteen years of age who is in the United States. Several hundred each year are filed on Form N-300, to take advantage of federal and state statutes that still confer advantages on intending citizens.[2] With the declaration no longer required in the transition from immigrant to citizen, how important is the idea of Americans in waiting that was the basis for the declaration in the first place? How influential is immigration as transition as a way of explaining what is fair and just about the treatment of lawful immigrants?

Transition in Alienage Laws

The idea of Americans in waiting survives in a variety of federal and state statutes that expressly distinguish lawful immigrants who are intending citizens or are otherwise regarded as en route to citizenship from noncitizens who are not. One of the most prominent examples is the federal Immigration Reform and Control Act, sometimes called IRCA. Enacted in 1986, IRCA was a complex effort to curb undocumented immigration. One part of IRCA strengthened border controls. The act also introduced civil and criminal penalties for employers who knowingly employ the undocumented, or who do not fill out and keep paperwork designed to deter and expose unlawful employment. Until IRCA, no federal law prohibited the mere hiring of a noncitizen who was not allowed to work. Another part of IRCA was a temporary agricultural worker program intended to reduce the demand for undocumented farm labor. Finally, IRCA granted amnesty in the form of eventual permanent residence for most noncitizens who had been unlawfully in the United States since 1982.[3]

The act's new penalties for employers raised concerns—which later studies confirmed as valid—that notwithstanding existing antidiscrimination laws, employers would discriminate against Latinos, Asian Americans, or others who "look foreign." The act tried to address these problems with civil penalties for employment discrimination based on an individual's national origin or lack of U.S. citizenship. This part of IRCA echoed Title VII of the Civil Rights Act of 1964, which prohibits employment discrimination on the basis of race, color, religion, sex, and national origin. But IRCA covers smaller employers, and unlike Title VII it bans discrimination on the basis of citizenship status.[4]

The original 1986 version of IRCA penalized employers only if they discriminated against citizens, or against intending citizens because they were not citizens. The statute defined intending citizens largely as I have—as permanent residents who have filed declarations of intent—but only if they applied for naturalization within six months of satisfying the residency requirement and became citizens within two years of applying. There were exceptions for processing delays and for those "actively pursuing naturalization."[5]

In 1990, Congress deleted the requirement of a declaration of intent before filing an antidiscrimination complaint under IRCA, but the basic idea remains. The statute now says that a noncitizen is not a "protected individual" unless she applies to naturalize within six months of satisfying the residency requirement and becomes a citizen within two years of applying. The exceptions remain for processing delays and actively pursuing naturalization. Like the Supreme Court's reasoning in *Harisiades* and *Carlson* that non-naturalizing lawful immigrants should not complain if they are treated less well than citizens, IRCA's antidiscrimination provisions protect lawful immigrants only if they are on their way to citizenship.[6]

The same idea of Americans in waiting also appears in a variety of other federal statutes that currently favor lawful immigrants who are intending citizens—defined as noncitizens who have filed a declaration of intent to naturalize—over noncitizens who are not. Some of these federal statutes were enacted back when a declaration of intent was a prerequisite for naturalization, and other statutes were enacted after a declaration became optional in 1952. Since the late 1800s, only citizens or intending citizens have been able to own mineral rights in the United States or to acquire land in U.S. territories. Under the Taylor Grazing Act, which became law in 1934, permits are issued only to citizens and noncitizens who have filed declarations of intent to become citizens "as required by the naturalization laws" (although as mentioned no such declarations are required today). Under more recently adopted provisions, the National Institute of Standards and Technology may hire intending citizens if it cannot find suitably qualified citizens, and the Board of Governors of the Federal Reserve System may hire only citizens or intending citizens. Federal restrictions on technology exports adopted in the 1990s do not rely on declarations of intent, but rather use the IRCA definition of "protected individual" to treat lawful immigrants like citizens unless they can naturalize but do not.[7]

Some state laws similarly reflect the idea of Americans in waiting by distinguishing explicitly between noncitizens who are headed toward citizenship and those who are not. For example, some states limit certain housing programs and property ownership to citizens and intending citizens. Under a California statute, only citizens and intending citizens may file mining claims. Other state laws treat intending citizens like citizens for certain types of state public employment, for admission to the bar, and for access to state public works contracts. The Washington State Supreme Court has upheld the constitutionality of a state statute that imposes criminal penalties for unlicensed firearm possession only on noncitizens who are not intending citizens.[8]

Other state laws go further and treat a lawful immigrant like a citizen only if he has applied for naturalization, or in some cases actually naturalized. The U.S. Supreme Court decision in *Ambach v. Norwick* upheld a New York statute that barred noncitizens from public school teaching unless they had applied for naturalization and naturalized within a certain time period. Similarly, New Jersey will issue a teaching certificate to a lawful immigrant only if she has filed a declaration of intent to naturalize. The certificate will be revoked if she has not naturalized five years later or becomes ineligible to naturalize.[9]

Some state welfare statutes also require more than a declaration of intent. In New Jersey, lawful immigrants and some other lawfully present noncitizens are eligible for state food stamps. They lose their eligibility if they meet the residency requirement for naturalization but do not apply to naturalize within sixty days. Several other states also condition a lawful immigrant's welfare eligibility on applying for naturalization once he can. Other states require their agencies to encourage eligible noncitizens to naturalize. Of course, states tie benefits to naturalization because they can cut costs by turning lawful immigrants who cannot draw federal aid into citizens who can. But regardless of motivation, these laws distinguish noncitizens who will naturalize from noncitizens who will not.[10]

Although federal and state statutes address a wide variety of topics and show that the idea of Americans in waiting sometimes matters, the statutes are so scattered that collectively they show that viewing immigration as transition is *not* as pervasive as it once was. After all, declarations of intent were once required before naturalization and served as the key to the fundamental matter of noncitizen voting eligibility. Both of these chief signs of immigration as transition are gone. At the same time, however, laws that incorporate the idea of Americans in waiting remain familiar enough that legislators could revive the idea, if they so choose.

Transition in Permanent Residence

Assessing the real influence of immigration as transition today requires looking beyond statutes that expressly treat intending citizens differently, and analyzing aspects of immigration and citizenship that are more fundamental and even taken for granted. One important sign that immigration as transition remains influential is the very existence of the status of permanent residence. In each of the six years from 1998 through 2003, an average of about 830,000 noncitizens became lawful immigrants and thus acquired the status of permanent resident of the United States. This status is not tied to a particular job, school, or locale. It entitles lawful immigrants to stay indefinitely, and it qualifies its holder for citizenship a few years later.[11] Conferring this status on a large group of noncitizens when they first arrive in the United States seems so natural that it is easy to overlook the important choice that it represents—to identify a group of potential future citizens.

Looking at some other countries that do not confer precitizenship status upon initial admission makes clear that permanent resident status in the United States reflects immigration as transition. Countries where the traditional self-image is *not* one of a nation of immigrants—where immigration is not seen as a transition to citizenship—typically have no immigration law status equivalent to permanent residence in the United States. Consider Germany, where the longtime official government policy was that it is not "a country of immigration." Germany historically *sent* migrants to the United States, Canada, Latin America, and elsewhere. But the reality in Germany has changed over the past few decades as more and more immigrants have arrived. The German government has acknowledged officially that Germany is indeed a country of immigration, although one of the two largest political parties has cautioned that it is not a *classic* country of immigration.[12]

Consistent with this traditional German attitude toward immigration, it is not surprising that German law has historically admitted noncitizens for fixed admission periods rather than for the indefinite stay that is the hallmark of permanent residence in the United States. Noncitizens in Germany generally can acquire an indefinite residence permit like U.S. permanent residence only after they renew their residence permits for five years and satisfy other conditions, including knowledge of the German language and payments into a Social Security–type program.[13]

The evolution of this German counterpart to permanent residence shows that it is not based on any notion that lawful immigrants should be treated from arrival as future citizens. Rather, the German indefinite resident permit is based on immigration as affiliation and the idea that equality is more earned than presumed. Before 1978, residence permits were issued for a limited duration, though they could be renewed. Two decisions of the German Constitutional Court in the 1970s limited state discretion to deny renewal of residence permits or to deport noncitizens.

These decisions reflected the idea that with long-term residence, noncitizens gain a measure of constitutional protection. This recognition of ties then became the conceptual basis for the indefinite residence permits that Germany began to issue in 1978.[14]

There are signs of change in both Germany and the United States. As of 2005, a new German law for the first time authorizes a U.S.-style indefinite residence permit from the date of initial admission. Against the backdrop of prior official refusal to acknowledge immigration, the existence of something resembling permanent residence in the United States has at least symbolic significance. So far, however, admission in this new category is too restricted and extraordinary to signal a reorientation of basic German policy toward anything close to "Germans in waiting."[15]

In the United States, change is more pronounced, and it is in the opposite direction, away from treating lawful immigrants on arrival as Americans in waiting and toward the assumptions more typical of Germany. New U.S. laws and policies have reduced emphasis on admitting noncitizens as lawful immigrants when they first arrive, and thus diminished the influence of immigration as transition. It has become more typical over the past generation for noncitizens to arrive in the United States either lawfully as nonimmigrants or even unlawfully, but then to acquire family and community ties that make them eligible to become lawful immigrants. The number of noncitizens who came as lawful immigrants or in an asylum or refugee status that converts automatically to permanent residence has decreased steadily in recent years, from 66 percent in the two-year period 1998–99 to 38 percent in 2004.[16]

Several new nonimmigrant categories expressly allow for this later affiliation-based, German-style conversion to permanent residence. Proposals under serious discussion in Congress would admit workers temporarily (especially in agriculture) but let them become lawful immigrants after they work for several years. The apparent trend is that more newcomers to the United States are *not* treated on arrival as Americans in waiting. Although newcomers may become lawful immigrants, this is based on ties that they acquire—immigration as affiliation. The idea of Americans in waiting has become less central to what it means to come to America.[17]

And as the idea of Americans in waiting has waned, being a permanent resident has become closer to other forms of lawful presence in the United States. It has long been true that courts have rejected the constitutional arguments of permanent residents, treating them no better than other noncitizens. But it is noteworthy when an important U.S. Supreme Court decision *in favor* of noncitizens does not rely on the fact that the noncitizens in question had been permanent residents. This happened in the 2001 decision in *Zadvydas v. Davis*, which held that the government may not indefinitely detain noncitizens who cannot be removed from the United States. The Court noted that Zadvydas and Ma had been lawfully admitted and were physical present in the United States, but it mentioned only in passing that they had been permanent residents.[18]

Legal scholar David Martin is correct that Zadvydas and Ma's prior permanent resident status is a "more thorough explanation" for the outcome than any rationale that the Court actually articulated.[19] But as a matter of ways to think and talk about immigration and citizenship, the absence of permanent residence in the Court's explanation is highly noteworthy—and yet not a complete surprise, for it is consistent with the subtle but clear trend. Permanent resident status has become less central to what it means to come to the United States. It has become commonplace to talk about lawful immigrants as if they were no different from noncitizens who are not lawful immigrants. Immigration as transition and the idea of Americans in waiting matters less, and the line that really matters is becoming the line that divides all citizens from all noncitizens.

Transition in Citizenship Laws

Examining naturalization in the United States is another important way to assess the current influence of immigration as transition and the idea of Americans in waiting. First, consider the basic requirements. Naturalization is generally open only to lawful immigrants, and closed to many other noncitizens who live and work in the United States. The only noncitizens who are not lawful immigrants but still can naturalize are noncitizen U.S. nationals and some noncitizens who have served in the U.S. armed forces. Otherwise, naturalization applicants must have been permanent residents for five years, though this requirement is only three years if they are spouses of U.S. citizens, and even less if they have worked for certain U.S. government agencies and nonprofit organizations. A minimum period of physical presence in the United States is also required. Applicants must be at least eighteen years old. Applicants must be persons "of good moral character," a requirement that can disqualify a noncitizen with a criminal conviction.[20]

Since 1906, naturalization applicants also have had to pass an English language test. The current statute requires "an understanding of the English language, including an ability to read, write, and speak words in ordinary usage in the English language." There is a test for "knowledge and understanding of the fundamentals of the history, and of the principles and form of government, of the United States." These English and civics requirements may be waived due to age or disability, and there is a special exemption for refugees from Laos who fought for the United States during the war in Vietnam. Naturalization applicants must be "attached to the principles of the Constitution of the United States and well disposed to the good order and happiness of the United States." All applicants except the disabled must take an oath of allegiance to the United States. At times, Congress has considered proposals for stiffer requirements, such as bills introduced in the 1880s and 1890s that would have required ten or even twenty-one years of residence before applying. But these and similar proposals have not become law.[21]

The current naturalization requirements are undemanding for many who apply, and for them the transition to citizenship can be easy and routine. For other potential citizens, however, the requirements and procedures pose serious obstacles. Though the government approves most applications, it denies many others. Some applicants fail the civics test, even though the government has relied since 1986 on a set of one hundred possible questions available for study in advance along with the answers. Other denials are based on lack of good moral character because of criminal convictions, sometimes for crimes that may seem minor.

The denial rate for naturalization applications was once quite low, but it increased dramatically in the late 1990s. Denials in the six-year period from 1998 through 2003 were about 35 percent of the number of applications. This figure is hard to interpret, since an application counted as denied in any given year could have been filed in a previous year. But the contrast with prior eras is clear; the average denial rate for the thirty years from 1961 to 1990 was much lower—less than 3 percent.[22]

The government once officially reported the reasons for denials. The overwhelming majority were for withdrawal or failure to follow through with the application. These reports stopped in the early 1980s, leaving observers to informed speculation. Some denials reflect criminal convictions or failure to pass the English or civics tests, but much of the recent rise in the denial rate is related to processing delays. In the late 1990s, naturalization applicants often had to wait several years for a decision. Delays raise the denial rate by making more likely that applicants fail to respond to government correspondence, miss interviews, or even die while waiting. The real denial rate for the past ten years is probably lower than the high figures for the late 1990s, and closer to the 3 percent that prevailed before 1990. But the denial rate only partly answers the question whether naturalization requirements reflect immigration as transition. The prospect of denial deters many potential citizens from applying. Respondents in one survey most often pointed to insufficient English-language ability as the reason they had not applied. Long processing delays undoubtedly dampen interest among some eligible applicants, and others are hard-pressed to come up with the application fees, $400 per person as of 2006.[23]

From 1991 through 2004, an average of about 550,000 new U.S. citizens naturalized annually, in spite of significant processing delays during much of this period. The naturalization rate differs widely by nationality. Lawful immigrants from Vietnam and Taiwan have been more than five times as likely to naturalize as those from Germany and Canada. In 2003, more than 42 percent of naturalizing new citizens were born in Asia. Overall, about 60 percent of the noncitizens who have been permanent residents long enough to naturalize have done so, and 40 percent have not.[24] The naturalization requirements and rate as a whole show that the United States is open to naturalization by lawful immigrants, but not unequivocally so. Immigration as transition is influential, but it could be more influential. There is room to move in either direction.

Naturalization requirements and naturalization rates do not tell the whole story, of course. Any look at naturalization to assess the influence of immigration as transition needs to dig deeper than the acquisition of formal citizenship status. At least as important are complex questions about degrees of social, political, and economic participation in American society, as well as equally daunting questions about belonging to America and feeling American. At this level, naturalization is far from routine for many lawful immigrants who might become U.S. citizens. This may explain why the naturalization rate is not higher, since an eligible immigrant may decide against naturalization if it will not mean belonging.

In spite of these complexities, encouraging naturalization is a frequently articulated U.S. government goal, as a number of court decisions in recent decades have acknowledged. Moreover, eligible immigrants have a right to be naturalized if they meet the requirements. Government officials do not have open-ended discretion to deny or approve naturalization applications; they must apply legal rules and standards set out in statutes and regulations. This contrasts with what a legislative report called "a very loose, unsatisfactory, and careless method of naturalization" in state courts before 1906, when Congress changed the name of the federal Bureau of Immigration to the Bureau of Immigration and Naturalization and federal authorities assumed the power to decide naturalization applications.[25]

The United States is, by law and tradition, more open to naturalization than many other countries are. Though some individuals may face social and psychological barriers to naturalization, such barriers tend to be lower in the United States than elsewhere. Naturalization in the United States is comparatively unremarkable and even routine. These differences between naturalization in various countries are consistent with their traditional views of immigration. For example, the same contrast that is evident in immigration laws of the United States and Germany has its counterpart in naturalization.

Naturalization in Germany: A Comparative Side-Glance

For much of modern German history, to "be German" has not been rooted in membership in any single political state, but rather has been "prepolitical" in the sense that no German state included all those who traditionally called themselves Germans. This was true before German unification in 1870, remained true after 1870 because of the diaspora of persons of German descent into eastern Europe and the former Soviet Union, and continued in a different form during the era of East and West Germanys—effectively from the end of World War II until 1990. It is therefore unsurprising that the traditional German understanding of naturalization assumes more than membership in a "German" political entity. Rather, naturalization historically has meant that the applicant becomes German in a profound way, through something of a change of identity. An Austrian colleague who lives in Germany once quipped, "You can become a German, but it takes longer than a lifetime." At an even more fundamental level, the traditional function of naturalization is not to foster an individual's integration into German society, but rather to affirm or even consecrate integration after it has occurred, as legal scholar Kay Hailbronner has put it.[26]

In contrast to naturalization as of right in the United States, naturalization applicants in Germany traditionally had no expectation of approval based on objective legal standards. Until 1990, German law gave government officials a great deal of discretion to approve or deny naturalization in individual cases. The German government's 1977 naturalization guidelines noted that resident aliens enjoyed "far-reaching rights and liberties" without becoming citizens. Elevating resident aliens to citizenship through naturalization depended on the touchstone of cultural assimilation, as measured by each applicant's "basic attitude toward German culture," his or her "voluntary and lasting orientation" (*Hinwendung*) to Germany, and whether naturalization would be in the "public interest."[27]

In the United States, the acquisition of the *formal* status of citizen through naturalization is comparatively unburdened by deep issues of ethnocultural identity. (I defer for several pages the more complex question whether this formal citizenship status leads to full sense of belonging to America, or instead to a version of what is sometimes called "second-class citizenship.") One key contributor to this separation between blood and citizenship is that acquiring citizenship by birth under U.S. law depends on birth on U.S. soil (*jus soli*), not the citizenship of a child's parents (*jus sanguinis*). It is no accident that countries that rely mainly on *jus soli* for birthright citizenship tend to be open to naturalization, and that countries—including Germany—that rely mainly on *jus sanguinis* have relatively restrictive naturalization laws.

This makes sense, for both *jus sanguinis* and restrictive naturalization laws reflect the knowledge—and perhaps the intent—that citizenship laws preserve the ethnic origins of the population, much as the National Origins Act did in U.S. immigration law. In contrast, both *jus soli* and open naturalization policies reflect the knowledge—and perhaps the intent—that citizenship laws broaden the ethnic origins of the population. In this way, *jus soli* belongs to a view of citizenship that includes routine naturalization, which is turn is a hallmark of immigration as transition.[28]

Jus soli birthright citizenship also reflects immigration as transition in another, equally crucial way. *Jus soli* reflects transition for *families*, by assuring first-generation immigrant parents that their children born in the United States will be citizens. Historically, this was especially important for Asian immigrants, who were barred from naturalization, but whose

U.S.-born children became citizens under the U.S. Supreme Court's 1898 decision in *Wong Kim Ark*. More fundamentally, *jus soli* recognizes that transition can be a multigenerational process. The United States has no second-generation or third-generation noncitizens. Similar thinking explains why the U.S. Constitution counts all persons for constitutional redistricting regardless of their immigration status. This rule recognizes that legislators represent not just current residents, but also a district's future residents, many of whom will be citizens by virtue of *jus soli*.[29]

Understandings of immigration and citizenship in Germany are evolving, as they are elsewhere. Legal scholar Ruth Rubio-Marin has observed that the reunification of Germany and the return of the German diaspora eliminated two key supports for an ethnocultural definition of German citizenship. And immigration itself is another chief agent of change, notably in significant amendments to German naturalization law that took effect in 1990, 1992, and 2000. (Developments in European Union citizenship have done little in the short term to undermine the centrality of national citizenship.)[30]

Though the 1990 amendments did not adopt naturalization "as of right," they did adopt naturalization "as a general rule" for first-generation immigrants born outside Germany with fifteen years of residence in Germany. The 1990 amendments also dropped the residence requirement to eight years for immigrant families' second- and third-generation children—born in Germany to immigrant parents or grandparents but without citizen status because of *jus sanguinis* citizenship laws. At least as important, the 1990 amendments, by making naturalization available "as a general rule," meant that government officials could deny applications only in exceptional cases. The 1990 amendments also lowered the fees considerably.[31]

The 1992 amendments turned "as a general rule" naturalization into "as of right" naturalization. Assimilation tests were replaced by a presumption of assimilation based on length of residence and other objective criteria. The 1992 changes also eased naturalization by allowing applicants to retain prior citizenship in some circumstances. Amendments in 2000 reduced the residence requirement to eight years for all applicants. Though this is considerably longer than the five or three years required in the United States, the number of naturalizations in Germany is much higher now than it was ten or fifteen years ago. And as a sign that the naturalization changes marked a broader shift in German citizenship law, the 2000 amendments also introduced a limited form of *jus soli* citizenship.[32]

Although these recent changes signal a shift in direction, it takes time to change deeply rooted attitudes. Naturalization in Germany shows that naturalization in the United States is comparatively routine and unremarkable. The effects of the German amendments have been limited. Reducing the residency requirement from fifteen to eight years did nothing for the large number of potential applicants who had already lived in Germany for more than fifteen years but had not naturalized for other reasons. The new *jus soli* provisions are subject to significant conditions. A child born in Germany acquires *jus soli* citizenship only if one parent has lived in Germany for eight years with certain types of residence permits. Moreover, the child must choose before his twenty-third birthday between German and any other citizenship that she may hold. This key aspect of the new *jus soli* rules reveals the one area in which German citizenship law seems most resistant to change: dual citizenship.

Dual Citizenship and Transition

Whether any individual is a dual citizen depends on the interaction of two (or more) national laws. Consider two typical scenarios. Ralf is born in New York City. Both his mother and his father are German citizens. Ralf will be a German citizen by *jus sanguinis*. He will be a U.S. citizen by *jus soli*. As this example shows, dual citizenship often results when a child is born in a *jus soli* country to parents from a *jus sanguinis* country. In a second scenario, Maria, a citizen of imaginary Ruritania, naturalizes as a U.S. citizen. If Ruritanian law allows her to keep Ruritanian citizenship, Maria would be both a Ruritanian and U.S. citizen. But if Ruritania disallows this—perhaps because it sees naturalization in another country as severing ties to Ruritania—Maria will be a U.S. citizen only, even if the United States accepts dual citizenship.[33]

Attitudes toward dual citizenship measure the influence of immigration as transition because forcing an applicant to relinquish her former citizenship makes naturalization that much less routine. Germany tolerates dual citizenship, but generally only for ethnic Germans, children of binational couples, and children born to German parents in countries with *jus soli* citizenship. The official position is that these are exceptions, and that dual citizenship is disallowed, for example for immigrant parents' children who acquire citizenship through the new *jus soli* rules, or where dual citizenship would arise from naturalization in Germany. This attitude against dual citizenship is consistent with German hesitation to accept naturalization as routine.[34]

In comparative perspective, U.S. acceptance of dual citizenship is tied in three ways to making naturalization unexceptional and thus consistent with immigration as transition. First, allowing a new U.S. citizen to keep her former citizenship can eliminate practical disincentives to naturalize. For example, until 1998 Mexican citizens who naturalized in the United States automatically lost Mexican citizenship and thus their right to inherit property in Mexico. When Mexico began to accept a limited form of dual nationality, more permanent residents from Mexico became U.S. citizens. Second, dual citizenship is tied to routine naturalization because it suggests that naturalization need not involve the sort of identity transformation that might burden naturalization in other countries. Prospective citizens are more likely to want this thinner version of naturalization. Third, dual citizenship makes naturalization seem more ordinary because applicants may believe that they will be more welcome as new citizens in a country that accepts dual citizenship.[35]

At a Crossroads

A mixed picture emerges from this chapter's search for immigration as transition and the idea of Americans in waiting. Today, the formal status of intending citizen has legal consequences, with some laws expressly distinguishing lawful immigrants who are intending citizens from all other noncitizens. Perhaps more important, immigration as transition is evident in some of the basic structure of immigration and citizenship law: the very status of permanent residence, *jus soli* citizenship, and routine naturalization.

On the whole, however, being an intending citizen makes a difference too seldom to signal that the idea of Americans in waiting has anything close to the central role that the idea once played in thinking and talking about immigration. This has been the trend since the declaration of intent became optional in 1952. Permanent residence means less than it once did as a status for persons admitted from their first day in the United States as a group of potential citizens. Naturalization requirements are more demanding, and naturalization rates are lower than they could be.

An even more basic sign that the influence of immigration as transition has diminished is the language of current debates. The core of immigration as contract, affiliation, or transition is not a particular result (which might be explained in other ways), but rather a certain rhetorical style and appeal to fairness and justice. The language of current debates largely reflects immigration as contract and immigration as affiliation. Some people insist that lawful immigrants and other noncitizens need not be treated as the equal of citizens, and that fair and just results may be achieved without equality as long as immigrants have proper notice and their expectations are protected. This is immigration as contract. The rebuttal typically urges the recognition of the ties that lawful immigrants and other noncitizens have acquired during their lives in the United States. This is the affiliation-based view that fair and just results require a form of earned equality.

All of this reflects a trend toward accepting two competing approaches to immigration. In debates over welfare eligibility and deportation, contract and affiliation have assumed center stage, and immigration as transition is much less seen or heard. Though reports of the demise of the idea that lawful immigrants are Americans in waiting may be exaggerated, immigration as transition is clearly at a crossroads.

CHAPTER 8

The Meaning of Transition

★

What would it mean to take transition seriously and treat and talk about immigrants as Americans in waiting? And why, if at all, should this happen? To answer these questions, I start with some key similarities between immigration as transition and immigration as affiliation. Both reflect a welcome of lawful immigrants. Both assume that democracy is impaired by having a permanent group of marginalized residents who are governed but cannot acquire a voice in governing. The risk to democratic processes and to confidence in those processes is especially grave if this excluded population is large and has complied with the requirements for lawful presence.

Compare these assumptions to immigration as contract, which instead assumes that fairness and justice are attainable by replacing a version of equality for lawful immigrants with adequate notice and protection of expectations. Contract sees the terms of belonging as part of the original understanding associated with a noncitizen's arrival. This understanding may be exclusionary, as the early plenary power cases show. More recent examples show that immigration as contract can sometimes protect noncitizens, if the government has changed the laws that apply to noncitizens or otherwise upset their expectations. As a general rule, however, immigration as contract assumes that even lawful immigrants will not acquire rights under U.S. law as time passes. Instead, immigration as contract justifies limits on immigrants' rights, with proper notice.

Like contract, both affiliation and transition recognize that not *all* lawful immigrants are equal to citizens, and in this sense both treat permanent residence as a probationary period. Unlike contract, both affiliation and transition try to give some meaning to equality, but by treating only *some* lawful immigrants like citizens. Immigration as affiliation treats those with ties like citizens; transition treats the lawful immigrants who are on their way to citizenship like citizens.[1]

The key to equality in both affiliation and transition is that they redefine equality to mean *access* to equality. Immigration as affiliation allows lawful immigrants to earn a degree of equality as they develop ties in the United States. Immigration as transition presumes that lawful immigrants and citizens are equal until the immigrants decline to naturalize. As a corollary, both affiliation and transition find acceptable a *temporary* difference between lawful immigrants and citizens, even if permanent second-class status is unacceptable. The key is each individual lawful immigrant's access to equality, which both affiliation and transition provide. But fundamental problems arise if lawful immigrants face impenetrable barriers to equality of treatment, for this would create a permanently marginalized group.[2]

Beyond Territorial Personhood and International Human Rights

Both affiliation and transition go beyond the protections for lawful immigrants that derive from territorial personhood or international human rights, which provide only a minimum degree of recognition for noncitizens in the United States. Both territorial personhood and international human rights stop short of recognizing that noncitizens, especially lawful immigrants, have many connections to the United States beyond physical presence or being a person. This is why territorial personhood and human rights figure most prominently in arguments by refugees and asylum seekers, who often have no connection to the United States other than getting here, and less in arguments by lawful immigrants.

To show how both affiliation and transition go beyond territorial personhood and human rights, consider two main arguments in the mid-1990s against the restrictions in California's Proposition 187 on public benefits for the undocumented. The first argument was that all persons, citizens or not, are entitled to a minimum standard of living that includes adequate health care, food, and financial security. One possible source of such a standard is the Universal Declaration of Human Rights, adopted by the United Nations General Assembly in 1948. The declaration proclaimed that persons have a "right to a standard of living adequate for the health and well-being of himself and of his family, including food, clothing, housing and medical care and necessary social services." However, this document was not intended as a binding instrument, nor is it customary international law.[3] Other international law instruments that are intended to be binding have similar provisions. The International Covenant on Economic, Social and Cultural Rights, which the United States has signed but not ratified, recognizes "the right of everyone to the enjoyment of the highest attainable standard of physical and mental health." But even if the United States were a party, this standard is too vague to support a serious challenge to Proposition 187.[4]

Human rights–based criticism of Proposition 187 relies much more heavily on the argument that any country has only limited authority to discriminate between citizens and noncitizens. The Universal Declaration of Human Rights provides: "All are equal before the law and are entitled without any discrimination to equal protection of the law." The International Covenant for Civil and Political Rights is virtually identical: "All persons are equal before the law and are entitled without any discrimination to the equal protection of the law." But even staunch human rights proponents concede that no nondiscrimination principle can be absolute in immigration and citizenship as long as some persons are citizens, other persons are not, and citizenship has meaning. Any nondiscrimination argument begs the question: When is different treatment *too* different?[5]

Those who rely on territorial personhood or human rights–based nondiscrimination arguments to challenge the unequal treatment of lawful immigrants risk serious unintended consequences. The easy refutation of these arguments can make discrimination against lawful immigrants seem justified and thus dilute protections for them to a lowest common denominator for *all* noncitizens in the United States. A cautionary tale is Germany's Basic Law, key provisions of which protect human rights of individuals whether they are German citizens or not. Though this was an understandable reflection of the immediate post-World War II reaction to the recent Nazi past, the heavy reliance on human rights may allow citizenship to be more exclusive. Put more generally, a focus on territorial personhood or human rights may make it too easy to minimize rights. Affiliation and transition recognize that noncitizens, especially lawful immigrants, should sometimes be treated like citizens for reasons that go beyond territorial personhood and human rights.[6]

Transition and Affiliation: The Differences

The differences between transition and affiliation emerge most clearly in the ways that they distinguish among noncitizens. Immigration as affiliation does not confer citizen-like treatment on all lawful immigrants. Affiliation says that new arrivals have only minimal ties but should be treated more like citizens as they build a life in the United States. Affiliation-based equality is to be earned. Permanent residence gradually resembles citizenship but does not equal it, although a few advocates of immigration as affiliation urge what amounts to automatic naturalization of longtime permanent residents.[7] Immigration as affiliation recognizes that a group of newly arrived lawful immigrants will always be treated unlike citizens, but addresses the problem of defining equality in immigration and citizenship by letting individual lawful immigrants gradually earn near-equality through an approximation of citizenship.

Affiliation is the real foundation for some arguments on behalf of noncitizens that are phrased in human rights terms. One argument against Proposition 187 was that it violates human rights to deny public benefits to anyone—lawfully or unlawfully present—who has come to the United States and become a productive member of society. This is human rights rhetoric, but affiliation-based substance. It argues for protections for noncitizens who live and work in the United States far more persuasively than human rights or territorial personhood arguments, which are the only arguments that new arrivals can make before they develop ties.[8]

From a lawful immigrant's perspective, the problem with affiliation (and with contract, for that matter) is that even if affiliation-based laws and policies recognize his ties, America's welcome is uncertain and deferred. A lawful immigrant may be a near-citizen permanent resident indefinitely. Part of the problem is that affiliation gives no special protection to lawful immigrants over other noncitizens in the United States who develop ties.[9] Moreover, affiliation and contract ignore the significance of permanent residence as a step toward naturalization. Neither contract nor affiliation views the citizen-noncitizen line as porous, temporary, and routinely overcome. For this reason, it is wrong to think that recognizing noncitizens' ties is a sign of generosity in U.S. immigration law.

This skepticism of immigration as affiliation finds support in Mae Ngai's historical work showing that the avenues of relief created after the

National Origins Act to allow deportable noncitizens to stay lawfully in the United States were practically (and sometimes formally) unavailable to Mexicans. This troubling episode shows that *whose* ties and *which* ties were recognized to allow noncitizens to avoid deportation on a case-by-case basis was not an objective or neutral matter. Even after the end of the national origins system's explicit discrimination, the recognition of ties depends on the considerable discretion that remains in immigration law enforcement.[10]

In contrast, immigration as transition means treating lawful immigrants as Americans in waiting from their first day in this country. This means weakening distinctions between them and citizens. Generally, taking transition seriously means that equality is presumed and that lawful immigrants should be treated like citizens until they have been here long enough to naturalize. As a corollary, immigration as transition also allows sharper distinctions between prenaturalization lawful immigrants and other noncitizens, whether lawfully or unlawfully present.

The real difference between affiliation and transition thus lies in their end points. Affiliation works gradually toward equal citizenship but does not get all the way there. In this sense, immigration as affiliation represents a way to treat lawful immigrants well without citizenship. Though immigration as transition gives new lawful immigrants immediate near-equality with citizens, that is not transition's conceptual essence. Rather, immigration as transition recognizes that even the best treatment of lawful immigrants is always something less than citizenship, and instead tries to give them the best chance to reach complete equality in the future through the acquisition of citizenship itself.

This basic difference between affiliation and transition flips the relevance of time. Affiliation gives a lawful immigrant nothing on arrival, but gradually confers a favored status that approaches but never equals citizenship. Transition protects them during an earlier period—when they are Americans in waiting—that starts with arrival and ends with eligibility to naturalize.

Naturalization

Naturalization is the first area in which immigration as transition would influence the treatment of lawful immigrants. Though the heart of transition is routine access to citizenship through naturalization, routine does not mean immediate or automatic. There may be a waiting period and a process with meaningful requirements. However, undue impediments to naturalization are inconsistent with immigration as transition. One key measure of immigration as transition is the naturalization rate, which could be much higher than it is today. Many lawful immigrants may choose not to naturalize, but that choice must be theirs to make freely.

The current naturalization statute requires only basic English-language competence in "simple words and phrases," and further provides that "no extraordinary or unreasonable condition shall be imposed." Any tougher language requirement would be inconsistent with transition. Similarly, immigration as transition supports the exemptions to the English, civics, and oath requirements for those lacking mental capacity. Transition also supports relaxing the current bars for a lawful immigrant with criminal convictions if the convictions do not make him deportable. He should not be left in limbo where he can neither naturalize nor be deported.[11]

Some waiting period for naturalization is consistent with immigration as transition, especially if lawful immigrants enjoy an immediate but provisional equality. Even with a wait, routine naturalization preserves the access to equality that is key to immigration as transition. Any period that a noncitizen spends waiting for his application for permanent residence to be approved should count toward the residency requirement for naturalization. Since he has met all of the requirements to become a lawful immigrant, credit for this time implements transition's strong preference for easing access to citizenship.

Immigration as transition means that naturalization decisions must be standardized and predictable, and thus not subject to the unreviewable discretion of individual government officials. Naturalization should be a matter of right in that it must be granted to any noncitizen who fulfills the requirements. Any denial of naturalization must be subject to review within an administrative agency, and the highest level of agency decision making must then be reviewable in the federal courts.[12]

Immigration as transition also suggests that the five-year prenaturalization period should be more than probation that ends with screening devices. It should also be a period to integrate future new citizens into American society. This suggests using the civics and history requirements to educate rather than purely to test. Current practice already reflects some of this by restricting the examination to one hundred questions that applicants can get (with official answers) in advance. The opportunity to study shifts the emphasis to the lawful immigrant's desire and commitment to become a citizen. Federal, state, and local governments can play important roles by affirmatively helping lawful immigrants become citizens, either directly or through nongovernmental organizations. The federal government already provides some help of this sort, as do some state and local governments and nongovernmental organizations.[13]

In contrast to transition, immigration as affiliation does not place great value on naturalization. In fact, it allows naturalization to be selective, since affiliation gives longtime lawful immigrants a bundle of rights that approach citizenship. Even if they don't naturalize, they are protected as near-citizens. It therefore matters less to a lawful immigrant if she can naturalize routinely, or if the process is standardized and predictable, or if applicants get government help.

For this reason, affiliation-based rights of noncitizens should be more extensive if naturalization is comparatively difficult. What lawful immigrants do not get through naturalization, they can get at least partly through affiliation-based protections.[14] For example, citizens of European Union member countries can vote as resident noncitizens in local elections in some other EU countries. This makes more sense in Europe, where naturalization is generally harder, than it would in the United States, where most arguments for noncitizen voting are made on behalf of longtime permanent residents who could naturalize. Their ability to gain the vote by naturalizing may help explain why the movement for noncitizen voting has not been especially successful in the United States.

Families

The treatment of families sheds important light on why immigration as transition matters. Imagine a lawful immigrant, Feng Jiang, who was admitted from China three years ago in one of the employment-based admission categories. He has learned to speak English fluently, and he is active in his community in suburban Seattle, where he works as a researcher at a cancer institute. Feng wants to become a U.S. citizen as soon as possible, but he will not be eligible for two more years, and the naturalization paperwork will take some time after that. Feng recently married a widow from Singapore who has a six-year-old son. His new wife and stepson want to join Feng in the United States as soon as possible.

If Feng had had a wife and child when he was admitted, the entire family could have immigrated together. But because he married after becoming a lawful immigrant, his wife and stepson cannot simply join him, but rather face a long wait. In May 2006, spouses and unmarried children of permanent residents were admitted as permanent residents themselves only after waiting almost four years—since March 2002. And because no more than about twenty-five thousand lawful immigrants may come from any single country each year, natives of Mexico who were admitted in May 2006 had been waiting seven years—since June 1999. Anyone who applied in mid-2006 as a permanent resident's spouse or child would almost certainly wait longer than four years, since demand exceeds supply, making the waiting list longer every month.[15]

If Feng were a citizen, his wife and stepchild would qualify for permanent residence as "immediate relatives." This category has no numerical cap, so immigrant visas would be available immediately, though the paperwork can take time. Citizens—but not permanent residents—can also petition for married and adult offspring and for siblings. Rather than petition as a permanent resident for his wife and stepchild, Feng will likely get faster results if he naturalizes as soon as he can and then petitions as a citizen for his spouse and stepson as immediate relatives.[16]

The question is whether Feng should be forced to choose as a new immigrant between separation from his family and separation from the United States. Constitutional protection of family unity draws support from the 1977 U.S. Supreme Court decision in *Moore v. City of East Cleveland*, which invalidated a zoning ordinance that barred a homeowner and her grandson from living under the same roof. The Court reasoned that the ordinance unconstitutionally interfered with the integrity of the family. The Court's 1972 decision in *Stanley v. Illinois* struck down an Illinois statute that made children of unwed fathers wards of the state if their mother dies. According to the Supreme Court, the statute unconstitutionally infringed on a father's interest in child custody.[17]

But *Moore* and *Stanley* were not immigration decisions. The plenary power doctrine probably lets Congress regulate family-based immigration without regard to constitutional protections for family unity in the domestic context. The closest precedent to Feng's case is not *Moore* or *Stanley*, but the Supreme Court's 1977 decision in *Fiallo v. Bell*. Recall from chapter 4 that *Fiallo* upheld the statutory definition of "child," which at

that time recognized the relationship between a child born out of wedlock with her mother but not her father. The government argued that the
statute guarded against false claims by unwed fathers and recognized the
probability that a child born out of wedlock would have a closer relationship with its mother than its father. The plaintiffs cited scientific methods
to prove paternity and pointed to the overbreadth in the statute's gender-
related assumptions about unwed parents and their children.[18]

In cases that do not involve noncitizens, judges closely examine the
constitutionality of gender and legitimacy classifications. Judges typically
apply intermediate scrutiny, requiring more than mere rational basis for
the statute, but less than the compelling governmental interest demanded
by strict scrutiny. *Fiallo*, however, reasoned that this was an immigration
law case within plenary power and upheld the statute without adopting
intermediate scrutiny. Family-based admission categories evidently may
discriminate against noncitizens by drawing lines that would unconstitutionally intrude on family unity outside of immigration law.[19]

Even if the Constitution allows long waits for spouses and children
of lawful immigrants, the next question is whether Congress should
shorten the waiting periods as a matter of policy. Contract, affiliation,
and transition give different answers. Immigration as contract says Feng
must accept any obstacles to family reunification that existed when he
became a lawful immigrant. Because the long waits for spouses and children are common knowledge and a matter of public record, Feng cannot
be heard to complain now. In fact, one restrictionist commentator has
made a contract-based argument against family reunification for lawful
immigrants.[20]

Viewing family reunification as a matter of immigration as affiliation,
new lawful immigrants typically lack the ties to ask for much by way of
family sponsorship opportunities. Affiliation says that after some time in
the United States, they should be able to sponsor close relatives just as citizens can. The current system so operates in practice, in that lawful immigrants can sponsor their close relatives under the limited annual allotment
for spouses and children, but only after a long waiting period. Alterna-
tively, they can satisfy the residency period, naturalize, and then petition
as citizens. Both long waits are consistent with immigration as affiliation.

Neither contract nor affiliation explains why long waits for a lawful
immigrant's spouse and children to come to America are highly troubling, but immigration as transition does. These long waits seriously

disrupt family life. Families do without everything that a missing spouse and parent would bring to family life, from money to love. It is hard for a lawful immigrant to feel that he can establish much of a life in America if his wife and children are not here. Or they come unlawfully, often at great physical risk en route, and once here live under threat of exploitation by employers and arrest and deportation by the government. Immigration as transition suggests that until lawful immigrants can naturalize, they should have the same family sponsorship opportunities as citizens.

Public Education

Imagine a law that denies public elementary and secondary education to all lawful immigrant children in the United States. Though no such law is likely to be enacted or even proposed, it reveals key features of immigration as contract, affiliation, and transition. Immigration as contract has very little to say about this law. Contract would preserve for lawful immigrants any access to public education that was available when they arrived. For future arrivals, a bar on public education would not be inconsistent with contract. Any arguments against this law must have some other basis.

The affiliation-based argument against this law would be that even the newest newcomer comes to America with enough ties to demand access to public education, since education is fundamental to participation in American society. But ascribing such affiliation at the moment of admission gets away from the foundation of immigration as affiliation—*acquired* ties. Affiliation supports the argument that public schools must be open to lawful immigrant children who have lived in America for some time. But this does not explain why barring *new* lawful immigrant children is wrong.

Immigration as transition provides the strongest argument against this imaginary law. Transition emphasizes a lawful immigrant's integration, starting even before he has enough ties here to warrant affiliation-based protections. Denying basic education would profoundly impede a lawful immigrant's economic and social integration, without which formal citizenship, if and when later acquired, would mean little. Though some could attend private schools or otherwise compensate for lack of public education, virtually nothing is more important than education for enabling immigrant children to participate in American society.

While this argument may seem to be based on territorial personhood or international human rights, its persuasive power comes not from the child's presence as a person in the United States, but from the child's future prospects in U.S. society. This concern is at the heart of immigration as transition.

Denying education seems especially objectionable in light of the familiar American national self-image as a society of upward mobility in which education should count for more than class, race, or inherited wealth. In 2003, about 28 percent of new lawful immigrants were under twenty-one years of age, and 71 percent were under forty. These are young immigrants who need education for themselves and for their involvement in their children's education. Though some observers evaluate the wisdom of current immigration policy by focusing on immigrants' education levels on arrival, the education that immigrants and their children get in the United States will matter more in the long run.[21]

The transition-based argument against this imaginary law is a matter of policy, not of constitutional command, but the main ideas that tie education to transition are evident in constitutional court decisions on noncitizens and public education. The U.S. Supreme Court's decision in *Plyler v. Doe* struck down as unconstitutional a Texas state law that effectively barred undocumented children from public schools. The *Plyler* reasoning would not necessarily invalidate such a federal law, since *Mathews v. Diaz* (discussed in chapter 4) recognized that the federal government has far more latitude to enact alienage laws than states and localities do. Still, the Court was deeply disturbed by the denial of public education, even to children unlawfully present.

Quoting from *Brown v. Board of Education*, the Supreme Court in *Plyler* explained the link between transition and education: "it is doubtful that any child may reasonably be expected to succeed in life if he is denied the opportunity of an education." Noting the "special constitutional sensitivity" of education, the Court was troubled that the Texas law would create a permanent underclass. Concurring separately, Justice Blackmun added that "classifications involving the complete denial of education are in a sense unique, for they strike at the heart of equal protection values by involving the State in the creation of permanent class distinctions."[22] These concerns about excluding a group from full participation in society would no doubt intensify if the children were lawful immigrants.

Transition, Integration, and Inclusive Citizenship

Admittedly, two key assumptions underlie the arguments made in this chapter that transition includes an educational component to naturalization testing and calls for treating new lawful immigrants like citizens in family reunification and public education. The first is that transition should reach beyond mere formal citizenship as a legal status to a fuller sense of belonging through family, education, and economic opportunity. The difficult question is why I am defining "transition" so broadly. After all, many *citizens* have dysfunctional families, substandard educations, and little real economic opportunity, and these problems often compound each other. Are transition-based immigration laws justified in giving lawful immigrants not just formal citizenship, but also a fuller sense of citizenship through participation, integration, and opportunity?[23]

The answer is that transition would be an illusory welcome for lawful immigrants if it were limited to formal citizenship through naturalization. We usually think of family, education, and economic opportunity as *means* of admission. Family and employment are two of the main avenues of lawful immigration, and employment-based admission depends heavily on an immigrant's education. And after admission, affiliation-based recognition is based chiefly on family and work. At the same time, family, education, work, and economic opportunity are *objects* of admission, crucial aspects of belonging. Though many lawful immigrants are highly educated and not in serious jeopardy of ending up at the bottom of the socioeconomic ladder, others have limited access to economic opportunity and yet have great potential to contribute to America. For this group, transition without the chance to integrate through family, education, and work creates a serious risk—borne out by empirical studies—of being relegated to the sort of underclass that deeply troubled the *Plyler* Court. Instead, our treatment of lawful immigrants as Americans in waiting must reflect hope that they do better than our least fortunate citizens, whose plight must be the focus of separate remedies.[24]

My second assumption is that transition calls for citizens and lawful immigrants to be treated *equally*. This assumption of equality may seem in tension with my observation that immigration as transition strives for *access* to equality rather than equality itself. If that is true, then why give lawful immigrants sponsorship opportunities that are *equal* to those of citizens until the lawful immigrants can naturalize? Why not just shorten their waits for family reunification without treating them just like citizens?

One possible reason for equal treatment is practical. If lawful immigrants and citizens are not treated equally, the way to adhere to transition's core principles would be a case-by-case inquiry into each example of different treatment. The question then would become whether family reunification or a welfare safety net is really necessary for transition to citizenship. In the safety net context, the U.S. Supreme Court hinted at such a minimum standard as a matter of constitutional law when *Graham v. Richardson* struck down state laws that required citizenship for welfare eligibility. The Court observed: "in the ordinary case an alien, becoming indigent and unable to work, will be unable to live where, because of discriminatory denial of public assistance, he cannot 'secure the necessities of life, including food, clothing and shelter.'" A few years later in *Foley v. Connelie*, the Court said that strict scrutiny of alienage classifications applies only to "exclusions [that] struck at the noncitizens' ability to exist in the community."[25] It is difficult to know when impediments to a lawful immigrant's transition to citizenship are undue. Are education and employment *necessities* of life? On balance, however, this practical criticism of a minimum necessities-of-life approach seems unpersuasive, since case-by-case inquiries are commonplace under rules of law that initially seem vague but gradually acquire definition as courts apply them.

The real reason why equal treatment is important for giving meaning to immigration as transition is more fundamental. The question is not whether equal treatment is *necessary* for integration. If that were the question, then it might adequately reflect immigration as transition to give new lawful immigrants something less than full equality, by eliminating only the impediments that deprive immigrants of the necessities of life. In fact, this is how immigration as affiliation fosters integration during the prenaturalization period. Affiliation recognizes ties as the basis for giving lawful immigrants something less than full equality, and that treatment in turn can be expected to foster some integration. But affiliation does not treat lawful immigrants and citizens equally, and so it does not make the most of the prenaturalization years as an opportunity to integrate newcomers into American society. In contrast, immigration as transition treats new lawful immigrants and citizens equally not just to send a clear message of welcome but also to make the most of the prenaturalization years as an integration period.

By integration I do not mean the sorts of assimilation that at times in American history have reflected pressure by the native majority for immigrants to cut ties with their own cultures, languages, or societies. I mean a reciprocal process in which immigrants change America as much as America changes them, and yet a process that keeps this nation of immigrants one nation. This is close to what sociologist Alan Wolfe calls "benign multiculturalism" and what historian David Hollinger has associated with "post-ethnic America."[26] Treating immigrants as Americans in waiting is the most effective way to weave this reciprocity into the fabric of American law and policy.

In this process, immigration as transition suggests an understanding of naturalization that is far removed from the traditional German view that naturalization is the end point of integration or even its consecration.[27] In contrast, immigration as transition views naturalization as part of an integration process that will continue beyond the formal acquisition of citizenship through naturalization. Naturalization is neither a start nor an end point, but an important milestone along the way.

This integration period is important. With about a million new lawful immigrants arriving annually, these years before naturalization are a crucial time for immigration's collective impact on the United States, a formative period full of fragile but pivotal moments. New immigrants can find a framework for participating in society in ways that embody mutual respect for immigrants and their new country, and that do not demand conformity to the Anglo-Saxon ideal that dominated thinking about assimilation for much of American history. Or, as was commonplace in earlier eras, new immigrants can hear messages of exclusion that make them reluctant to participate. Precisely because formal citizenship is no guarantee of equality, immigration as transition tries to make the most of this period for integration.

A skeptic might caution that generosity toward immigrants is a precious commodity. This is true, but what we can offer to lawful immigrants should neither be hoarded nor spent only penny-wise. Instead, it should be leveraged as a national investment in light of two key assumptions of immigration as transition. First, integration is a reciprocal process, so it is important that lawful immigrants perceive control over the terms of their future lives. The fact that permanent resident status is not necessarily permanent is a core assumption of immigration as transition. From this perspective, the Supreme Court's characterization of lawful immigrants in *Graham v. Richardson* as a discrete and insular minority seems exaggerated because they can become citizens. By redefining equality to mean access to equality, and then making the treatment of a lawful immigrant turn on her choice to naturalize, she gains some control over how she is treated. Naturalization becomes more like voluntary integration and less like coercive assimilation.[28]

A second core assumption of immigration as transition is that giving new lawful immigrants meaningful choice about naturalization and integration means asking how they should be treated, assuming that they will become citizens. In contrast, immigration as affiliation assumes that permanent residence may be permanent and that the noncitizen may never naturalize. Affiliation therefore asks a very different question: How should a permanent resident be treated, assuming that he will *not* become a citizen? But this is not the right question for noncitizens whom we hope will naturalize and attain a sense of belonging to America.

These two assumptions underscore not only how transition goes beyond affiliation, but also how immigration as transition goes beyond the minimum floor of protections based on territorial personhood or human rights, which do not assume that noncitizens become citizens. Permanent residence in the United States leads routinely to citizenship, and thus is fundamentally different from superficially similar statuses elsewhere, such as a long-term residence permit in Germany. Immigration as transition thus reflects something distinctive about immigration and citizenship in the United States that affiliation, territorial personhood, and human rights all fail to capture. It is no accident that thinking about immigration and immigrants in human rights terms is more common in countries like Germany, where transition has had little or no influence on immigration traditions.[29]

This analysis of what it would mean to recover the lost story of Americans in waiting casts doubt on what has become the conventional way of thinking and talking about immigration and citizenship in the United States as a matter of tension and accommodation between immigration as affiliation and immigration as contract. Exploring immigration as transition shows that an analytical framework consisting only of contract and affiliation is incomplete.

Considering the meaning of transition also casts doubt on the conventional view that affiliation-based recognition of ties in America is the main conceptual vehicle for the generous treatment of lawful immigrants. Immigration as contract can protect lawful immigrants by protecting their expectations. More fundamentally, immigration as affiliation supports only a tentative welcome of immigrants, compared to the welcome that immigration as transition offered during much of U.S. history. With the decline of the idea of Americans in waiting, America has rescinded much of its equal treatment of lawful immigrants based on the expectation of full membership.

This decline of the idea of Americans in waiting is partly a matter of devaluing the status of lawful immigrants by failing to distinguish strongly between them and other noncitizens in the United States. In addition, this decline has limited the potential of U.S. citizenship to be a viable context for a sense of belonging, and for participation in civic, political, social, and economic life that is inclusive and ultimately respectful of all individuals. Affiliation-based treatment of longtime permanent residents as near-citizens reduces naturalization incentives and makes citizenship less meaningful. The less it means to be a citizen, the more other forms of belonging will emerge, many of them more parochial and less cosmopolitan or democratic, and more closely tied to the exclusionary workings of race, ethnicity, or class.

This problem of devaluing citizenship diminishes with immigration as transition, because it calls for new lawful immigrants to be treated like citizens. Incentives work *for* naturalization, not against it. Immigration as transition thus enables citizenship to strike a balance between two extremes: forcing immigrants to give up their culture and traditions or allowing them to live so totally apart as to jeopardize a cohesive American society. Treating immigrants as Americans in waiting is the best way to assure that America remains faithful to its tradition as a nation of immigrants—as welcoming immigrants while still remaining one nation.

The introduction to this book observed that equality is elusive in immigration and citizenship, where outsiders are inherently unequal. But if equality has any meaning in legal and popular culture, it is the message, at its most succinct and eloquent in *Brown v. Board of Education*, that the permanent subordination of any group has no place in America. This message has as much meaning in immigration and citizenship as elsewhere, but it is easy for messages of exclusion to reach the ears of newcomers. Reciprocity, choice, and the offer of complete membership are all important because it is a hard road to come to America and arrive at any sense of belonging. The danger is that the framework for immigration and citizenship in the United States will marginalize newcomers permanently in ways that are inconsistent with America's commitment to equality.

CHAPTER 9

Race, Belonging, and Transition

★

The idea of Americans in waiting and a prenaturalization period of integration for new lawful immigrants are especially important in light of the long history of racial and ethnic discrimination in U.S. immigration and citizenship. With the great shift in the second half of the twentieth century toward immigration from Asia, Latin America, and Africa, immigration as transition has become an essential vehicle for making national citizenship inclusive.

Race, Ethnicity, and Belonging

Historian John Higham once observed with characteristic insight: "virtually the whole American response to foreign minorities was contained in two general attitudes: on the one hand, rejection and withdrawal; on the other, a confident faith in the natural, easy melting of many peoples into one." The traditional melting pot image comes from Israel Zangwill's 1908 Broadway hit play of the same name, based on *Romeo and Juliet* and set in turn-of-the-century immigrant America. Today the once-dominant image of immigration and assimilation in the melting pot seems hopelessly oversimplified. Every immigrant group, generation, and individual feels some tension between assimilation and separatism.[1]

Much of this tension arises against the complex backdrop of race and ethnicity in immigration. As many writers have observed, the immigrant experience in America has traditionally included some expectation of conformity to a white, Anglo-Saxon, Protestant majority. As Alex Aleinikoff has noted, sanguine views of immigrant integration emerged during the second quarter of the twentieth century, when immigration declined dramatically as a result of the national origins system, the Great Depression, and World War II. This dynamic is exceedingly complex, largely because immigration itself changed the majority culture.[2]

The role of race and ethnicity in immigration entered a new phase when broader civil rights developments led to the passage of the 1965 amendments to the Immigration and Nationality Act. As immigration from Asia and Latin America increased dramatically, public discourse on immigration and on ethnicity and race began to merge. It became naïve to discuss immigration and citizenship without considering its racial and ethnic implications, or to discuss race and ethnicity without considering immigration and citizenship. Perhaps this realization was long overdue. As Michael Omi and Howard Winant observed in their seminal work on concepts of race in the United States, "Race will *always* be at the center of the American experience."[3]

Some who urge reducing immigration blame ethnic, linguistic, and cultural identities among immigrants for what they call the failure of immigrants to integrate into American society. As in earlier eras, this skepticism largely responds to the geographic concentration of immigrants in states including California, Texas, and Florida, and in smaller enclaves such as Miami's Little Havana. Modern modes of transportation and communication allow immigrants to stay in close touch with their countries of origin. Coming to America can look more equivocal, especially if dual citizenship is available.

According to the direst predictions, newcomers will tear America apart with ethnic and racial separatism. The writer Peter Brimelow went so far as to call explicitly for America to return to its white, European roots. Similar views came from Patrick Buchanan, sometimes presidential candidate and senior advisor to three U.S. presidents. Political scientist Samuel Huntington, though not basing his views explicitly on race, has argued that failure to assimilate immigrants to a core Anglo-Saxon Protestant culture in the United States is a threat to U.S. national existence.[4]

Others counter by applauding the coming of immigrants who can maintain home country ties, including dual citizenship, while putting down roots in America. Similarly, some argue that cultural diversity is in fact an important source of national unity in the long run. Consistent with these views, some social scientists have observed that ethnic, linguistic, and cultural identities have not fostered any enduring separatism, but rather have given immigrants a base from which they have expanded their participation in the American economy, society, and politics.[5]

Closely related to the ethnic aspects of immigration and citizenship is language. It was common for immigrant parents to educate their children in their native languages throughout the 1800s and up to World War I, when fervent nationalism provoked the first major efforts to suppress school instruction in languages other than English. Unsurprisingly, the main target was German. In 1919, Nebraska adopted a law forbidding public, private, and religious schools from teaching in any language other than English through the first eight grades. More than twenty other states had similar laws. The governor of Iowa issued a proclamation banning the use of any non-English language in schools, church services, and conversations in public places or over the telephone. The U.S. Supreme Court struck down the Nebraska law as a violation of due process, but attempts to elevate English to official or exclusive status continued.[6]

This early-twentieth-century version of the English-language movement had two overlapping aspects. One argued that lack of English fluency was a sign of lower intelligence. This was persuasive at a time when eugenics was influential in U.S. immigration policy. Another argument, more familiar today, expressed the fear that the use of other languages threatened national cohesion and that language homogeneity was essential to American identity. President Theodore Roosevelt declared: "Hereafter we must see that the melting pot really does not melt. There should be but one language in this country—the English." It was only natural that the same forces that tried to suppress non-English school instruction also tried to bring English-language requirements into the requirements for admission to the United States.[7]

Generations later, similar movements tried to suppress the use of other languages, especially when linguistic diversity broadened exponentially near the end of the twentieth century. Skeptics condemned the use of other languages on election ballots and in other official settings. In the 1980s, California's U.S. Senator S. I. Hayakawa campaigned for a constitutional amendment to declare English the official language of the United States. In 1986, California passed Proposition 63, an initiative that made English the state's official language, and similar measures have been adopted in more than twenty other states. In 1998, California voters adopted Proposition 227, which virtually eliminated public bilingual education.[8]

Critics of these efforts typically acknowledge the practical need to learn English but decry its elevation to official status as coercion to abandon other languages. Many of these critics dispute the commonplace accusation that immigrants or their children lack interest in learning English. This view draws support from the 2000 census, which shows that English remains the language of choice among the children and grandchildren of Hispanic immigrants, and that most Americans of Hispanic descent were moving steadily toward English monolingualism.[9]

My purpose here is not to provide detailed accounts of these highly contentious debates about immigration, race, ethnicity, and language, but to observe that they raise very basic questions about American identity. These controversies arise against a background of reciprocal skepticism, which in turn has several elements. One is the long history of racial restrictions in immigration and citizenship. Another is the role that race and ethnicity continues to play today, albeit a much more subtle role than in the past. Also important is the link between race and the decline of immigration as transition.

Transition and Race

The American dream seemed to become more open to all with the end of racial naturalization bars in 1952 and the end of the national origins system in 1965. Today's lawful immigrants are a much more diverse group than the white Europeans who dominated the flow from the nation's earliest years to the late 1960s. These trends explain the conventional wisdom that an egalitarian and inclusive vision of immigration and citizenship emerged in the second half of the twentieth century out of a past marked by explicit racial discrimination.

I am not so sanguine. One sobering lesson from the lost story of Americans in waiting is that at the same time that immigration and citizenship law freed itself from express racial restrictions, immigration became less of a transition to citizenship. As immigration became more open, being an immigrant began to mean less. The decline of immigration as transition, together with the growing emphasis on contract and affiliation, replaced a recognition of immigrants as future citizens with a much more tentative welcome. Affiliation emerged as the basis for whatever equality newcomers could earn. Immigrants were no longer Americans in waiting.

This was not just historical coincidence. Immigration as transition declined largely because of fears that the wrong immigrants could become intending citizens. In the late 1800s, skepticism of voting by intending citizens partly reflected alarm that nonwhite immigrants could vote. Gerald Neuman has observed that the practice of noncitizen voting by intending citizens "rested on an empirical view of European immigrants as future U.S. citizens." In an arresting speech from the 1873–74 Ohio Constitutional Convention reported by historian Alexander Keyssar, one delegate objected to a proposal for intending citizen voting because it would give the vote

> not only to the unnaturalized foreigner who comes here from European countries, but also to the unnaturalized African who might be brought over . . . by Dr. Livingstone; and should he capture in the jungles of that benighted land . . . a specimen of the connecting link between man and the animal, as described by the theory of Darwin, and bring him to Ohio, that link could not only claim to become a citizen of the United States, but without naturalization . . . claim to be a sovereign, a voter and an office-holder. . . . The Chinese, the Japanese, and even the Ashantees, who are now at war with England . . . could become voters.

Several states with intending citizen voting limited it to white men, but most did not, and gradually the practice as a whole died out.[10]

Consider also Justice Fuller's dissent in the U.S. Supreme Court's 1898 decision in *Wong Kim Ark*, which held that persons of Chinese descent born in the United States are citizens by virtue of the Fourteenth Amendment to the Constitution. Fuller expressed the sentiment that the status of the intending citizen and the idea of Americans in waiting was tied to the expectation of full assimilation:

> Expatriation included not simply the leaving of one's native country, but the becoming naturalized in the country adopted as a future residence. The emigration which the United States encouraged was that of those who could become incorporate with its people; make its flag their own; and aid in the accomplishment of a common destiny.[11]

As chapter 1 explained, this expectation did not apply to Chinese immigrants. This view of naturalization made it increasingly untenable to view immigrants as Americans in waiting once immigration broadened beyond its original Anglo-Saxon, Protestant core to other Europeans, and after

World War II to more and more immigrants from Asia and Latin America.

This brings me back to the idea that immigration as transition is concerned not with what is necessary for integration, but rather what can make the most of a lawful immigrant's prenaturalization years. If new lawful immigrants are not treated with the expectation of naturalization, an important opportunity is lost to make them feel safe to reach outside their immigrant enclaves and to integrate into American society. Given the history of discrimination in immigration law, immigrants from Latin America, Asia, and Africa are especially likely to respond to an ambivalent or skeptical welcome with their own reticence. What may seem like immigrants' resistance to integration may be their natural reaction to America's attitude toward immigrants. As Austrian political scientist Rainer Bauböck has observed: "Where immigrants feel that the receiving state actively discriminates against them or does not protect them against social discrimination they will hardly develop commitment towards it." Treating new lawful immigrants as Americans in waiting is important to combat the feeling among Latin American, Asian, and African immigrants that no matter what they do, they will always remain strangers in the land—perpetual foreigners based on name, skin color, language, or accent. This is a concern prompted not only by history, but also by recent developments.[12]

Race and Ethnicity After September 11

Developments since the September 11 terrorist attacks show that the implications of race and ethnicity for integration remain central to immigration and citizenship. On December 12, 2001, a *New York Times* survey revealed broad approval of two separate systems of justice, one for "them" and one for "us."[13] The facts that emerged about the hijackers confirmed the same image of terrorists as foreigners that had quickly but falsely emerged after the 1995 bombing of the Oklahoma City federal building by Timothy McVeigh and Terry Nichols.

Much of the war on terrorism soon became a story of a separate system of justice for suspected terrorists. Some were prosecuted under criminal law in the federal courts, but a far greater number were apprehended outside the United States and held pending military tribunals as "enemy combatants" at Guantánamo Naval Base. Although the U.S. Supreme Court held that some constitutional protections apply to these detainees, they remain beyond the protections of traditional criminal procedure.[14]

Part of the sentiment for a separate system of justice reflects the idea that the delicate balance between law enforcement and civil liberties should tip toward law enforcement when noncitizens rather than citizens are affected. But the sentiment also reflects the fear that criminal law cannot do the job alone because it generally investigates and prosecutes after crimes have been committed. Criminal law tries only exceptionally to identify those likely to commit future crimes. After September 11, however, public officials repeatedly emphasized their goal of preventing future terrorist attacks.[15]

In addition to a separate system for enemy combatants, immigration law also emerged as a type of antiterrorism law. As far back as the Alien and Sedition Acts of 1798, and then in the early federal immigration statutes of the late 1800s, immigration law has barred and deported noncitizens from the United States on ideological and national security grounds. Noncitizens can be arrested, detained, and deported under immigration law with little recourse to the constitutional protections that would limit the government outside of immigration. For this reason, the government found it easier after September 11 to proceed against noncitizens in the United States who were suspected of terrorist ties by enforcing immigration laws, rather than initiating criminal prosecutions.

Immigration Law as Antiterrorism Law

Starting right after the attacks, the federal government arrested and detained more than one thousand noncitizens, mostly men. Though the apparent purpose was to investigate acts of terrorism that had already occurred and to prevent further acts of terrorism, the arrests and detentions were mostly for immigration law violations. As would become typical, the focus was on noncitizens from Arab and Muslim countries. About one-third were Pakistanis. The rest came from Egypt, Turkey, Jordan, Yemen, India, Saudi Arabia, Morocco, Tunisia, Syria, Lebanon, Israel, and Iran.

Many detainees were held for long periods, some exceeding one year. Almost immediately, allegations surfaced that the detainees were being held improperly and mistreated. The government denied the allegations, but an investigation by the Office of the Inspector General in the Department of

Justice later confirmed not only that the allegations had merit but also that some government officers and employees had tried to conceal the mistreatment. Some detainees were physically and verbally abused by guards. The inspector general also found that the conditions of confinement were unduly harsh and prevented detainees from obtaining legal counsel. The government did not properly notify many of the detainees of the charges against them. The process for checking detainees for terrorism connections dragged on for eighty days on average. Almost all detainees were cleared of terrorism connections, although many were removed for immigration law violations.[16]

The government also concentrated its deportation resources after September 11 on noncitizens from Arab and Muslim countries. Entry-exit controls and visa application procedures for these countries were tightened significantly. And as chapter 4 mentioned, immigration proceedings were closed to all observers, including family members and the press, in more than one thousand "special interest" cases, mostly involving removal of noncitizens from predominantly Arab or Muslim countries. In November 2001, the Department of Justice initiated a project to interview almost eight thousand noncitizens who were in the United States as nonimmigrants, focusing on Middle Eastern men ages eighteen to forty-six. The purpose was to determine what knowledge these interviewees had of terrorists and planned terrorist activities.[17]

Starting in November 2002, the government required males at least sixteen years of age from twenty-five predominantly Arab or Muslim countries (plus North Korea) who were not permanent residents to appear at Immigration and Naturalization Service offices as part of a "call-in special registration" program to be photographed, fingerprinted, and interviewed under oath. They were sometimes asked for personal information, for example regarding political affiliations, places of worship, and roommates, and for credit card and banking information. About twelve hundred men were arrested and detained when they appeared for special registration, often on the basis of immigration violations that normally would go undetected or overlooked. Some were held for several days or even longer in squalid conditions and without access to attorneys, family, and friends. By mid-2003, about eighty-five thousand noncitizens had complied with call-in registration, of whom more than thirteen thousand were in the country unlawfully and thus faced possible removal. The government reported identifying eleven noncitizens with links to terrorism through this process, plus about four hundred persons sought on criminal charges or barred from the United States. Later, at the start of the war against Iraq in March 2003, the FBI commenced an interview program for about eleven thousand Iraqi-born individuals in the United States, including citizens and noncitizens, "to elicit information that may be useful to the U.S. government in the event of hostilities in Iraq."[18]

Race and ethnicity, not any individualized indication that the targeted persons deserved investigation, became a central ingredient of these immigration law enforcement initiatives. This mode of law enforcement is what I define as racial or ethnic profiling, as distinct from a description of a particular suspect that includes race or ethnicity. These individuals were caught up in post–September 11 enforcement measures because they were from predominantly Arab or Muslim countries, not because there was any specific evidence of terrorist links that brought them to the attention of authorities. Many of these noncitizens were not undocumented immigrants or students or other temporary visitors, but rather lawful immigrants, some of whom had lived in the United States for many years.

Assessing the government's use of race and ethnicity in post–September 11 immigration enforcement should begin by asking how these antiterrorism measures differ from the racial profiling of African Americans—sometimes called "DWB," or "driving while black"—that had drawn criticism from a wide array of public officials, including President George W. Bush and Attorney General Ashcroft.[19] The complex question that arises from this turn of events is why the prior consensus against racial profiling seemed to flip so quickly toward widespread acceptance of racial profiling after September 11. Answering this question begins with a close look at the role of discretion in immigration law enforcement.

Discretion in Immigration Law Enforcement

Defenders of the Bush administration's use of immigration law as antiterrorism law after September 11 responded in several ways to accusations of racial and ethnic profiling. First, many of the targeted individuals had violated immigration laws, so the government was just enforcing the law. Second, the administration used immigration law as antiterrorism law against noncitizens, who can justifiably be handled under a system of justice that is separate from citizens.

Assessing the response that the government was just enforcing the law requires looking at the role of discretion in immigration law. Immigration enforcement has never been a simple matter of identifying and deporting violators. Many noncitizens in the United States are here in violation of immigration laws. Some violations are highly technical, such as a gap between two valid periods of student status, while others are more obvious, such as ignoring a final removal order. This state of immigration under-enforcement opens up a great deal of discretion for government officials, and enforcement focus and zeal have fluctuated. The main use of immigration law as antiterrorism law after September 11 has not involved new laws, such as the Patriot Act, but new patterns of enforcing laws that have long been on the books.[20]

This history of discretionary enforcement reflects tacit agreement among politically powerful groups, including employers who need foreign workers and the consumers who want to keep down the price of groceries, hotel rooms, and everything else. Many citizens have a close personal interest in underenforcement, to allow their relatives to join them here before they qualify for lawful status. This underenforcement has been built into the immigration statutes themselves. For many years, no federal law made it unlawful to hire a noncitizen who lacked work authorization. In 1952, Congress did make it a felony to "harbor" an alien unlawfully in the United States and expanded the Border Patrol's enforcement authority. But at the insistence of southwestern growers and other agricultural interests, Congress added the so-called Texas Proviso, which defined harboring to *not* include employing an unauthorized worker.[21]

This state of affairs was supposed to change in 1986, when the Immigration Reform and Control Act (IRCA) introduced penalties for employers who knowingly hire or continue to hire unauthorized workers, but the scheme has been predictably ineffective. The law requires employers only to see if identity and work authorization documents reasonably *appear* to be genuine. Any further probing, such as asking for more documents, exposes employers to liability for discrimination. Fake green cards and other false work authorization documents soon became readily available. As long as employers check documents and do the paperwork, they risk no liability. Enforcement efforts are sporadic, and penalties on the very few employers who are caught are too light to deter future violations. Overall, IRCA failed to eliminate unauthorized employment as a magnet for undocumented immigration. This is not a surprise. Too many powerful interests opposed any law that would actually stanch the flow of undocumented workers into jobs that employers could not fill with lawful workers at the wages offered.[22]

The history of IRCA is just one episode in the story of enforcement ambivalence in immigration law. Enforcement puts on a strong public face, but in reality laws go underenforced or unenforced. A powerful consensus says that strict immigration law enforcement would drag down the U.S. economy, block the reunification of families, and otherwise hurt broad segments of American society. Chronic but broadly accepted tolerance of illegal immigration prevails, even if politics demands an occasional show of force.

Because IRCA has been an ineffective strategy for enlisting the private sector to check immigration documents, immigration law enforcement against unauthorized work depends on direct enforcement through workplace raids. The government can decide that political fallout would be too intense if it rounded up too many undocumented workers, and the number of raids has steadily decreased in recent years. As a revealing contrast, the Internal Revenue Service has created a mechanism for undocumented noncitizens to pay federal income taxes.[23]

With regard to Mexican immigration, which now accounts for an estimated 69 percent of the undocumented population in the United States, discretion has played a big role going back at least as far as the National Origins Act of 1924. As chapter 6 noted, Congress did not impose a numerical cap on Western Hemisphere immigration. This left the public charge exclusion ground as one of the key limits on Mexican immigration, and its enforcement against Mexican immigrants by agency officials was highly discretionary.[24]

Broad discretion has also been a part of federal administration of temporary farmworker programs going back to 1917. The Bracero program admitted perhaps four hundred thousand Mexican temporary workers annually from 1942 to 1962, but its broader consequence was a pattern of reliance on Mexican farmworkers, which lawful admissions have often failed to satisfy. During the Bracero years, and much more afterward, there was a great deal of unlawful immigration, which the government could then tolerate or quash—for example in Operation Wetback in 1954—as economic conditions dictated and enforcement resources allowed. Temporary farmworker admissions continue today but admit too few workers to meet labor demands, especially in the western and southwestern states. Many migrants would rather come unlawfully than through a program that ties them to one employer, and many of those admitted under a program leave their contracts to escape oppressive working conditions. For their part, many employers prefer workers without lawful status.[25]

Besides the workplace, the other traditional venue for immigration enforcement is the Mexican border, but the same pattern of broad discretion to expand, reduce, or target enforcement exists there as well. In spite of highly publicized initiatives in population centers such as San Diego and El Paso, border enforcement as a whole remains chronically underfunded. This is likely to remain true as long as discretion in enforcement suits the imperatives of U.S. immigration, economic, and foreign policy, and as long as the American public remains reluctant to pay the fiscal and social costs of turning the physical border into a new Berlin Wall.[26]

Discretionary enforcement extends to other aspects of immigration law. Until the mid-1990s, the government only rarely deported even the many noncitizens who were deportable for criminal convictions. Today, even simple reporting requirements outpace government resources. Noncitizens in the United States are required to report every change of address to the government. But when the government announced that it would check for noncompliance, it could not keep up with the flood of forms, let alone what truly full compliance would produce. Again, the pattern of underenforcement leaves the enforcement that does occur highly dependent on the exercise of discretion.[27]

The degree of public acquiescence in incomplete enforcement is evident in the persistence of proposals to grant amnesty or earned legalization to many of the millions of undocumented noncitizens. These individuals have lived and will continue to live beyond the reach of immigration law enforcement. These uncertainties were the basis of the Supreme Court's suggestion in *Plyler v. Doe* that an unlawfully present noncitizen might not be unlawful after all: "An illegal entrant might be granted federal permission to continue to reside in this country, or even to become a citizen," and undocumented children have "inchoate federal permission to remain."[28]

Underenforcement coupled with broad enforcement discretion can let the undocumented live and work for years in the United States, if they are not so unlucky as to be caught. They establish toeholds that in turn generate further migration from their hometowns. Yet, they live in the shadows and margins of American society, fearing detection, detention, and deportation, even if the statistical probability of these misfortunes is low. They are victims of employer coercion. They must live with the knowledge that a downturn in the economy will reveal that their real value as workers is that they are not just cheap but expendable, to be hired when are needed and somehow made to disappear when they are not.[29]

This baseline of underenforcement has historically given the government much latitude to enforce some aspects of immigration law but not others, or to target certain industries, localities, groups, or individuals for enforcement. Government officials are under great pressure to balance competing demands, which can run against enforcement. For example, local and state police are often reluctant to enforce immigration laws because doing so would not only drain resources from other law enforcement functions, but also undermine community relationships that are essential for their work.[30]

At other times, economic downturns like California's recession in the early 1990s generate demands for more enforcement. In other historical periods, enforcement has responded to perceived foreign threats such as heightened enforcement against anarchists at the turn of the twentieth century and Communists during the McCarthy era. In the 1930s, U.S. consuls refused to exercise discretion to admit European refugees when their numbers exceeded the set limits. This cast a shadow over U.S. refugee policy for at least a generation after World War II, and U.S. officials responded by exercising enforcement discretion to protect European refugees by paroling them in the United States if admission slots were unavailable.[31]

September 11 heightened the tensions inherent in the exercise of discretion. For many Americans who already had been dissatisfied with chronic immigration law underenforcement, the war on terrorism underscored the need for stronger measures. In October 2001, Attorney General Ashcroft explicitly announced an antiterrorism strategy of detaining and removing noncitizens for minor immigration violations, citing Attorney General Robert Kennedy's pledge in the 1960s to prosecute mobsters if they so much as spit on the sidewalk. Discretion shifted the focus of immigration enforcement toward noncitizens from Arab and Muslim countries, against whom immigration law became antiterrorism law.[32]

Profiling, Rationality, and Citizenship

The role of discretion in immigration law enforcement is essential to analyzing whether the government can justify profiling. Though, since September 11, the government has defended its actions against noncitizens by saying that it is just enforcing the law, many violations seldom if ever lead to enforcement under normal circumstances. Many noncitizens who voluntarily reported during the special registration program had no lawful status but had met all of the requirements for permanent residence and were merely waiting for paperwork processing, which has taken more than two years to complete in some parts of the country.[33] Others were clearly in the United States unlawfully but would not have drawn government attention except for their ethnicity.

More fundamentally, the fact that someone violates the law should not end the inquiry into whether enforcement is objectionable. Assume, for example, that the district attorney of a large American city adopts a policy to concentrate resources for armed robbery prosecutions on cases in which the defendants are African Americans. No one would dispute that armed robbery is a serious crime, but it would still be wrong to prosecute only African Americans. Understanding why requires a closer look at profiling.

One troubling aspect of racial or ethnic profiling in law enforcement is that it can be irrational. It can lead to lazy enforcement that relies on unfounded suppositions rather than hard evidence. The thousands of detentions that resulted from the post–September 11 immigration law enforcement against Arabs and Muslims led to virtually no terrorism convictions. Racial or ethnic profiling can cause ethnic communities to mistrust enforcement agencies, and the failure to enlist these communities' assistance may be fatal to efforts to investigate terrorism.[34]

But irrationality is not the only problem with profiling. Even rational profiling may be wrong if it offends other values that matter. The law rightly lets the rational search for truth be impeded by other important values, such as the attorney-client privilege and the rule in criminal procedure that excludes from evidence the fruits of an unlawful search. The sentiment that it is better to let ten guilty persons go free than convict a single innocent one explains why a criminal prosecution must prove guilt beyond a reasonable doubt. Any search for rational truth takes place in a broader context of other values, and the search for those values in the profiling context requires analysis of the line between citizens and noncitizens.[35]

This brings me to the second response to the charges of racial and ethnic profiling, namely that the Bush administration's use of immigration law as antiterrorism law after September 11 was directed against noncitizens. The broad consensus against domestic profiling may have flipped in favor of immigration law enforcement against Arabs and Muslims because they were not U.S. citizens like the black and Latino targets of the profiling roundly criticized before September 11. Enforcing immigration law as antiterrorism law seemed to target noncitizens in a separate system of justice for "them."

The assumption was that profiling in immigration law enforcement hurts only the noncitizens who are arrested, detained, or deported. Even the administration's critics seemed to accept this assumption and did not press the point that post–September 11 enforcement tread too much on *citizens*' civil liberties.[36] This focus on noncitizens in assessing immigration law profiling is consistent with the dominant approach to constitutional rights in immigration law cases. Recall from chapter 4 how the Supreme Court decisions in *Mandel* and *Fiallo* quashed any serious look at how government immigration decisions affect the rights of citizens.

This way to frame the question—as whether U.S. law should recognize the interests of noncitizens to come and stay—is how many restrictionists have framed immigration and citizenship questions, which they then answer with a firm "no." Peter Brimelow, for example, has criticized U.S. immigration policy for treating "immigration as a sort of imitation civil right, extended to an indefinite group of foreigners who have been selected arbitrarily and with no regard to American interests."[37] Similarly, the Supreme Court's plenary power decisions generally have asked if noncitizens have judicially enforceable constitutional rights. The Court's answers have depended on the noncitizen and on the constitutional claim in question, but the dominant approach has been to assess the case from a noncitizen's rather than citizen's perspective. Those who are more sympathetic to immigration and immigrants often respond to the government and to restrictionists with the argument that noncitizens *do* have rights that courts, Congress, and the executive branch should recognize. Their response is natural, but it tacitly accepts an inquiry focused on noncitizens only.

If profiling by race and ethnicity affects only noncitizens, it is easy to limit the inquiry to the question of whether profiling is rational, for the profiling of noncitizens seems different from the profiling of citizens, and it seems reasonable to place noncitizens outside the scope of our inquiry into other values that might trump rationality. This distinction explains the December 2001 *New York Times* survey's endorsement of two separate systems of justice. If the profiling of noncitizens is rational, then it seems unobjectionable. In the long run, however, immigration policy must serve the national interest, and this depends on how immigration decisions affect citizens. Many noncitizens have close family, employment, or ethnic ties to U.S. citizens and to communities that include many citizens. The real test of profiling is how it affects citizens, and the worst aspect of plenary power is that it disregards the interests of citizens in choosing new citizens, and thus in shaping their national future.

Defining Discrimination in Immigration

How do immigration decisions affect citizens? Family reunification is especially important, for the effects are immediate and direct. Employers have a strong interest in having noncitizen employees. Moreover, noncitizens are vital members of ethnic communities made up of citizens and noncitizens. Beyond this, analysis gets harder. How might immigration laws harm communities, and does that harm amount to unconstitutional discrimination? The answers shed important light on the need for immigration as transition to counter the historical and current role of race and ethnicity in immigration and citizenship.

Explicit racial bars to citizenship ended in 1952, and the national origins system ended in 1965. The Refugee Act of 1980 is sometimes cited for the idea that uniform and neutral standards rather than the country of origin or U.S. foreign policy should govern asylum decisions. The U.S. Supreme Court's 1985 decision in *Jean v. Nelson* held that the provisions on immigration parole in the statute and regulations prohibit discrimination based on race or national origin, even if the provisions do not expressly address discrimination. But accusations persist that immigration laws are discriminatory in intent or practical effect. Some critics target expressly different treatment of people from specific countries. More subtly, laws or practices that are neutral on the surface may mask inequality when applied to countries that are very different by history, demographics, and geography. For example, current law limits annual immigration from any single country to about 25,600. This seems neutral, but it disproportionately affects countries like Mexico, where the demand for immigrant admission to the United States is huge, rooted in long historical entanglement (as explained in chapter 6) and a shared nineteen-hundred-mile border with the greatest per capita income differential of any national border in the world.[38]

In contrast to laws and policies that are neutral on the surface are those that expressly treat certain countries differently. In 1986, Congress adopted the diversity visa program to reinvigorate European immigration. Irish immigrants were singled out to receive sixteen thousand of the annual forty thousand visas distributed by lottery for several years. Currently, an annual lottery gives about fifty thousand diversity immigrant visas only to nationals of "low admission" countries. The program has been billed as promoting diversity, and in fact many of the visas go to African immigrants, whose share of the immigrant flow is historically low. But perhaps because its original purpose and early effects were to boost European immigration, critics have called it an antidiversity program.[39]

The hard question is how to define discrimination. One way to think about discrimination in immigration law is by analogy to the law governing legislative redistricting. Both types of law decide who belongs. Immigration law does so directly, while redistricting decides the political effects of belonging. Just as immigration law can stunt the growth of racial or ethnic groups, redistricting can exclude them politically. Officials who make immigration decisions have a sense of the race or ethnicity of those admitted or excluded, just as drafters of redistricting plans know who lives in the districts they create.[40]

But courts are unlikely to apply redistricting standards to immigration, partly because the plenary power doctrine inhibits constitutional challenges, and partly because it is very hard to prove the race-conscious intent that is an essential element of an unlawful discrimination claim. More fundamentally, confidence is extraordinarily elusive that a given immigration law is discriminatory. It is almost impossible to ascertain the normal number of Irish to be admitted to the United States as a baseline for deciding whether the diversity visa program discriminates unconstitutionally.[41]

At a deeper level, immigration law sometimes *should* consider country-specific factors rather than pursue complete uniformity and neutrality. It is not necessarily bad, let alone unconstitutional, to treat a specific country differently. Sound overall immigration policy may consist of the right balance of exceptional policies for single countries. Equality here may be, as legal philosopher Ronald Dworkin has explained more generally, a matter not of equal treatment, but treatment as an equal, which may lead justifiably to different policies or outcomes.[42]

For example, from 1981 to 1994 the U.S. government interdicted Haitians—but not Cubans—in the Caribbean before they could reach U.S. beaches or territorial waters and apply for asylum. Treatment of Haitians and Cubans became more alike in 1994, when the government responded to an influx of Cubans sailing to Florida on small homemade rafts by interdicting them as well. But Cubans still get uniquely favorable treatment, most notably under the "wet foot, dry foot" policy: if interdicted at sea they are returned to Cuba, but those who reach U.S. territory can become permanent residents after just one year without satisfying the usual admission criteria.[43]

Treating generally lighter skinned Cubans better than Haitians of African ancestry has prompted charges of racial discrimination, but streamlining the process for Cuban asylum seekers may be sensible if they are more likely to qualify for asylum.[44] Moreover, the treatment of Cubans reflects the U.S. government's desire to undermine Fidel Castro's communist regime. From this foreign policy perspective, it is just as fair to compare Haitians not with Cubans, but with Salvadorans and Guatemalans. They are nonblack asylum seekers from the Western Hemisphere who have not fared well under U.S. law, largely because they, like Haitians, come from noncommunist countries.

More generally, immigration is just one of many country-specific links between the United States and other countries. For example, immigration is an alternative to international trade in that the United States may send work to other countries if not enough workers come here. Immigrants send part of their earnings to relatives and others in their native countries, and this can add up to a large share of gross domestic product and thus is an alternative to direct foreign aid. Moreover, historical ties make U.S. immigration policy toward some countries justifiably different. Given the historical U.S.-Mexico relationship, it may be more nondiscriminatory to depart from formal equality and increase the annual cap on Mexican immigrant admissions beyond the standard 25,600, and to establish legalization programs that favor Mexicans over noncitizens from other countries. Noncitizens from several dozen countries are admitted without visas, but this is based on low rates of visa fraud by visitors from those countries. And taking in Southeast Asian refugees, some of whom directly helped U.S. forces in Vietnam, has been a way of accepting some responsibility for the war.[45]

Discrimination After September 11

The Bush administration's use of immigration law as antiterrorism law crossed over the line into inappropriate discrimination by race and ethnicity. Although the administration started with the premise that Al Qaeda is not a nation-state, it targeted noncitizens from almost three dozen countries chosen substantially by ethnicity and religion. Legal scholars Susan Akram and Kevin Johnson have contrasted the much narrower scope of the Carter administration's decision to single out Iranians for heightened scrutiny after the 1979 seizure of hostages at the U.S. embassy in Tehran.[46] And although the Bush administration's profiling targeted noncitizens, it was impossible to interview, detain, or deport noncitizens living and working in the United States without profoundly affecting citizens who are closely related. Calling them noncitizens makes it easy to forget that they are the fathers and husbands and mothers and wives of citizens. The effects on Arab-American and Muslim U.S. citizens go beyond the more complex scenarios in which it is hard to define discrimination, and more closely resemble historical situations in which discrimination is clearer and more troubling.

In earlier historical periods, laws that restricted Asian immigration and barred interracial marriage inhibited the growth and ultimate integration of Asian-American communities. The selective deportations of noncitizens who would not have been deported but for their ethnicity deeply damaged Arab and Muslim communities in the United States after September 11. Families were dissolved when family members were deported. An estimated one out of every eight residents—including some U.S. citizens—abandoned Brooklyn's Little Pakistan neighborhood in the eighteen months after September 11. Especially given perceptions in Arab and Muslim communities, even before September 11, of anti-Arab or anti-Muslim bias in American culture in general and in immigration law enforcement in particular, a climate of fear pervaded communities with post–September 11 government enforcement.[47]

Moreover, racial and ethnic profiling in immigration law enforcement burdens the citizens and communities who are closely tied to the targeted individuals with a stigma akin to the stigma that the U.S. Supreme Court described in *Brown v. Board of Education* as "a feeling of inferiority as to their status in the community that may affect their hearts and minds in a way unlikely ever to be undone." This stigma not only affronts the dignity of individuals and the idea of a society in which individuals are not subordinated by race or ethnicity; it also can spur private hatred. Soon after September 11, President Bush, Attorney General Ashcroft, and other high government officials spoke out against attacks against persons who were or appeared to be Arab or Muslim. Yet, the Department of Justice opened investigations into 546 post–September 11 cases of violence or threats against persons who were (or were believed by their attackers to be) of Muslim, Arab, Sikh, or South Asian religion or ethnicity. The FBI reported that hate crimes against Muslims and persons of Middle Eastern ethnicity increased sixteenfold over the previous year. The trend continued in 2003 and 2004.[48]

To use an image from the American frontier, after September 11 the government seemed to circle the wagons for self-protection, with the antiterrorism measures aimed at noncitizens, who are outside the circle. But looking at affected U.S. citizens and communities shows that the line defining the circle is not bright, and the circle tightens asymmetrically by race and ethnicity. The circled wagons image sheds light on how U.S. citizens of Japanese ancestry felt during World War II when they found themselves outside the circle, officially relabeled not as citizens but as "nonaliens" and sent to internment camps. A lesser known example of the same phenomenon is the Mexican-American repatriations of the 1930s, when noncitizens and citizens alike were forced to "return" to Mexico, though some in fact had never seen Mexico. Arab-American and Muslim citizens should be inside the circled wagons, but after September 11 the Bush administration overlooked one of the key lessons from the Japanese-American internment and Mexican-American repatriations: as soon as enforcement of immigration law relies on race and ethnicity, then a person's race and ethnicity will matter more than whether he is a citizen.

Beyond Race and Ethnicity

The role of race and ethnicity in U.S. immigration and citizenship law and the recent turn toward profiling in immigration law enforcement have made many Latin American, Asian, and African immigrants feel that their welcome in America is tentative and contingent. The message that they are less than fully American can extend beyond the immigrant generation. For example, many Asian Americans—having learned, as did their immigrant parents and grandparents, that their acceptance in America is ambivalent and fragile—report feeling like perpetual foreigners even though they are native English-speakers born in the United States. The need to view immigration as transition and to revive the idea of Americans in waiting reflects a continuing need to remedy messages of exclusion and instead foster voluntary integration into American life.

I am not suggesting, however, that these matters of race and ethnicity are the central—or even a central reason—for recovering the lost story of Americans in waiting. Although the historical role of race and ethnicity explains much of why immigration as transition lost its central influence, they are just the most obvious elements of a more pervasive phenomenon that exists even when race and ethnicity are not implicated. With all immigrants, there is a serious danger of what Alex Aleinikoff and sociologist Rubén Rumbaut have called a self-fulfilling prophecy, a circle that starts when the receiving society believes—often based partly on race and national origin—that immigrants are not integrating. This leads to laws and attitudes that make immigrants feel less welcome, which in turn makes immigrants naturally reluctant to integrate, which leads to more exclusionary practices. As Aleinikoff and Rumbaut have put it, "the way people are invited or welcomed to become members of the society influences their joining behavior which, in turn, influences how the society invites others to join it." The idea of Americans in waiting is the key to breaking this cycle for all immigrants, and to resurrecting the promise of citizenship as an inclusive vehicle for participation in civic, political, social, and economic life.[49]

CHAPTER 10

Taking Transition Seriously

The essence of immigration as transition is giving lawful immigrants the best chance to belong in America, in a broad sense that goes beyond formal citizenship to include integration into American society. The crucial focus is the time until lawful immigrants can naturalize. For new immigrants who are children and adolescents, this transition period should last at least until they are twenty-one years old, to let them decide as adults whether to naturalize. This transition period also should last beyond the five-year qualifying residency period to allow time for the naturalization procedure from application to oath. Current law allows lawful immigrants to apply for naturalization starting three months before they meet the residency requirement, but the process can take much longer. Congress recognized this delay in 1997 when it set up a public assistance eligibility scheme that reflected some transition-based thinking. Under that scheme, several groups of noncitizens granted protection from persecution are eligible for federal benefits, but only for the five years it takes to qualify for naturalization plus two more years for processing. This makes sense as a general approach, but an extra two years may not be enough processing time even for lawful immigrants who apply promptly.[1]

Being treated as an American in waiting should not require a new immigrant to file a declaration of intent to naturalize. Though this is how eligible noncitizens historically acquired—and still can acquire intending citizen status, it is not a declared intent to naturalize nor ultimately naturalizing that matters. The key to reviving the idea of Americans in waiting is the working assumption that any given lawful immigrant will become a citizen. This treatment should encourage many lawful immigrants not only to naturalize but also to integrate into American society more generally, no matter their original intentions.

The Safety Net

I have discussed the influence that two views of immigration—immigration as contract in chapter 2, and immigration as affiliation in chapter 4—exert on welfare eligibility for lawful immigrants. Immigration as transition has been strikingly absent from this debate, so it is fair to pose this question: Might a stronger role for transition change lawful immigrants' access to federal public assistance? Immigration as transition calls for equality with citizens in the prenaturalization period. This principle does not require any particular level of benefits, but rather is an equality principle that gives new lawful immigrants what citizens get. This would mean making new lawful immigrants eligible for federal Supplemental Security Income. They would also be eligible for food stamps without the current five-year waiting period.

These implications of transition may prompt questions as to why welfare eligibility should be expanded for lawful immigrants at a time when the federal government and many states and localities are trying to reduce the use of welfare programs by citizens. Put more broadly, the question is whether America can expect more of immigrants than of its own citizens. Does transition mean moving newcomers toward what citizens really are, or toward what we want citizens to be—to what I call "virtuous citizenship"? Someone who wants to limit food stamps for citizens might, with this notion of virtuous citizenship in mind, also oppose changing current law to give food stamps to new lawful immigrants.[2]

Limiting transition to virtuous citizenship has two serious problems. One is that the meaning of virtue in citizenship—what citizens should or should not be—is fiercely debated. Even if there were a broad consensus for reducing welfare dependence, there is no consensus on why and how to do so. Second and more fundamentally, transition's emphasis on integration makes it perverse to think only in terms of virtuous citizenship. Limiting transition by removing the safety net will only increase the number of new immigrants who may fall into poverty and remain there after they can naturalize. The only way to avoid this cycle is to take citizenship not in some virtuous form, but as citizenship in fact. Giving lawful immigrants access to public assistance, including skills training, increases the number of Americans in waiting who can achieve financial self-sufficiency or even prosperity. In this sense, public assistance functions like access to public education.

A related objection to welfare eligibility for new lawful immigrants is that it is fair to expect more financial self-sufficiency from them than from citizens. At least in categories other than refugees and asylum, it may be good policy to admit only immigrants who will not require public assistance. More generally, any group should be able to use selective admission criteria to shape its future membership, typically by demanding that new members meet higher standards than the least virtuous of its current members. There is nothing wrong with the inadmissibility ground for aliens likely to become a public charge, or with minimum education or job skills requirements. But these are initial admission criteria. In contrast, immigration as transition informs the treatment of lawful immigrants *after* admission, by articulating a commitment to their integration. Taking transition seriously means giving new lawful immigrants the same safety net as citizens if they fall into poverty in spite of the financial resources that they showed for admission.

Voting

Should lawful immigrants be allowed to vote? Taking transition seriously would mean rethinking current practice. As chapter 6 explained, noncitizen voting was widespread for much of the 1800s and the early 1900s. Many states and territories limited voting by noncitizens to those who filed declarations of intent to naturalize. The decline of noncitizen voting was part of broader changes in the link between voting and citizenship. Although *Minor v. Happersett* upheld a law denying the vote to citizen women by explaining that not all voters were citizens and not all citizens were voters, citizenship and voting gradually became more congruent. Other requirements—most prominently race and gender—were repealed, and voting came to be both extended and limited to citizens.[3]

Many of the same social and political forces that led to immigration restrictions around World War I contributed to the end of statewide noncitizen voting by the 1920s. Today, noncitizen voting is rare. Noncitizen parents of schoolchildren may vote in schools elections in Chicago, as they could in New York City school board elections from 1970 until the school boards were disbanded in 2002. Noncitizen voting in general elections is confined to a few small communities in Maryland. A few proposals for local noncitizen voting have surfaced recently, but none has passed.[4]

The long history of noncitizen voting makes clear that the U.S. Constitution allows it. But does the Constitution require that noncitizens, or at least some noncitizens, have the right to vote? The only published court decision on this issue is the 1973 Colorado Supreme Court decision in *Skafte v. Rorex*, which rejected a permanent resident's argument that denying him the vote in a local school district election violated his constitutional rights. *Skafte* relied in turn on the U.S. Supreme Court's decision earlier the same year in *Sugarman v. Dougall*, which had invalidated a citizenship requirement for all New York state employees but recognized "a State's interest in establishing its own form of government, and in limiting participation in that government to those who are within 'the basic conception of a political community.' " *Skafte* relied on this part of *Sugarman* to hold that voting can constitutionally be limited to citizens.[5]

In 1982, the U.S. Supreme Court elaborated on *Sugarman* in *Cabell v. Chavez-Salido*, which involved several noncitizens who wanted to become state probation officers. They challenged the constitutionality of California's requirement of U.S. citizenship for "public officers or employees declared by law to be peace officers." The Court upheld the requirement by relying on *Sugarman* to explain: "The exclusion of aliens from basic governmental processes is not a deficiency in the democratic system but a necessary consequence of the community's process of political self-definition."[6] While the Supreme Court's 1971 decision in *Graham v. Richardson* had kept states and localities from denying public assistance, *Sugarman* and *Cabell* established that the Constitution allows states and localities to limit voting and other political activity to citizens. *Skafte, Sugarman,* and *Cabell* combine to confirm that noncitizen voting is a legislative question, not a constitutional one.

Immigration as contract requires notice and implied consent, but it otherwise does not limit the terms of permanent residence for new arrivals. Since noncitizen voting ended as a general practice at least eighty years ago, no lawful immigrant today can make a plausible contract-based argument for voting. Instead, most proponents of noncitizen voting make affiliation-based arguments that cite the strength of noncitizens' ties, sometimes in contrast to their political vulnerability. The emphasis on ties explains why these arguments seem most frequent and persuasive in

local elections, where community ties are most immediate and compelling.[7]

The history of noncitizen voting by intending citizens highlights the
significance of voting as civic education and therefore a significant part of
the transition to citizenship. An 1863 Vermont Supreme Court decision
that interpreted state statutes to allow noncitizens to vote and serve on
school committees said this about noncitizen voting:

> While awaiting the time when they are to become entitled to the full
> rights of citizenship, it seems to us a wise policy in the Legislature
> to allow them to participate in the affairs of these minor municipal
> corporations, as in some degree a preparatory fitting and training
> for the exercise of the more important and extensive rights and du-
> ties of citizens.[8]

From this transition-based perspective, a proposal by political scientists Rodolfo de la Garza and Louis DeSipio makes good sense. They
would let permanent residents vote at least in local elections, but only for
the first five years (plus time for the naturalization process), when they
cannot naturalize. After that, they could no longer vote as lawful immigrants, but they could naturalize and vote as citizens. The idea that voting
is a form of civic education also suggests that voting by new immigrants
could be required as part of the naturalization civics exam, or that voting
could substitute for the exam as de la Garza and DeSipio have suggested.[9]

A skeptic might object that voting is necessary for neither a lawful immigrant's formal naturalization nor her integration into American society. Many citizens vote infrequently or not at all. Exclusion from the
voting booth would seem to impede integration far less than separating a
lawful immigrant from his wife and children, or leaving him destitute and
without medical care. The problem with this response is that taking transition seriously means more than removing undue obstacles to integration. As chapter 8 explained, the real question is not whether voting is
necessary, but rather how it would enhance integration.

Voting has special importance because it involves core political
rights. Lawful immigrants in the United States enjoy significant participation in social and economic life, so it is tempting to make citizenship
and political rights more exclusive and disallow voting by lawful immigrants. Alex Aleinikoff has observed that this distinction explains the
logic of the U.S. Supreme Court's alienage law decisions of the 1970s and

1980s.[10] *Graham* extended welfare eligibility to noncitizens, while *Sugarman* and *Cabell* emphasized that politics can be reserved for citizens. However, to tap the potential of voting to foster civic education and involvement as aspects of integration and transition to citizenship, it is important to include voting and other political rights in any transition-based treatment of new lawful immigrants.

Public Employment

Related to noncitizen voting is the question of whether public employment should be limited to citizens. Noncitizens are generally barred from federal civil service under the regulations issued after *Mow Sun Wong*, and it seems clear that a citizenship requirement for federal employment is constitutional. The U.S. Supreme Court has invalidated state laws requiring U.S. citizenship for licensing as notaries, civil engineers, and attorneys, and, in the case of *Sugarman*, for any state employment. In contrast, *Cabell* and several other decisions applied the *Sugarman* political functions exception to uphold state laws that probation officers, public school teachers, and state troopers must be U.S. citizens.[11]

Even if these court decisions give the constitutional answers, is it a good idea to bar lawful immigrants from all public employment? Immigration as transition suggests that it is not. Requiring citizenship for all public jobs severely limits access to the labor market, especially where the public sector is large. A job and paycheck are at stake, as the dissent in *Cabell* emphasized, in contrast to the majority's depiction of probation officers as policy makers and government representatives. Similarly, when the Supreme Court struck down a citizenship requirement for licensed civil engineers, it cast the issue as "the right to work for a living in the common occupations of the community." This is a transition-based emphasis on access to work, which is key to integration. This need to foster integration argues against excluding lawful immigrants from all federal and state public employment.[12]

A harder question is whether it is consistent with immigration as transition to exclude lawful immigrants from government policy-making positions. Policy making is hard to define, but even if there are close cases, this category surely includes elected officials. As with voting, if the goal is simply to remove serious obstacles to integration, there is no good reason to let lawful immigrants hold any policy-making jobs. But because taking transition seriously means not just removing obstacles to integration but also fostering integration affirmatively, new lawful immigrants should be eligible for policy-making positions including elected office. It is hard to imagine more intensive civic education. As a practical matter, new lawful immigrants may be less likely to be appointed or elected to these positions, but that is no reason to disqualify them categorically.

Deportation

Taking transition seriously would change the deportation scheme for lawful immigrants. Immigration as transition suggests that it should be more lenient for new lawful immigrants than for other noncitizens, so that new lawful immigrants would have something close to the absolute security of residence that citizens enjoy. The basic idea is that lawful immigrants have more at stake than other noncitizens. New lawful immigrants, even if they lack the sort of ties that affiliation-based deportation rules recognize, are Americans in waiting on their way to citizenship, and deportation takes away that opportunity.

Deportability based on criminal convictions is the only large category of lawful immigrant removals. Though more noncitizens are removed (formally or informally) after crossing the border surreptitiously or violating nonimmigrant admission terms, these two categories almost never involve lawful immigrants. Immigration as transition would mean abandoning the current practice of applying the same criminal deportability grounds to all noncitizens in the United States. New lawful immigrants should be deportable only for crimes that are more serious than crimes that make tourists, business travelers, or students deportable. It would make sense to provide that the deportability grounds for a single crime involving moral turpitude or controlled substances do not apply to new lawful immigrants. It should also be much harder for the government to remove a new lawful immigrant for the less serious crimes in the aggravated felony category.

Immigration as transition also suggests rethinking deportability grounds that are not based on crimes, applying the same basic principle that deportation for new lawful immigrants should be separate from the scheme for other noncitizens. For example, the *AADC* litigation involved the scope of First Amendment protection when the government tried to deport noncitizens on various grounds tied to national security and ideology. Such First

Amendment limits on the application of deportation grounds should reflect more deference to new lawful immigrants than to other noncitizens.

Immigration as transition does not suggest more deportation safe harbors such as the provision making noncitizens deportable for a single crime involving moral turpitude only if it is committed within five years of admission. This sort of rule protects longtime lawful immigrants from deportation but not the new lawful immigrants who are transition's chief concern. For the same reason, new lawful immigrants should be eligible for discretionary relief from removal without such residency prerequisites as the eligibility threshold for cancellation of removal—five years as a permanent resident and seven years after admission in any lawful status. The current distinction that makes discretionary relief from removal more available to lawful immigrants than to other noncitizens should be maintained.[13]

At a more basic level, taking transition seriously would prompt rethinking the traditional rule that deportation is a civil rather than criminal matter. Treating the deportation of lawful immigrants as criminal punishment for constitutional purposes would trigger important criminal procedure protections, including the right to counsel at government expense, as well as the prohibitions against retroactive punishment and cruel and unusual punishment.[14] Treating deportation as civil has drawn substantial criticism, typically reflecting an argument that lawful immigrants have ties in America and that severing those ties is such a harsh consequence that it amounts to criminal punishment. But this affiliation-based argument makes only half of the case for treating deportation as criminal punishment. The other essential half of the argument—based on immigration as transition—is that minimizing protections for lawful immigrants by calling deportation "civil" ignores the special status of new lawful immigrants as Americans in waiting.

The next question is why transition *ever* allows deportation of new lawful immigrants. Immigration as transition might seem to bar deportation of new lawful immigrants, but taking transition seriously does not go that far, and the government should be able to expel new lawful immigrants for serious crimes. The difficult question is why deportation is the one area where I do not advocate treating new lawful immigrants like citizens, even if it should be harder to deport new lawful immigrants than other noncitizens.

The answer lies in comparing deportation with other aspects of permanent residence. One apparent difference is that family reunification, public assistance, voting, and public employment pose the question of whether lawful immigrants and citizens have equal access to an affirmative right or benefit. Deportation seems different because the issue is rather immunity from removal. But this is not a real difference, for deportation can just as easily be characterized as depriving noncitizens of the "benefit" of living in the United States indefinitely.

A more promising way of distinguishing deportation is that family reunification, public assistance, voting, and public employment are all things that citizens have as a part of being citizens. Letting a lawful immigrant take advantage of these benefits merely accelerates the timing; immigration as transition lets her do now what she can do as a citizen later. Family reunification, public assistance, voting, and public employment are part of a lawful immigrant's integration. Committing crimes is different because citizens have no right to commit crimes.

This way of distinguishing deportation is also a bit too neat. Though lawful immigrants do not have a right to commit crimes, they may have a right not to be deported for doing so. Moreover, receiving welfare payments is a form of behavior that some may find troubling. I concede that this line defies entirely watertight justification, but on balance it seems reasonable to use the line between criminal behavior and other behavior to carve out an area in which new lawful immigrants need not be treated just like citizens. Taking transition seriously means treating new lawful immigrants like citizens as to things that are desirable in citizens like voting, or at least tolerable like getting public benefits. For unlawful activities, however, it is consistent with immigration as transition that permanent residence is a probationary period, when the wisdom of initial admission decisions can be verified and in exceptional cases *not* lead to naturalization. This makes sense because making permanent residence completely equal to citizenship would make admission of new permanent residents both more momentous and less informed. It would amount to choosing new citizens, but with much less information than would be available when new lawful immigrants want to naturalize several years after admission. Though it is important to take transition seriously, it should not mean the end of permanent residence as a stage between admission and naturalization.

Non-Naturalizing Permanent Residents

The general question that remains is what should happen if a permanent resident chooses not to naturalize. Imagine that Jill Dawson, permanent resident for the past twenty years, gets hurt in an accident at her job in a car assembly plant. She is permanently disabled and unable to work. If she were a citizen, she would be eligible for welfare benefits. And if she were in the period before she could naturalize, she would have a transition-based argument for eligibility. But having decided not to naturalize, she is no longer an American in waiting, and immigration as transition is no longer a basis for her eligibility.

As chapter 6 noted, the fact that a lawful immigrant had not naturalized was a transition-based aspect of the U.S. Supreme Court's reasoning in *Harisiades* and *Carlson*, two decisions from the 1950s. Both decisions cited non-naturalization in rejecting constitutional arguments against deportation, but this is troubling because it took the significance of non-naturalization to its logical but unnecessary extreme. Exclusive reliance on immigration as transition as a basis for immigration and citizenship decisions might suggest that Jill's decision not to naturalize should relegate her to the position of a complete stranger. But as the introduction explained, contract, affiliation, and transition are complementary—not mutually exclusive—rationales for the treatment of lawful immigrants. The treatment of any given noncitizen in the United States should reflect a blend of all three, considering the terms of her admission (contract), the length and character of her stay (affiliation), and where she stands regarding naturalization (transition). Transition suggests that a lawful immigrant should be treated almost like a citizen until she can naturalize. A non-naturalizing lawful immigrant should retain protections based on affiliation and contract that are less extensive than the virtual equality with citizenship that immigration as transition would give her before naturalization.

Immigration as affiliation can play an especially important ameliorating role for non-naturalizing lawful immigrants, because they almost always have been in the United States long enough to deserve protection based on ties here. Though U.S. law and policy should take transition more seriously, and thus enhance protections for lawful immigrants until they can naturalize, nothing suggests that those who do not naturalize should lose any of the protections that they now enjoy on the basis of the understandings under which they came to the United States, or on the basis of their ties here.

Affiliation and contract thus soften the effects of withdrawing transition-based protections from lawful immigrants who do not naturalize. This is important because, as I said at the end of chapter 8, lawful immigrants should not be coerced into citizenship. Coercion would undermine the reasons to view immigration as transition in the first place, especially the most compelling one—using transition to reimagine citizenship as an inclusive framework for participation in American society.

Coercion to naturalize is hard to define, and especially hard to distinguish from an incentive to naturalize. It may seem coercive for the government to respond to a lawful immigrant's decision not to naturalize by reducing or eliminating benefits or protections that she had been enjoying. Or it might be just as accurate to call it a benign incentive to naturalize. Defining incentive and coercion is not a search for the inherent meaning of these words, but rather an assessment of the rewards and penalties linked to naturalization. This assessment should begin by seeing that immigration as transition and immigration as affiliation offer different incentive patterns.

As chapter 4 explained, affiliation-based benefits and protections for longtime lawful immigrants reduce naturalization incentives. For example, a lawful immigrant currently gains Medicare and food stamp eligibility after five years, but at that point he has satisfied the naturalization residency requirement. A law that denies him Medicare and food stamp eligibility even after five years would give him a tangible incentive to naturalize. But if he can get the same benefits without naturalizing, he may decide not to. Immigration as transition produces a very different incentive pattern, because its logic confines near-equal treatment of citizens and lawful immigrants to the prenaturalization years. Once a lawful immigrant does not naturalize, he can no longer invoke transition-based rationales for treatment as an American in waiting. The prospect of losing near-equal treatment can create significant naturalization incentives.

If transition were the *only* rationale for protecting lawful immigrants, then those who do not naturalize would suffer a precipitous drop in protection. This threat might be enough to turn incentives into coercion. But transition is not the only rationale for protecting lawful immigrants, as long as immigration as affiliation and immigration as contract offer complementary protections for non-naturalizing permanent residents. They would lose the right to vote and other transition-based equality with citizens but not be treated as total strangers. They would still have the more limited, affiliation-based rules for family reunification, public benefits, public employment, and deportation that longtime permanent residents now enjoy. This leaves lawful immigrants with a meaningful choice to naturalize or not, which means that a transition-based scheme can provide incentives without coercion.

CONCLUSION

The Idea of Americans in Waiting

★

What does it mean to be a "nation of immigrants"? In this book I have tried to answer this question by looking carefully at how America treats lawful immigrants. Of course, there are other ways to take the pulse of our attitude toward newcomers—how we guard our borders, and how we choose immigrants in the first place. These are also important questions, but how we treat the noncitizens who are closest to citizens—the lawful immigrants who can stay in America indefinitely—tells us in the most basic terms how we see immigration as part of our national future.

In the introduction I observed that *Brown v. Board of Education* and its affirmation of this nation's commitment to equality poses a special dilemma in immigration and citizenship, where it is basic that citizens and noncitizens are not always equal. The line between citizens and the noncitizens who are most like citizens poses the most difficult version of this equality dilemma, because it is the line that we draw closest to home, at the place of greatest intimacy between outsider and insider. How we draw it reveals basic truths about our nation of immigrants.

The conventional account of immigration and citizenship law centers on attitudes that I have called immigration as contract and immigration as affiliation. Both of these views of immigration go beyond the minimum standards that derive from treating noncitizens as a matter of territorial personhood or international human rights. Immigration as contract reflects the notion that we can achieve fair and just outcomes without equality for noncitizens as long as we respect other values, such as notice and the protection of expectations. Immigration as affiliation lets lawful immigrants earn an approximation of equality as they gradually form ties in the United States. In this story of tension and accommodation between immigration as contract and immigration as affiliation, contract is often cast as less receptive to immigrants, and affiliation as more receptive. But these generalizations are much too simple, for immigration as contract can be a conceptual framework for protecting noncitizens. Perhaps less obviously, the emphasis on ties in immigration as affiliation means that it welcomes immigrants—especially new ones—less warmly than is commonly understood.

But the fundamental shortcoming of this conventional contract-versus-affiliation account is that neither contract nor affiliation treats new immigrants as if they will become citizens. Only by understanding that there is a third view of immigration—as transition to citizenship—does the full array of past, present, and future choices become clear. Immigration as transition recognizes the line between us and them as a permeable border that many lawful immigrants will cross in the natural course of time.

Transition once lay at the conceptual center of the treatment of lawful immigrants in the United States, but this was during an earlier historical period when immigration law was an unabashed tool for defining America along racial and ethnic lines. Immigration and citizenship criteria gradually became much more open, but as it did the meaning of immigration changed. The idea of Americans in waiting faded from the core of immigration and citizenship law and became its lost story.

The decline in the idea of Americans in waiting went largely unnoticed, perhaps because the position of noncitizens generally strengthened, reflecting not only the emergence of immigration as affiliation, but also the evolution of immigration as contract from a way to limit noncitizens' rights into a framework for protecting them. These developments meant more recognition of noncitizens' rights in general, but lawful immigrants became much more like all other noncitizens in the United States.

Seeing new immigrants once again as Americans in waiting would mean not only removing obstacles to naturalization, but also making the most of the time before a lawful immigrant can naturalize, treating it as a period of integration into American life. This would call for significant changes to current law, so that new lawful immigrants would be treated just like citizens in a number of key areas, including family reunification, public education, public assistance, voting, and public employment. The only difference between citizens and new lawful immigrants would be exposure to deportation for serious crimes, though they would be less exposed than other noncitizens. Otherwise, lawful immigrants would be treated like citizens until they can naturalize. If they do not, they would still have contract-based and affiliation-based protections that would put them in a better position than noncitizens who are not lawful immigrants at all, but not as good as the near-equality that new lawful immigrants enjoy as Americans in waiting.

Now I come full circle back to three ideas from the beginning of this book. The first concerns the role of law. The introduction explained that I would examine law as an archive of public values and a reflection of the premises that have undergirded attitudes about immigration and citizenship throughout U.S. history. In concluding my inquiry into the lost story of Americans in waiting, I have another comment on the role of law. In my envisioned recovery of immigration as transition, the law serves as a steering mechanism that creates the basic conditions for integration, but without the clumsy, coercive, direct state intervention that has characterized assimilation or integration programs in the past. If we take transition seriously, the law will create the conditions for lawful immigrants to make free, meaningful choices, and for nongovernmental organizations and individuals working in communities to help make them feel like Americans in waiting. This role for law and government is key to an inclusive vision of U.S. citizenship.

The role of law is closely related to another idea from the early parts of this book that merits revisiting. Much of the story of the Chinese exclusion laws was an account of the gradual shift from state to federal immigration laws. Most immigration and citizenship law has been federal law since the last part of the nineteenth century, and this has led to the general attitude that immigration and immigrants are a federal responsibility. This is a sound rule of thumb for immigration law enforcement, given that state and local involvement may become overzealous and mistaken-ridden, reflect an even wider array of discretionary choices than federal enforcement, and undermine the community trust that is necessary for effective law enforcement in a broader sense. In areas other than enforcement, however, states and localities should tap—as some are now doing— their tremendous resources for the integration of immigrants, by helping immigrants become Americans in the communities where they live and work. Transition is a broader view of immigration than the narrow set of legal issues in which it makes sense to think in terms of federal responsibility alone.[1]

The third idea to revisit from the beginning of this book is my starting assumption that national citizenship in the United States can be a viable context for a sense of belonging and for participation in civic, political, social, and economic life that is inclusive and respectful of all individuals. Any given law or policy, at any given moment in history, reflects a blend of the views of immigration that I have labeled contract, affiliation, and transition. At stake in this blend is the meaning of immigration and our nation of immigrants. The key ingredient is the idea of Americans in waiting, for it reflects a reception of immigrants that will encourage them to choose freely to think of themselves as Americans. Because it offers that choice, the idea of Americans in waiting is the key to realizing the promise of inclusive citizenship.

NOTES

INTRODUCTION *Immigrants in America*

1 347 U.S. 483 (1954).

2 See Immigration and Nationality Act (INA) § 101(a)(20), codified in 8 United States Code.

3 See Act of May 26, 1924, ch. 190, § 3, 43 Stat. 153, 154–55, Act of May 19, 1921, ch. 8, § 2, 42 Stat. 5, 5.

4 See INA §§ 201, 203, 207, 208, 241(b)(3); Thomas Alexander Aleinikoff, David A. Martin, and Hiroshi Motomura, Immigration and Citizenship: Process and Policy 282–84, 302–65, 790–1015 (West 5th ed. 2003); Ruth Ellen Wasem, Congressional Research Service, U.S. Immigration Policy on Permanent Admissions 6–11 (updated ed. 2005).

5 See INA §§ 101(a)(3), 320, 322; Aleinikoff, Martin, and Motomura, Immigration and Citizenship, at 32–53, 53–89. By way of exception, inhabitants of American Samoa and Swains Island are U.S. nationals but neither aliens nor citizens. See INA §§ 101(a)(22), (a)(29), 301; Aleinikoff, Martin, and Motomura, Immigration and Citizenship, at 13–14 n. 2.

6 See Nancy F. Rytina and Chunnong Saeger, Department of Homeland Security, Naturalizations in the United States: 2004, at 1 (2005); Nancy F. Rytina, Department of Homeland Security, Estimates of the Legal Permanent Resident Population and Population Eligible to Naturalize in 2003, at 3–4 (2005). See also Michael Fix, Jeffrey S. Passel, and Kenneth Sucher, Trends in Naturalization, 80 Interpreter Releases 1473, 1475 (2003).

7 See Act of Jan. 29, 1795, ch. 20, § 1, 1 Stat. 414, 414.

8 See Act of May 20, 1862, ch. 75, § 1, 12 Stat. 392, 392.

9 See Leon E. Aylsworth, The Passing of Alien Suffrage, 25 Am. Pol. Sci. Rev. 114, 114–16 (1931).

10 See Michael Walzer, Spheres of Justice: A Defense of Pluralism and Equality 39 (Basic Books 1983) (citing Henry Sidgwick, The Elements of Politics 295–96 [Macmillan 1891]).

CHAPTER 1 *Contract and Classical Immigration Law*

1 Chae Chan Ping v. United States (the *Chinese Exclusion Case*), 130 U.S. 581 (1889).

2 On Chinese immigration, reactions, and legislation in this period, see Tomas Almaguer, Racial Fault Lines: The Historical Origins of White Supremacy in California 154–82 (Univ. of California Press 1994); Gabriel J. Chin, *Chae Chan Ping* and *Fong Yue Ting*: The Origins of Plenary Power, in Immigration Stories 7–29 (David A. Martin and Peter H. Schuck eds., Foundation Press 2005); Roger Daniels, Asian America: Chinese and Japanese in the United States since 1850, at 9–66 (Univ. of Washington Press 1988); Roger Daniels, Coming to America: A History of Immigration and Ethnicity in American Life 239–43 (2d ed. Perennial 2002); Roger Daniels, Guarding the Golden Door: American Immigration Policy and Immigrants since 1882, at 11–26 (Hill and Wang 2004); Andrew Gyory, Closing the Gate: Race, Politics, and the Chinese Exclusion Act 212–59 (Univ. of North Carolina Press 1998); Bill Ong Hing, Making and Remaking Asian America Through Immigration Policy 1850–1990, at 20–26 (Stanford Univ. Press 1993); Patricia Nelson Limerick, The Legacy of Conquest: The Unbroken Past of the American West 261–69 (Norton 1987); Charles J. McClain, In Search of Equality: The Chinese Struggle against Discrimination in Nineteenth-Century America 9–76, 201–06 (Univ. of California Press 1994); Lucy E. Salyer, Laws Harsh as Tigers: Chinese Immigrants and the Shaping of Modern Immigration Law 8–18, 43–58 (Univ. of North Carolina Press 1995); Ronald Takaki, Strangers from a Different Shore: A History of Asian Americans 79–131 (updated & rev. ed. Little Brown 1998); Daniel J. Tichenor, Dividing Lines: The Politics of Immigration Control in America 87–108 (Princeton Univ. Press 2002). For California's population, see U.S. Bureau of the Census, Historical Statistics of the U.S.: Colonial Times to 1970, Bicentennial Edition Part I, 25 (1975).

3 Treaty of Trade, Consuls and Emigration between China and the United States, signed at Washington, July 28, 1868, Art. V, 137 Consolidated Treaty Series 469. On China's emigration ban, see Mae M. Ngai, Impossible Subjects: Illegal Aliens and the Making of Modern America 280 n. 32 (Princeton Univ. Press 2004); Wang Gungwu, The Chinese Overseas: From Earthbound China to the Quest for Autonomy 42–47 (Harvard Univ. Press 2000).

4 See Act of May 4, 1852, ch. 37, 1852 Cal. Stat. 84, repealed and superseded by Act of Mar. 30, 1853, ch. 44, 1853 Cal. Stat. 62 (officially repealed by Act of Apr. 26, 1939, ch. 93, 1939 Cal. Stat. 1067, 1215); Randall E. Rohe, After the Gold Rush: Chinese Mining in the Far West, 1850–1890, in Chinese on the American Frontier 3, 6 (Arif Dirlik ed., Rowman and Littlefield 2001).

5 See U.S. Cong., Joint Special Committee on Chinese Immigration, 44th Cong., 2d Sess., S. Rep. No. 689, at viii (1876).

6 *Chae Chan Ping*, 130 U.S. at 596–97 (citing treaty).

7 U.S. Const. art. II, § 1, cl. 5; see Noah Pickus, True Faith and Allegiance: Immigration and American Civic Nationalism 25–28 (Princeton Univ. Press 2005); Tichenor, Dividing Lines, at 51–52.

8 See U.S. Const. art. I, § 8, cl. 4; § 8, cl. 3; § 9, cl. 1. See generally Aleinikoff, Martin, and Motomura, Immigration and Citizenship, at 177–80, 184–86; Daniels, Coming to America, at 112–13; Rogers M. Smith, Civic Ideals: Conflicting Visions of Citizenship in U.S. History 115–36 (Yale Univ. Press 1997).

9 Act of June 25, 1798, ch. 58, § 1, 1 Stat. 570, 571; Act of July 6, 1798, ch. 66, § 1, 1 Stat. 577, 577, codified at 50 U.S.C. § 21 (1988). See John Higham, Strangers in the Land: Patterns of American Nativism 1860–1925, at 7–9 (Atheneum 2d ed. 1963); Smith, Civic Ideals, at 162–63.

10 On states, see Higham, Strangers in the Land, at 175; Michael C. LeMay, From Open Door to Dutch Door: An Analysis of U.S. Immigration Policy since 1820, at 23–24 (Praeger 1987); Tichenor, Dividing Lines, at 35, 59, 66. On assimilation, see Higham, Strangers in the Land, at 20–21, 108–09; Tichenor, Dividing Lines, at 84.

11 On immigration in this period, see Daniels, Coming to America, at 126–64; Higham, Strangers in the Land, at 10–15; Matthew Frye Jacobson, Whiteness of a Different Color: European Immigrants and the Alchemy of Race 41–52 (Harvard Univ. Press 1998); Desmond King, Making Americans: Immigration, Race, and the Origins of the Diverse Democracy 20–22 (Harvard Univ. Press 2000).

12 See U.S. Census Bureau, Luke J. Larsen, U.S. Census Bureau, The Foreign-Born Population in the United States: 2003 (2004).

13 Higham, Strangers in the Land, at 4–8.

14 See John W. Chambers II, To Raise an Army: The Draft Comes to Modern America 48–49 (Free Press 1987).

15 See Mary Sarah Bilder, The Struggle over Immigration: Indentured Servants, Slaves, and Articles of Commerce, 61 Mo. L. Rev. 743, 793–98 (1996); Gabriel J. Chin, Regulating Race: Asian Exclusion and the Administrative State, 37 Harv. C.R.-C.L. L. Rev. 1, 12 (2002); James W. Fox, Jr., Citizenship, Poverty, and Federalism: 1787–1882, 60 U. Pitt. L. Rev. 421, 559–65 (1999); Gerald L. Neuman, The Lost Century of Immigration Law (1776–1875), 93 Colum. L. Rev. 1833 (1993). See also Gerald L. Neuman, Strangers to the Constitution: Immigrants, Borders, and Fundamental Law 19–51 (Princeton Univ. Press 1996); Salyer, Laws Harsh as Tigers, at 4.

16 22 U.S. (9 Wheat.) 1, 203, 235 (1824).

17 36 U.S. (11 Pet.) 102, 132, 141 (1837).

18 Act of Mar. 2, 1819, ch. 46, 3 Stat. 488, 488; Act of Feb. 28, 1803, ch. 10, 2 Stat. 205, 205; Act of Feb. 19, 1862, ch. 27, 12 Stat. 340, 340.

19 Smith v. Turner (Passenger Cases), 48 U.S. (7 How.) 283, 409, 410–12, 447, 463–64 (1849), invalidating Act of Apr. 20, 1837, ch. 238, §§ 2,3, 1837 Mass. Laws 270, 270; Act of Mar. 30, 1798, ch. 67, § 5, 1797 N.Y. Laws 93, 94.

20 See N.Y. Act of Apr. 11, 1849, ch. 350, § 2; People v. Downer, 7 Cal. 169, 171 (1857), invalidating Act of Apr. 28, 1855, ch. 153, 1855 Cal. Stat. 194, 194–95; Lin Sing v. Washburn, 20 Cal. 534 (1862), invalidating Act of Apr. 26, 1862, ch. 313, 1858 Cal. Stat. 295.

21 See Henderson, 92 U.S. 259, 270, 275 (1876); Chy Lung, 92 U.S. 275, 279–81 (1876); Edye v. Robertson (Head Money Cases), 112 U.S. 580, 593–96 (1884) (upholding Act of Aug. 3, 1882, ch. 376, §§ 1, 2, 22 Stat. 214, 214).

22 See Compagnie Francaise de Navigation a Vapeur v. Louisiana State Bd. of Health, 186 U.S. 380, 387 (1902); Morgan's S.S. Co. v. Louisiana Bd. of Health, 118 U.S. 455, 465–66 (1886).

23 Act of Aug. 3, 1882, ch. 376, § 2, 22 Stat. 214, 214. See Tichenor, Dividing Lines, at 67; Daniels, Coming to America, at 272.

24 On immigration preemption, see Hiroshi Motomura, Federalism, International Human Rights, and Immigration Exceptionalism, 70 U. Colo. L. Rev. 1361, 1369–75 (1999); Hiroshi Motomura, Whose Immigration Law? Citizens, Aliens, and the Constitution, 97 Colum. L. Rev. 1567, 1587–1601 (1997); Hiroshi Motomura, Whose Alien Nation? Two Models of Constitutional Immigration Law, 94 Mich. L. Rev. 1927, 1945–46 (1996). On modern pleas by states, see Chiles v. United States, 69 F.3d 1094, 1096 (11th Cir. 1995), cert. denied, 517 U.S. 1188 (1996); California v. United States, 104 F.3d 1086 (9th Cir.), cert. denied, 522 U.S. 806 (1997).

25 Act of Mar. 3, 1875, ch. 141, §§ 1, 5, 18 Stat. 477, 477. On the Page Act, see Kerry Abrams, Polygamy, Prostitution, and the Federalization of Immigration Law, 105 Colum. L. Rev. 641, 690–715 (2005); Sucheng Chan, The Exclusion of Chinese Women, 1870–1943, in Entry Denied: Exclusion and the Chinese Community in America, 1882–1943, at 94, 94–146 (Sucheng Chan ed., Temple Univ. Press 1991); Kevin R. Johnson, The Huddled Masses Myth: Immigration and Civil Rights 126 (Temple Univ. Press 2004); Leti Volpp, Divesting Citizenship: On Asian American History and the Loss of Citizenship Through Marriage, 53 UCLA L. Rev. 405, 458–69 (2005). For the Chinese exclusion laws, see Act of May 6, 1882, ch. 126, 22 Stat. 58; Act of Apr. 27, 1904, ch. 1630, § 5, 33 Stat. 392, 428; repealed by Act of Dec. 17, 1943, ch. 344, 57 Stat. 600, 600. See also An act to execute certain treaty stipulations relating to the Chinese, S. 196(71), 47th Cong. (1882); 13 Cong. Rec., S. 2551 (Apr. 4, 1882) (veto message).

26 See Act of May 6, 1882, ch. 126, §§ 4–6, 22 Stat. 58, 59–60.

27 On enforcement and response, see Kitty Calavita, The Paradoxes of Race, Class, Identity, and "Passing": Enforcing the Chinese Exclusion Acts, 1882–1910, 25 Law & Soc. Inquiry 1, 14–31 (2000); Erika Lee, At America's Gates: Chinese Immigration during the Exclusion Era, 1882–1943, at 77–109 (Univ. of North Carolina Press 2003); Salyer, Laws Harsh as Tigers, at 37–93.

28 See Act of July 5, 1884, ch. 220, 23 Stat. 115, 116; Chew Heong v. United States, 112 U.S. 536, 559–60 (1884).

29 See Act of Oct. 1, 1888, ch. 1064, §§ 1, 2, 25 Stat. 504, 504.

30 See T. Alexander Aleinikoff, Semblances of Sovereignty: The Constitution, the State, and American Citizenship 155–65 (Harvard Univ. Press 2002); Stephen H. Legomsky, Immigration Law and the Principle of Plenary Congressional Power, 1984 Sup. Ct. Rev. 255; Hiroshi Motomura, The Curious Evolution of Immigration Law: Procedural Surrogates for Substantive Constitutional Rights, 92 Colum. L. Rev. 1625 (1992); Hiroshi Motomura, Immigration Law After a Century of Plenary Power: Phantom Constitutional Norms and Statutory Interpretation, 100 Yale L.J. 545 (1990); Peter H. Schuck, The Transformation of Immigration Law, 84 Colum. L. Rev. 1 (1984), republished essentially in original

form in Peter H. Schuck, Citizens, Strangers, and In-Betweens: Essays on Immigration and Citizenship 19 (Westview Press 1998).

31 See 130 U.S. at 584, 589, 600, 603.

32 See Lees v. United States, 150 U.S. 476, 480 (1893); Plessy v. Ferguson, 163 U.S. 537 (1896). On equal protection and the federal government, see Bolling v. Sharpe, 347 U.S. 497, 500 (1954); Korematsu v. United States, 323 U.S. 214, 216 (1944); Hirabayashi v. United States, 320 U.S. 81, 83, 100 (1943).

33 130 U.S. at 603–06, 609.

34 Id. at 606. See Fong Yue Ting v. United States, 149 U.S. 698, 743 (1893) (Brewer, J., dissenting); *Plessy*, 163 U.S. at 561; Aleinikoff, Semblances of Sovereignty, at 23–32; Sarah H. Cleveland, Powers Inherent in Sovereignty: Indians, Aliens, Territories, and the Nineteenth Century Origins of Plenary Power over Foreign Affairs, 81 Tex. L. Rev. 1, 256–67 (2002); Higham, Strangers in the Land, at 168–70; Jacobson, Whiteness, at 157–59, 205–13; Smith, Civic Ideals, at 429–41.

35 Consistent with plenary power as contract are Legomsky, Plenary Congressional Power, at 269–70 (guest theory); Ruth Rubio-Marin, Immigration as a Democratic Challenge: Citizenship and Inclusion in Germany and the United States 140 (Cambridge Univ. Press 2000) (on Lem Moon Sing v. United States, 158 U.S. 538 [1895]).

36 130 U.S. at 609.

37 See In re Chae Chan Ping, 36 F. 431, 433–34 (C.C.N.D. Cal. 1888); Salyer, Laws Harsh as Tigers, at 263 n. 125.

38 On Japanese immigration and reactions, see Daniels, Asian America, at 100–29; Daniels, Coming to America, at 250–58; Daniels, Golden Door, at 41–45; Roger Daniels, The Politics of Prejudice: The Anti-Japanese Movement in California, and the Struggle for Japanese Exclusion 1–15 (Univ. of California Press 1977); Higham, Strangers in the Land, at 166, 171–72; Hing, Asian America, at 26–29, 53–55; Limerick, Legacy of Conquest, at 269–73; Ngai, Impossible Subjects, at 39–40; Salyer, Laws Harsh as Tigers, at 126–28; Tichenor, Dividing Lines, at 123; Yuji Ichioka, The Issei: The World of the First Generation Japanese Immigrants, 1885–1924, at 1–90 (Free Press 1988).

39 Act of Aug. 3, 1882, ch. 376, § 2, 22 Stat. 214, 214, followed by Act of Mar. 3, 1891, ch. 551, §§ 1, 11, 26 Stat. 1084, 1084, 1086.

40 See Exec. Order no. 589, Mar. 14, 1907. On Chinese bachelor society, see Daniels, Asian America, at 16–17; Hing, Asian America, at 44–45; Todd Stevens, Tender Ties: Husbands' Rights and Racial Exclusion in Chinese Marriage Cases, 1882–1924, 27 L. & Soc. Inquiry 271 (2002).

41 See Act of Mar. 3, 1891, ch. 551, §§ 7, 8, 26 Stat. 1084, 1085–86. On statutes in this period, see Daniels, Golden Door, at 29–30; Salyer, Laws Harsh as Tigers, at 23–32, 69–93; Tichenor, Dividing Lines, at 70.

42 See Act of Mar. 3, 1891, ch. 551, § 8, 26 Stat. 1084, 1085.

43 See Act of Aug. 3, 1882, ch. 376, § 2, 22 Stat. 214, 214.

44 142 U.S. 651, 656, 659–60 (1892).

45 Id. at 659 (emphasis added).

46 See Act of May 5, 1892, ch. 60, § 6, 27 Stat. 25, 25–26; Fong Yue Ting v. United States, 149 U.S. 698 (1893).

47 People v. Hall, 4 Cal. 399, 404–05 (1854), interpreting Act of Apr. 16, 1850, ch. 99, 1850 Cal. Stat. 229, 230. See Daniels, Asian America, at 34.

48 149 U.S. 698, 707, 713, 730 (1893) (emphasis added). See Daniel Kanstroom, Deportation, Social Control, and Punishment: Some Thoughts About Why Hard Laws Make Bad Cases, 113 Harv. L. Rev. 1889, 1898, 1907–08 (2000) (calling the Fong reasoning "contractual").

49 See Schuck, The Transformation of Immigration Law, at 3.

50 See id. at 7. See also David Abraham, The Good of Banality? The Emergence of Cost-Benefit Analysis and Proportionality in the Treatment of Aliens in the US and Germany, 4 Citizenship Studies 237, 243 (2000); Legomsky, Plenary Congressional Power, at 269.

51 See Morton J. Horwitz, The Transformation of American Law, 1870–1960: The Crisis of Legal Orthodoxy 4 (Oxford Univ. Press 1992); Pennoyer v. Neff, 95 U.S. 714 (1877).

52 On categorical reasoning in constitutional law in this period, see T. Alexander Aleinikoff, Constitutional Law in the Age of Balancing, 96 Yale L.J. 943, 949–52 (1987).

53 See James H. Kettner, The Development of American Citizenship, 1608–1870, at 8–9, 44, 55, 143 (Univ. of North Carolina Press 1978).

CHAPTER 2 *Promises, Promises*

1 See INA §§ 212(a)(3), 237(a)(4). See also Aleinikoff, Martin, and Motomura, Immigration and Citizenship, at 1184–1209; Higham, Strangers in the Land, at 30–31, 52–56, 111–13; Johnson, Huddled Masses, at 55–90; Tichenor, Dividing Lines, at 71.

2 Act of Mar. 3, 1903, ch. 1012, §§ 2, 38 32 Stat. 1213, 1214, 1221. *Public Opinion* is quoted in Higham, Strangers in the Land, at 55.

3 See Act of Mar. 3, 1875, ch. 141, § 5, 18 Stat. 477, 477; Act of Aug. 3, 1882, ch. 376, § 2, 22 Stat. 214, 214; Act of Feb. 26, 1885, ch. 164, § 1, 23 Stat. 332, 332; Act of Mar. 3, 1891, ch. 551, § 1, 26 Stat. 1084, 1084. For current grounds, see INA § 212(a); Aleinikoff, Martin, and Motomura, Immigration and Citizenship, at 431–32, 440–52, 1209–26.

4 See Act of May 6, 1882, ch. 126, § 12, 22 Stat. 58, 61; Act of Oct. 19, 1888, ch. 1210, 25 Stat. 565, 566; Act of Mar. 3, 1891, ch. 551, § 11, 26 Stat. 1084, 1086; May 5, 1892, ch. 60, § 6, 27 Stat. 25, 25–26; Act of Mar. 3, 1903, ch. 1012, §§ 20, 21, 32 Stat. 1213, 1218; Act of Feb. 20, 1907, ch. 1134, §§ 3, 20, 21, 34 Stat. 898, 899–900, 904–05; Act of Feb. 5, 1917, ch. 29, § 19, 39 Stat. 874, 889–90; Act of May 26, 1924, ch. 190, § 14, 43 Stat. 153, 162.

5 On deportation numbers, see Ngai, Impossible Subjects, at 59.

6 See Aleinikoff, Martin, and Motomura, Immigration and Citizenship, at 1189–1202; Harlan Grant Cohen, Note, The (Un)favorable Judgment of History:

Deportation Hearings, The Palmer Raids, and the Meaning of History, 78 N.Y.U. L. Rev. 1431, 1452–66 (2003); Higham, Strangers in the Land, at 229–63; Edwin P. Hoyt, The Palmer Raids 1919–1920: An Attempt to Suppress Dissent (Seabury Press 1969); King, Making Americans, at 19–27, 85–126; William Preston, Jr., Aliens and Dissenters: Federal Suppression of Radicals 1903–1933, at 208–37 (Harvard Univ. Press 1963); Salyer, Laws Harsh as Tigers, at 233–39; Tichenor, Dividing Lines, at 140. On Americanization, see Pickus, True Faith and Allegiance, at 107–23.

7 Act of Oct. 16, 1918, ch. 186, § 2, 40 Stat. 1012, 1012; Abrams v. United States, 250 U.S. 616 (1919); Richard Polenberg, Fighting Faiths: The Abrams Case, the Supreme Court, and Free Speech (Viking 1987); Richard Polenberg, Progressivism and Anarchism: Judge Henry D. Clayton and the Abrams Trial, 3 L. & Hist. Rev. 397, 407 (1985).

8 S. Rep. No. 1796, 76th Cong., 3d Sess. 3 (1940). See Act of June 5, 1920, ch. 251, 41 Stat. 1008, 1008–09; Kessler v. Strecker, 307 U.S. 22, 29–31 (1939); Act of June 28, 1940, Pub. L. No. 670, ch. 439, § 23, 54 Stat. 670, 673.

9 Act of Sept. 22, 1950, ch. 1024, §§ 7, 8, 64 Stat. 987, 993–95; Act of June 27, 1952, ch. 477, § 340, 66 Stat. 163, 260.

10 Harisiades v. Shaughnessy, 342 U.S. 580, 586–87, 589 (1952). See also Burt Neuborne, *Harisiades v. Shaughnessy*: A Case Study in the Vulnerability of Resident Aliens, in Immigration Stories, at 87–112.

11 See Grayned v. City of Rockford, 408 U.S. 104, 109 (1972) (citing Baggett v. Bullitt, 377 U.S. 360, 372 [1964]).

12 341 U.S. 223, 231 (1951). See *Fong*, 149 U.S. at 730. Cf. Boutilier v. INS, 387 U.S. 118, 123–24 (1967) (rejecting vagueness challenge).

13 795 F. Supp. 13, 23 (D.D.C. 1992) (invalidating INA § 212(a)(27), repealed by Act of Nov. 29, 1990, Pub. L. No. 101–649, § 601(a), 104 Stat. 4978, 5067. A similar current provision is INA § 212(a)(3)(B).

14 915 F. Supp. 681 (D.N.J. 1996), rev'd on jurisdictional grounds, 91 F.3d 416 (3d Cir. 1996). See INA § 237(a)(4)(C)(i), then § 241(a)(4)(C)(i).

15 915 F. Supp. at 699, 701.

16 See Anne Fadiman, The Spirit Catches You and You Fall Down: A Hmong Child, Her American Doctors, and the Collision of Two Cultures 201 (Farrar, Straus, and Giroux 1997).

17 See Hoffman Plastic Compounds, Inc. v. NLRB, 535 U.S. 137 (2002) (NLRA); Patel v. Quality Inn South, 846 F.2d 700, 704–05 (11th Cir. 1988), cert. denied, 489 U.S. 1011 (1989) (FLSA).

18 See 42 U.S.C. § 1971 (federal elections); 28 U.S.C. §§ 1861, 1865 (federal jurors); Perkins v. Smith, 370 F. Supp. 134, 134–38 (D. Md. 1974), aff'd, 426 U.S. 913 (1976) (federal jurors); Colo. Rev. Stat. § 13-71-105 (juries); Vt. Stat. Ann. tit. 4 § 962 (1997) (juries); 42 U.S.C. § 402(t) (Social Security); 7 U.S.C. § 1941 (agricultural loans); Moving Phones Partnership L.P. v. FCC, 998 F.2d 1051, 1055 (D.C. Cir. 1993), cert. denied, 511 U.S. 1004 (1994) (cell phone systems); La. Rev. Stat. Ann. § 56:8, La. Rev. Stat. Ann. § 56:252; Cal. Ins. Code § 11010.

19 See 7 C.F.R. § 764.4(a)(2) (agricultural emergency loans); 45 C.F.R. § 2522.200 (Americorps); 12 C.F.R. § 403.7 (declassification), 46 App. U.S.C. § 688 (maritime service); 42 U.S.C. § 13313 (renewable energy); Ark. Code Ann. § 6-50-206 (loans); Colo. Rev. Stat. § 24-32-2003 (youth corps); Ga. Code. Ann. § 20-3-519.1 (financial aid); 110 Ill. Comp. Stat. 947/65.50, § 925/3.06, § 205/9.16 (financial aid); Ind. Code. Ann. § 20-12-21.1-1 (financial aid). On tax liability, see 26 U.S.C. § 7701(a)(30)(A), 26 U.S.C. § 7701(b)(1)(A); Treas. Reg. § 1.1-1(a), (b); David M. Hudson, Tax Problems for Departing Aliens, 97–03; Immigration Briefings 1–3 (1997). On the draft, see 50 App. U.S.C. § 454, proclamation No. 2915.

20 Act of Aug. 3, 1882, ch. 376, § 2, 22 Stat. 214, 214; Act of Mar. 3, 1891, ch. 551, § 11, 26 Stat. 1084, 1086.

21 See Higham, Strangers in the Land, at 68–77, 163–64; Tichenor, Dividing Lines, at 69–70, 118. On organized labor, see Daniels, Golden Door, at 17. For counterexamples, see Christian Joppke, Immigration and the Nation-State: The United States, Germany, and Great Britain 43–44 (Oxford Univ. Press 2000); Tichenor, Dividing Lines, at 20–23.

22 See Daniels, Golden Door, at 62–63; Douglas S. Massey, Jorge Durand, and Nolan J. Malone, Beyond Smoke and Mirrors: Mexican Immigration in an Era of Economic Integration 26–33 (Russell Sage Foundation 2002); Earl Shorris, Latinos: A Biography of the People 42 (W.W. Norton 1992).

23 On employer control of unlawful workers, see Limerick, Legacy of Conquest, at 243–51; Ngai, Impossible Subjects, at 64, 136; Tichenor, Dividing Lines, at 151, 167–75, 211. The H-2A program is based on INA § 101(a)(15)(H). See also Kitty Calavita, Immigrants at the Margins: Law, Race, and Exclusion in Southern Europe (Cambridge Univ. Press 2005). Chapter 6 also discusses the Bracero program.

24 Francis A. Walker, Restriction of Immigration, 77 Atlantic Monthly 828 (1896). See Higham, Strangers in the Land, at 36–42, 56–68, 87, 106–30, 159, 168, 187, 232, 244; Jacobson, Whiteness, at 158–60.

25 See INA § 212(a)(4); 22 C.F.R. § 40.41; Matter of A—, 19 I&N Dec. 867, 869 (Comm'r 1988); Matter of Perez, 15 I&N Dec. 136, 137 (BIA 1974). On affidavits, see Matter of Kohama, 17 I&N Dec. 257, 258 (Assoc. Comm'r 1978). On immigrant visa refusals, see U.S. Department of State, Report of the Visa Office 2002, at 148–49 (2004). For historical perspective, see Daniels, Golden Door, at 61; Ngai, Impossible Subjects, at 54–55, 70–71.

26 See INA § 237(a)(5); 64 Fed. Reg. 28,679 (1999); Matter of B—, 3 I&N Dec. 323, 326–27 (AG & BIA 1948). On public charge removals, see Department of Homeland Security, 2003 Yearbook of Immigration Statistics 170 (2004).

27 See 42 U.S.C. § 1382j (SSI); 7 U.S.C. § 2014(i) (food stamps); Aziz v. Sullivan, 800 F. Supp. 1374, 1379–81 (E.D. Va. 1992).

28 See INA §§ 212(a)(4), 213A; 8 U.S.C. § 1631; 8 C.F.R. part 213a; 69 Fed. Reg. 7336 (2004); Aleinikoff, Martin, and Motomura, Immigration and Citizenship, at 443–51.

29 See 8 U.S.C. §§ 1611–1613, 1641. On the savings from noncitizen cuts, see Aleinikoff, Semblances of Sovereignty, at 165; Johnson, Huddled Masses, at 104;

Congressional Budget Office, Federal Budgetary Implications of H.R. 3734, The Personal Responsibility and Work Opportunity Reconciliation Act of 1996, at 14–15 (1996).

30 8 U.S.C. § 1601(1) (preamble); Remarks by the President to the Joint Session of the Michigan Legislature, 1997 WL 8030646, Mar. 10, 1997; S. Rep. No. 249, at 5–7 (1996), excerpted in Aleinikoff, Martin, and Motomura, Immigration and Citizenship, at 447.

31 See id. at 450; Leslie Pickering Francis, Elderly Immigrants: What Should They Expect of the Social Safety Net?, 5 Elder L.J. 229, 243–44 (1997).

32 See Abreu v. Callahan, 971 F. Supp. 799, 804–05 (S.D.N.Y. 1997); Kiev v. Glickman, 991 F. Supp. 1090, 1091 (D. Minn. 1998).

33 Rodriguez v. United States, 169 F.3d 1342, 1352 (11th Cir. 1999).

34 See Pub. L. No. 105-33, § 5302(a), 111 Stat. 251; Pub. L. No. 105-185, §§ 503, 504, 112 Stat. 523, 578 (1998); Pub. L. No. 105-306, 112 Stat. 2926 (1998); Pub. L. No. 105-185, Title V, § 508, 112 Stat. 578, 579 (1998).

35 143 Cong. Rec. S8319 (daily ed. July 30, 1997); Editorial, Restore Benefits to Legal Immigrants, San Francisco Chronicle, Apr. 10, 1997, at A24; James R. Edwards, Jr., Guest Editorial: Welfare Retreat Sends Mixed Messages, Investor's Business Daily, July 24, 1998.

36 On banishment and pardons, see Cooper v. Telfair, 4 U.S. 14, 19 (1800); Neuman, Strangers to the Constitution, at 22–23. On loss of citizenship and deportation, see Trop v. Dulles, 356 U.S. 86, 101–02 (1958). On denaturalization, see INA § 340; Aleinikoff, Martin, and Motomura, Immigration and Citizenship, at 107–13. On expatriation, see INA § 349; 61 Fed. Reg. 29,651 (1996); Aleinikoff, Martin, and Motomura, Immigration and Citizenship, at 113–44.

37 On loss of permanent residence, see Aleem v. Perryman, 114 F.3d 672, 676–79 (7th Cir. 1997); Matter of Huang, 19 I&N Dec. 749, 752–54 (BIA 1988); Aleinikoff, Martin, and Motomura, Immigration and Citizenship, at 479. For deportability, see INA § 237; Aleinikoff, Martin, and Motomura, Immigration and Citizenship, at 552–80, 1209–26. For crime-based removals, see 2003 Immigration Statistics, at 160.

38 See Pub. L. No. 100-690, § 7344(a), 102 Stat. 4181, 4470; Pub. L. No. 104-208, Div. C § 321, 110 Stat. 3009-627 (1996); Pub. L. No. 104-132, Title IV, §§ 414(a), 435(a), 110 Stat. 1214, 1274 (1996); Pub. L. No. 103-416, § 222, 108 Stat. 4305, 4320 (1994); Pub. L. No. 101-649, § 501, 104 Stat. 4978, 5048 (1990). For the current version, see INA § 101(a)(43).

39 See INA § 212(c), repealed by Pub. L. No. 104-208, Div. C, Title III, § 304(b), Sept. 30, 1996, 110 Stat. 3009-597.

40 See INA §§ 101(a)(43)(M), 237(a)(2)(A)(iii), 240A(a)(3).

41 See INA § 237(a)(2)(B). *St. Cyr* arose in a period when cancellation of removal had not yet displaced its precursor, waiver under former § 212(c), but the statute already provided that an aggravated felony, a drug offense, or two crimes involving moral turpitude disqualified permanent residents. Pub. L. No. 104-132, § 440(d), 110 Stat. 1214, 1277 (1996).

42 See INS v. St. Cyr, 533 U.S. 289 (2001); Nancy Morawetz, *INS v. St. Cyr*: The Campaign to Preserve Court Review and Stop Retroactive Application of Deportation Laws, in Immigration Stories, at 279–309. See also Fong Yue Ting v. United States, 149 U.S. 698, 707, 730 (1893); Landgraf v. USI Film Products, 511 U.S. 244, 266 (1994); Nancy Morawetz, Rethinking Retroactive Deportation Laws and the Due Process Clause, 73 N.Y.U. L. Rev. 97, 106–22 (1998); Anjali Parekh Prakash, Note, Changing the Rules: Arguing against Retroactive Application of Deportation Statutes, 72 N.Y.U. L. Rev. 1420 (1997).

43 Reno v. American-Arab Anti-Discrimination Committee, 525 U.S. 471, 491 (1999) (emphasis added). See also INS v. Yang, 519 U.S. 26, 30 (1996) (similarly calling one type of discretionary relief "an act of grace" at the attorney general's "unfettered discretion").

44 See *St. Cyr*, 533 U.S. at 296; Jideonwo v. INS, 224 F.3d 692, 697 (7th Cir. 2000); Mattis v. Reno, 212 F.3d 31, 35–40 (1st Cir. 2000). For factors, see Matter of Marin, 16 I&N Dec. 581, 584–85 (BIA 1978).

45 See 533 U.S. at 321–26 (quoting *Landgraf*). See also Ponnapula v. Ashcroft, 373 F.3d 480 (3d Cir. 2004) (convictions after trial).

46 See Rubio-Marin, Democratic Challenge, at 36–37.

47 See INA § 101(a)(43).

48 See INA § 212(d)(5); Aleinikoff, Martin, and Motomura, Immigration and Citizenship, at 506–09; Leng May Ma v. Barber, 357 U.S. 185, 188 (1958).

49 See Rainer Bauböck, Transnational Citizenship: Membership and Rights in International Migration 87–88 (Aldershot 1994) (citing Walzer, Spheres of Justice, at 58).

50 On what terms should be recognized, see Legomsky, Plenary Congressional Power, at 270; Gerald M. Rosberg, The Protection of Aliens From Discriminatory Treatment by the National Government, 1977 Sup. Ct. Rev. 275, 329; Rubio-Marin, Democratic Challenge, at 140. On food stamps after five years, see Act of May 13, 2002, Pub. L. No. 107-171, Title IV, § 4401, 116 Stat. 134, amending 8 U.S.C. § 1612(a)(2).

51 See U.S. Commission on Immigration Reform, Becoming an American: Immigration and Immigrant Policy 94–95 (1997); U.S. Commission on Immigration Reform, Legal Immigration: Setting Priorities 173 (1995).

52 Max Frisch, Überfremdung I, in Schweiz Als Heimat? 219 (1990). On losing ties, see Rubio-Marin, Democratic Challenge, at 182.

CHAPTER 3 *All Persons Within the Territorial Jurisdiction*

1 See Sucheng Chan, Asian Americans: An Interpretive History 33 (Twayne 1991); Daniels, Asian America, at 79–81; McClain, In Search of Equality, at 47–48; Takaki, Strangers from a Different Shore, at 93.

2 See Jacobson, Whiteness, at 159–70.

3 See Ho Ah Kow v. Nunan, 12 Fed. Cas. 252 (C. Cal. 1879). On anti-Chinese measures, see Higham, Strangers in the Land, at 31; McClain, In Search of Equality,

at 43–76, 79–97; Tichenor, Dividing Lines, at 90–92, 103 (citing Calif. Const. art. 1, § 17; art. 2 §§ 1, 19).

4 On *Yick Wo* and other cases, see Hing, Asian America, at 51; McClain, In Search of Equality, at 98–132; Thomas Wuil Joo, New "Conspiracy Theory" of the Fourteenth Amendment: Nineteenth Century Chinese Civil Rights Cases and the Development of Substantive Due Process Jurisprudence, 29 U.S.F. L. Rev. 353 (1995).

5 See Slaughter-House Cases, 83 U.S. 36, 81 (1873).

6 118 U.S. 356, 369, 370, 374 (1886).

7 See 163 U.S. 228, 237–38 (1896); Act of May 5, 1892, ch. 60, § 4, 27 Stat. 25, 25; Plessy v. Ferguson, 163 U.S. 537 (1896). See also Gerald L. Neuman, *Wong Wing v. United States*: The Bill of Rights Protects Illegal Aliens, in Immigration Stories, at 31–50.

8 149 U.S. 698, 725 (1893).

9 See Joo, New "Conspiracy Theory" of the Fourteenth Amendment.

10 See 149 U.S. at 738 (Brewer, J., dissenting); id. at 746 (Field, J., dissenting); id. at 762 (Fuller, C.J., dissenting).

11 Yamataya v. Fisher, 189 U.S. 86, 97–98, 101 (1903), applying Act of Mar. 3, 1891, ch. 551, §§ 1, 11, 26 Stat. 1084, 1084, 1086. This statute also made immigration inspectors' decisions final, subject only to review by the secretary of the treasury. See id. § 8; Salyer, Laws Harsh as Tigers, at 172–74.

12 189 U.S. at 101.

13 Courts continued to defer to government decisions in exclusion cases without hearing procedural due process claims at all. See Oceanic Steam Navigation Co. v. Stranahan, 214 U.S. 320, 343 (1909).

14 See Joo, New "Conspiracy Theory" of the Fourteenth Amendment.

15 239 U.S. 33, 41–43 (1915).

16 On economic rights as the basis for *Truax*, see Kevin R. Johnson, An Essay on Immigration Politics, Popular Democracy, and California's Proposition 187: The Political Relevance and Legal Irrelevance of Race, 70 Wash. L. Rev. 629, 648–49 n. 93 (1995); Irene Scharf, Tired of Your Masses: A History of and Judicial Responses to Early-Twentieth-Century Century Anti-Immigrant Legislation, 21 U. Haw. L. Rev. 131, 155 n. 172 (1999). See also Patsone v. Pennsylvania, 232 U.S. 138, 143–46 (1914); Crane v. New York, 239 U.S. 195 (1915), aff'g 214 N.Y. 154, 161–63 (1915).

17 See Rupert N. Richardson, Adrian Anderson, Cary D. Wintz, and Ernest Wallace, Texas: The Lone Star State 50–79 (9th ed. Pearson Prentice Hall 2005).

18 See Daniels, Coming to America, at 96–7; Daniels, Golden Door, at 62–63, 142; Limerick, Legacy of Conquest, at 228–32; Ngai, Impossible Subjects, at 50–51; Shorris, Latinos, at 35, 37; Treaty of Peace, Friendship, Limits, and Settlement between the United States of America and the Mexican Republic (Treaty of Guadalupe-Hidalgo), July 4, 1848, U.S.-Mex., art. VIII–X, 9 Stat. 922, 929–30.

19 See Almaguer, Racial Fault Lines, at 17–24; Limerick, Legacy of Conquest, at 238–41; Ngai, Impossible Subjects, at 51–52; Tichenor, Dividing Lines, at 89.

20 See Jacobson, Whiteness, at 25, 135; Pickus, True Faith and Allegiance, at 52–63; Act of Mar. 26, 1790, ch. 3, § 1, 1 Stat. 103, 103.

21 See INA §§ 301, 309; Aleinikoff, Martin, and Motomura, Immigration and Citizenship, at 32–53; Patrick Weil, Access to Citizenship: A Comparison of Twenty-Five Nationality Laws, in Citizenship Today: Global Perspectives and Practices 17 (T. Alexander Aleinikoff and Douglas Klusmeyer eds., Carnegie Endowment for Int'l Peace 2001).

22 60 U.S. 393 (1857). See Peter H. Schuck and Rogers M. Smith, Citizenship without Consent: Illegal Aliens in the American Polity 66–76 (Yale Univ. Press 1985); Smith, Civic Ideals, at 253–71.

23 See Elk v. Wilkins, 112 U.S. 94, 109 (1884), Aleinikoff, Martin, and Motomura, Immigration and Citizenship, at 15–16.

24 169 U.S. 649, 694–96 (1898). See also Lee, At America's Gates, at 103–05; Lucy E. Salyer, Wong Kim Ark: The Contest Over Birthright Citizenship, in Immigration Stories, at 51–85; Salyer, Laws Harsh as Tigers, at 98–99; Schuck and Smith, Citizenship Without Consent, at 77–79.

25 See Act of July 14, 1870, ch. 254, § 7, 16 Stat. 254, 256; Jacobson, Whiteness, at 22–31, 68–73.

26 Treaty of Trade, Consuls and Emigration between China and the United States, signed at Washington, July 28, 1868, Art. VI, 137 Consolidated Treaty Series 470.

27 See Act of July 14, 1870, ch. 254, § 7, 16 Stat. 254, 256; Cong. Globe, 41st Cong., 1st Sess. Part 1, 13, Dec. 6, 1869 (remarks of Pres. Grant); Act of Feb. 19, 1862, ch. 27, 12 Stat. 340, 340; Daniels, Golden Door, at 11–16; Hing, Asian America, at 23; Ngai, Impossible Subjects, at 38; Pickus, True Faith and Allegiance, at 65–66; Tichenor, Dividing Lines, at 95–97.

28 See In re Ah Yup, 5 Sawyer 155 (1878); Act of May 6, 1882, ch. 126, § 14, 22 Stat. 58, 61; Fong Yue Ting v. United States, 149 U.S. 698, 716 (1893).

29 260 U.S. 178, 197–99 (1922). See Ian F. Haney-Lopez, White by Law: The Legal Construction of Race 67–77, 80–92 (New York Univ. Press 1996); Ichioka, Issei, at 219–26; Jacobson, Whiteness, at 223–45; McClain, In Search of Equality, at 70–73; Ngai, Impossible Subjects, at 41–45, 96–126; Salyer, Laws Harsh as Tigers, at 13; Smith, Civic Ideals, at 369–70, 446–47; Takaki, Strangers from a Different Shore, at 208–09. On naturalization by Asian immigrants before Ozawa, see Pickus, True Faith and Allegiance, at 67, 108.

30 United States v. Thind, 261 U.S. 204, 210, 214–15 (1923). On Middle Eastern immigrants, see United States v. Cartozian, 6 F.2d 919, 919–22 (D. Ore. 1925); Dow v. United States, 226 F. 145, 145–48 (4th Cir. 1915); In re Halladjian, 174 Fed. 834, 835–45 (C.C.D. Mass. 1909); Matter of Najour, 174 Fed. 735, 735 (N.D. Ga. 1909).

31 See Act of Mar. 24, 1934, ch. 84, § 8, 48 Stat. 456, 462; Act of Oct. 14, 1940, ch. 876, § 303, 54 Stat. 1137, 1140; Act of Dec. 17, 1943, ch. 344, § 3, 57 Stat. 600, 60; Act of July 2, 1946, ch. 534, § 1, 60 Stat. 416, 416; Act of Mar. 20, 1952, Pub. L. No. 82-414, ch. 477, § 311, 66 Stat. 163, 239 codified at INA § 311. On civil rights and foreign policy, see Mary L. Dudziak, Cold War Civil Rights: Race and the Image of American Democracy (Princeton Univ. Press 2000).

32 See 110 The Nation no. 2849, 161, 162 (Feb. 7, 1920); Chinese Colony at Foot of Van Ness: The Plan to Remove Celestials to San Mateo County Is Opposed, San Francisco Chronicle, Apr. 27, 1906, at 9; Rejoices at the Fall of Schmitz in 'Frisco: Says Jap Trouble Is Only Labor Question: Will Not Tolerate Invasion of California Even if It Is Peaceful, Boston Sunday Herald, June 16, 1907.

33 Webb is quoted in Milton Konvitz, The Alien and the Asiatic in American Law 159 (Cornell Univ. Press 1946); and Sidney L. Gulick, The American Japanese Problem: A Study of the Racial Relations of the East and the West 189 (C. Scribner's Sons 1914). See also Keith Aoki, No Right to Own? The Early Twentieth-Century "Alien Land Laws" as a Prelude to Internment, 40 B.C. L. Rev. 37, 55–68 (1998); Gabriel J. Chin, Citizenship and Exclusion: Wyoming's Anti-Japanese Alien Land Law in Context, 1 Wyo. L. Rev. 497, 500–05 (2001); Daniels, Asian America, at 138–47; Ichioka, Issei, at 153–56, 226–43; Brant T. Lee, A Racial Trust: The Japanese YMCA and the Alien Land Law, 7 UCLA Asian Pac. Am. L.J. 1, 14–21 (2001); Ngai, Impossible Subjects, at 39–40, 46–47; Scharf, Tired of Your Masses, at 162–67; Takaki, Strangers from a Different Shore, at 208–10.

34 See Russian Volunteer Fleet v. United States, 282 U.S. 481, 489 (1931); Frick v. Webb, 263 U.S. 326 (1923); Webb v. O'Brien, 263 U.S. 313 (1923); Porterfield v. Webb, 263 U.S. 225 (1923); Terrace v. Thompson, 263 U.S. 197 (1923).

35 334 U.S. 410, 420, 422 (1948).

36 See Masaoka v. California, 39 Cal. 2d 883, 883 (1952); Fujii v. California, 38 Cal. 2d 718, 725–38 (1952).

37 457 U.S. 202, 210–30 (1982); Michael A. Olivas, Plyler v. Doe, the Education of Undocumented Children, and the Polity, in Immigration Stories, at 197–220; Paul Feldman, Texas Case Looms Over Prop. 187's Legal Future, L.A. Times, Oct. 23, 1994, at A1.

38 457 U.S. at 226; Linda S. Bosniak, Membership, Equality, and the Difference That Alienage Makes, 69 N.Y.U. L. Rev. 1047, 1121–23 (1994).

39 See 1 Lassa Oppenheim, International Law: A Treatise 640–41 (Hersch Lauterpacht ed., 8th ed. Longmans, Green 1955); T. Alexander Aleinikoff, Federal Regulation of Aliens and the Constitution, 83 Am. J. Int'l L. 862, 864 (1989).

40 See Joan Fitzpatrick and William McKay Bennett, A Lion in the Path? The Influence of International Law on the Immigration Policy of the United States, 70 Wash. L. Rev. 589 (1995); James A.R. Nafziger, The General Admission of Aliens Under International Law, 77 Am. J. Int'l L. 804 (1983); Saskia Sassen, Guests and Aliens xvii (1999). On Westphalia, see Joppke, Nation-State, at 265. On transnational and postnational, see Linda S. Bosniak, Opposing Prop. 187: Undocumented Immigrants and the National Imagination, 28 Conn. L. Rev. 555, 559 (1996); Peter J. Spiro, The Citizenship Dilemma, 51 Stan. L. Rev. 597, 623–24 n. 133 (1999). On human rights, see Linda S. Bosniak, Human Rights, State Sovereignty and the Protection of Undocumented Migrants under the International Migrant Workers Convention, 25 Int'l Migration Rev. 737 (1991); Berta Esperanza Hernandez-Truyol, Reconciling Rights in Collision, An International Human Rights Strategy, in Immigrants Out! The New Nativism and the Anti-Immigrant

Impulse in the United States 254 (Juan F. Perea ed., New York Univ. Press 1997).

41 See T. Alexander Aleinikoff, Citizens, Aliens, Membership and the Constitution, 7 Const. Comm. 9, 19 (1990).

CHAPTER 4 *Alienage and the Ties That Bind*

1 403 U.S. 365, 376–80 (1971).

2 403 U.S. at 372 (citing United States v. Carolene Prods. Co., 304 U.S. 144, 152–53 n. 4 [1938]).

3 403 U.S. at 376.

4 Id.

5 See Sugarman v. Dougall, 413 U.S. 634, 645, 646 (1973); Matter of Griffiths, 413 U.S. 717, 722 (1973).

6 See Schuck, The Transformation of Immigration Law, at 4 (calling territorial personhood and ties "communitarian"). Cf. Linda S. Bosniak, Exclusion and Membership: The Dual Identity of the Undocumented Worker Under United States Law, 1988 Wis. L. Rev. 955, 983 (noncitizens' ties within sphere created by personhood and territorial presence).

7 See 42 U.S.C. § 1395o(2)(B).

8 426 U.S. at 84–85. See Harold Hongju Koh, Equality with a Human Face: Justice Blackmun and the Equal Protection of Aliens, 8 Hamline L. Rev. 51, 70, 72, 99–102 (1985); Hiroshi Motomura, Immigration and Alienage, Federalism and Proposition 187, 35 Va. J. Int'l L. 201, 205–11 (1994); Rosberg, Protection of Aliens, at 284, 331. Cf. Michael J. Perry, Modern Equal Protection: A Conceptualization and Appraisal, 79 Colum. L. Rev. 1023, 1060–65 (1979) (*Diaz* as preemption).

9 426 U.S. 67, 77 (1976).

10 Id. at 78 n. 12, 79–80.

11 430 U.S. 787 (1977). See Aleinikoff, Semblances of Sovereignty, at 156.

12 *Diaz*, 426 U.S. at 77; *Plyler*, 457 U.S. at 210.

13 *Diaz*, 426 U.S. at 80.

14 Id. at 80, 82–83, cited in Abraham, The Good of Banality?, at 243.

15 See 8 U.S.C. § 1612(a)(2)(B).

16 189 F.3d 598 (7th Cir. 1999), cert. denied, 529 U.S. 1036 (2000).

17 426 U.S. 88, 101–03, 105, 114–16 (1976). See Mow Sun Wong v. Campbell, 626 F.2d 739, 744–45 (9th Cir. 1980), cert. denied, 450 U.S. 959 (1981); 5 C.F.R. §§ 7.3, 338.101.

18 See 189 F.3d at 606–08.

19 See id. at 603 n. 10, 608–09. See also Rodriguez v. United States, 169 F.3d 1342, 1351 (11th Cir. 1999); Rodriguez v. United States, 983 F. Supp. 1445, 1454–55 (S.D. Fla. 1997), aff'd, 169 F.3d 1342 (11th Cir. 1999); Abreu v. Callahan, 971 F. Supp. 799, 807, 816–17 (S.D.N.Y. 1997); Kiev v. Glickman, 991 F. Supp. 1090, 1095–96 (D. Minn. 1998).

20 See Schuck, The Transformation of Immigration Law, at 47–53; Horwitz, The Transformation of American Law, 1870–1960, at 213–46.

21 See id. at 49, 59–60.

22 See International Shoe Co. v. Washington, 326 U.S. 310, 316–19 (1945); Ngai, Impossible Subjects, at 78.

23 See Aleinikoff, Semblances of Sovereignty, at 173; Rubio-Marin, Democratic Challenge, at 31, 37.

24 See Kennedy v. Mendoza-Martinez, 372 U.S. 144, 160–61 (1963); Perez v. Brownell, 356 U.S. 44, 64–65 (1958); Aleinikoff, Semblances of Sovereignty, at 41; T. Alexander Aleinikoff, Theories of Loss of Citizenship, 84 Mich. L. Rev. 1471, 1494–98 (1986); Hannah Arendt, The Origins of Totalitarianism 290–302 (new ed. Harcourt 1994); Ronald Beiner, Why Citizenship Constitutes a Theoretical Problem in the Last Decade of the Twentieth Century, in Theorizing Citizenship 1, 15 (Ronald Beiner ed., State Univ. of New York Press 1995).

25 INA § 212(a)(28)(D), (G)(v), repealed by Act of Nov. 29, 1990, Pub. L. No. 101-649, § 601(a), 104 Stat. 4978, 5067.

26 408 U.S. 753, 762, 765–70 (1972). See also Peter H. Schuck, *Kleindienst v. Mandel*: Plenary Power v. the Professors, in Immigration Stories, at 169–96.

27 Since a 1986 amendment, an unwed father relationship counts "if the father has or had a bona fide parent-child relationship" with the child. See INA § 101(b)(1)(D).

28 430 U.S. 787, 792, 794–95 (1977). See also Ben-Issa v. Reagan, 645 F. Supp. 1556, 1559–62 (W.D. Mich. 1986); Manwani v. U.S. Dept. of Justice, 736 F. Supp. 1367, 1379–82 (W.D.N.C. 1990). Cf. Adams v. Baker, 909 F.2d 643, 647 n. 1 (1st Cir. 1990) (a citizen's perspective does not strengthen a challenge to a government decision, since a citizen has no basis for such a challenge). On citizen rights in immigration cases, see Adam B. Cox, Citizenship, Standing, and Immigration Law, 92 Calif. L. Rev. 373 (2004); Motomura, Whose Alien Nation?, at 1942–45; Frank H. Wu, The Limits of Borders: A Moderate Proposal for Immigration Reform, 7 Stan. L. & Pol'y Rev. 35, 45–46, 49–50 (1996).

29 953 F.2d 1498, 1511–15 (11th Cir.), cert. denied, 502 U.S. 1122 (1992). See also Ukrainian-American Bar Ass'n v. Baker, 893 F.2d 1374, 1381–82 (D.C. Cir. 1990).

30 See Memorandum from Chief Immigration Judge Michael Creppy, to All Immigration Judges (Sept. 21, 2001); North Jersey Media Group, Inc. v. Ashcroft, 308 F.3d 198 (3d Cir. 2002), cert. denied, 538 U.S. 1056 (2003); Detroit Free Press v. Ashcroft, 303 F.3d 681 (6th Cir. 2002).

31 See T. Alexander Aleinikoff and Rubén G. Rumbaut, Terms of Belonging: Are Models of Membership Self-Fulfilling Prophecies? 13 Geo. Immigr. L.J. 1, 14–21 (1998); Bauböck, Transnational Citizenship, at 111–12; William Rogers Brubaker, Membership without Citizenship: The Economic and Social Rights of Noncitizens, in Immigration and the Politics of Citizenship in Europe and North America 145, 162 (William Rogers Brubaker ed., Univ. Press of America 1989); Tomas Hammar, Democracy and the Nation State: Aliens, Denizens and Citizens in a World of International Migration 99–100 (Avebury 1990); Peter H. Schuck, The Treatment of Aliens in the United States, in Paths to Inclusion: The Integration of Migrants in the United States and Germany 203, 222 (Peter H. Schuck and Rainer Münz eds., Berghahn Books 1998).

32 See 2003 Immigration Statistics, at 137; In Greater Numbers, They Pledge Allegiance, Philadelphia Inquirer, Feb. 1, 2002, at B1.

33 On less meaningful citizenship, see Abraham, The Good of Banality? at 239, 240; Rubio-Marin, Democratic Challenge, at 101; Frederick Schauer, Community, Citizenship, and the Search for National Identity, 84 Mich. L. Rev. 1504, 1516 (1986); Schuck and Smith, Citizenship without Consent, at 106–08; Peter H. Schuck, Membership in the Liberal Polity: The Devaluation of American Citizenship, 3 Geo. Immigr. L.J. 1, 13–18 (1989). On lack of political participation, see Rubio-Marin, Democratic Challenge, at 3–4, 151.

CHAPTER 5 *The Most Tender Connections*

1 See Fong Yue Ting v. United States, 149 U.S. 698, 707, 713 (1893); Nishimura Ekiu v. United States, 142 U.S. 651, 659 (1892); H.R. Rep. No. 1365, 82d Cong., 2d Sess. 5 (1952). See also S. Rep. No. 1515, 81st Cong., 2d Sess. 44 (1951); Schuck, The Transformation of Immigration Law, at 27.

2 Act of Feb. 20, 1907, ch. 1134, § 3, 34 Stat. 898, 899–900. See U.S. President's Comm'n on Immigration and Naturalization, Report—Whom We Shall Welcome 202 (1953); Will Maslow, Recasting Our Deportation Laws: Proposals for Reform, 56 Colum. L. Rev. 309, 321–24 (1956).

3 See INA §§ 237(a)(1)(E)(i), (2)(A)(i), (5).

4 See INA § 237(a)(2)(B)(i). Affiliation-based exceptions treat some returning lawful immigrants as if they never left. See INA § 101(a)(13)(C); Aleinikoff, Martin, and Motomura, Immigration and Citizenship, at 429–30.

5 See INA § 212(h); Aleinikoff, Martin, and Motomura, Immigration and Citizenship, at 600–06.

6 See INA § 240A(a). For background, see Thomas Alexander Aleinikoff, David A. Martin, and Hiroshi Motomura, Immigration: Process and Policy 689–97 (West 3d ed. 1995); Act of Feb. 5, 1917, ch. 29, § 3, 39 Stat. 874, 878, repealed by Act of Jun. 27, 1952, Pub. L. No. 414, ch. 477, Title IV, § 403(13), 66 Stat. 163, 279; Ngai, Impossible Subjects, at 76–82.

7 See INA § 240A(a); Matter of C-V-T-, 22 I&N Dec. 7 (BIA 1998); Matter of Marin, 16 I&N Dec. 581, 584–85 (BIA 1978). For a proposal to expand cancellation eligibility, see Family Reunification Act of 2005, H.R. 2055, 109th Cong., 1st Sess. §§ 2, 3 (2005). For proposals to limit removal of noncitizens who arrived as children, see Development, Relief, and Education for Alien Minors Act (DREAM Act), S. 2075, 109th Cong., 1st Sess. § 4 (2005); Family Reunification Act, H.R. 2055, 109th Cong., 1st Sess. § 6 (2005). On international human rights, see Beharry v. Reno, 183 F. Supp. 2d 584, 595–604 (E.D.N.Y. 2002), rev'd on other grounds sub nom. Beharry v. Ashcroft, 329 F.3d 51 (2d Cir. 2003); Mojica v. Reno, 970 F. Supp. 130, 146–52 (E.D.N.Y. 1997), aff'd in part and dismissed in part sub nom. Henderson v. INS, 157 F.3d 106 (2d Cir. 1998).

8 See INA § 241(b)(2), repealed by Pub. L. No. 101-649, § 505(a), 104 Stat. 4978,

5050 (1990); Margaret H. Taylor and Ronald F. Wright, The Sentencing Judge as Immigration Judge, 51 Emory L.J. 1131, 1143–57 (2002).

9 149 U.S. at 740, 743 (Brewer, J., dissenting); id. at 749 (Field, J., dissenting); 4 Elliott's Debates 546, 555 (1836). See also Scheidemann v. INS, 83 F.3d 1517, 1527 (3d Cir. 1996) (Sarokin, J., concurring); Siegfried Hesse, The Constitutional Status of the Lawfully Admitted Permanent Resident Alien: The Inherent Limits of the Power to Expel, 69 Yale L.J. 262, 291 (1959); Bill Ong Hing, Detention to Deportation: Rethinking the Removal of Cambodia Refugees, 38 U.C. Davis L. Rev. 891, 949–68 (2005); Kanstroom, Deportation, at 1914–26; Maslow, Recasting Our Deportation Laws, at 323; Stephen H. Legomsky, The Alien Criminal Defendant: Sentencing Considerations, 15 San Diego L. Rev. 105, 118–29 (1977); Robert Pauw, A New Look at Deportation as Punishment: Why at Least Some of the Constitution's Criminal Procedure Protections Apply, 52 Admin. L. Rev. 305, 332, 337 (2000); Schuck, The Transformation of Immigration Law, at 25–27.

10 See INA §§ 210, 240A(b), 245A, 249; Pres. Bush Renews Call for a Temporary Worker Program, 82 Interpreter Releases 274 (2005); Alan Lee, The Bush Temporary Worker Proposal and Comparative Pending Legislation: An Analysis, 81 Interpreter Releases 477 (2004).

11 See Act of Dec. 28, 1945, ch. 591, §§ 1, 2, 59 Stat. 659, 659 (War Brides Act); 8 C.F.R. § 175.57(b) (1945).

12 338 U.S. 537, 542–44 (1950).

13 See Ellen R. Knauff, The Ellen Knauff Story 194–202, 218, 221–22 app. at 1–18 (W.W. Norton 1952); Charles Weisselberg, The Exclusion and Detention of Aliens: Lessons from the Lives of Ellen Knauff and Ignatz Mezei, 143 U. Pa. L. Rev. 933, 958–64 (1995).

14 Shaughnessy v. United States ex rel. Mezei, 345 U.S. 206, 208 (1953); Weisselberg, The Exclusion and Detention of Aliens, at 970–84.

15 345 U.S. at 208–15. On the aftermath, see Trop v. Dulles, 356 U.S. 86, 102 n. 36 (1957).

16 Kwong Hai Chew v. Colding, 344 U.S. 590 (1953). See also John Hayakawa Török, Ideological Deportation: The Case of Kwong Hai Chew, http://ssrn.com/abstract=462500 (Jan. 9, 2004).

17 Yamataya v. Fisher, 189 U.S. 86, 97–98, 101 (1903).

18 344 U.S. at 592, 600–01; Mezei, 345 U.S. at 214.

19 339 U.S. 763, 770–71 (1950), quoted in Chew, 344 U.S. at 596 n. 5.

20 326 U.S. 135, 148, 154 (1945); id. at 161 (Murphy, J., concurring).

21 See Woodby v. INS, 385 U.S. 276, 285–86 (1976).

22 See Carlson v. Landon, 342 U.S. 524, 542–44 (1952); Galvan v. Press, 347 U.S. 522, 531 (1952).

23 424 U.S. 319, 335 (1976). See also Goldberg v. Kelly, 397 U.S. 254 (1970).

24 459 U.S. 21, 32 (1982) (citing Eisentrager, 339 U.S. at 770). See Kevin R. Johnson, Maria and Joseph Plasencia's Lost Weekend: The Case of Landon v. Plasencia, in Immigration Stories, 221–44. See also David A. Martin, Due Process and Membership in the National Community: Political Asylum and Beyond, 44 U. Pitt.

L. Rev. 165, 210 (1983); T. Alexander Aleinikoff, Aliens, Due Process and "Community Ties": A Response to Martin, 44 U. Pitt. L. Rev. 237, 245 (1983).

25 See Hesse, Constitutional Status, at 276–87.

26 See Peter H. King, Lives of Worry, Sadness, "Why?" L.A. Times, June 30, 2005, at A1; Peter H. King, 18 Years Waiting for a Gavel to Fall, L.A. Times, June 30, 2005, at A1.

27 INA § 241(a)(6)(D), repealed by Act of Sept. 30, 1996, Pub. L. No. 104-208, Div. C, Title III, § 308(d)(2), 110 Stat. 3009, 3009-617; Hearings before the Senate Select Committee on Intelligence on the Nomination of William H. Webster, to be Director of Central Intelligence, 100th Cong. 94, 95 (1987), quoted in American-Arab Anti-Discrimination Comm. v. Reno, 70 F.3d 1045, 1053 (9th Cir. 1995), rev'd on other grounds, 525 U.S. 471 (1999).

28 INA § 241(a)(6)(F)(ii)-(iii), repealed by Act of Sept. 30, 1996, Pub. L. No. 104-208, Div. C, Title III, § 308(d)(2), 110 Stat. 3009, 3009-617. For the First Amendment argument, see American-Arab Anti-Discrimination Comm. v. Meese, 714 F. Supp. 1060, 1082 (C.D. Cal. 1989), aff'd in part and rev'd in part, American-Arab Anti-Discrimination Comm. v. Thornburgh, 970 F.2d 501 (9th Cir. 1991).

29 INA § 237(a)(4)(B).

30 American-Arab Anti-Discrimination Comm., 70 F.3d at 1063–66.

31 341 U.S. 494 (1951), cited in *Harisiades*, 342 U.S. at 592.

32 395 U.S. 444, 447 (1969). See also Hess v. Indiana, 414 U.S. 105, 108 (1973).

33 70 F.3d at 1063–64. See generally Hiroshi Motomura, Judicial Review in Immigration Cases After *AADC*: Lessons From Civil Procedure, 14 Geo. Immigr. L.J. 385, 394–96 (2000).

34 70 F.3d at 1064 (quoting United States v. Verdugo-Urquidez, 494 U.S. 259, 265 [1990]). The U.S. Supreme Court later reversed the appeals court, but on jurisdictional grounds. See 525 U.S. 471 (1999).

35 Act of Nov. 10, 1986, Pub. L. No. 99-639, § 5, 100 Stat. 3537, 3543. See Manwani v. United States Dep't of Justice, 736 F. Supp. 1367 (W.D.N.C. 1990); Motomura, Procedural Surrogates, at 1632–38, 1659–65. On the erosion of plenary power, Stephen H. Legomsky, Ten More Years of Plenary Power: Immigration, Congress, and the Courts, 22 Hastings Const. L.Q. 925 (1995); Legomsky, Plenary Congressional Power, at 296–306; Schuck, The Transformation of Immigration Law, at 34–73.

36 461 U.S. 574 (1983). See 26 U.S.C. § 501(c)(3).

37 461 U.S. at 592–93. See also Jones v. United States, 526 U.S. 227, 239 (1999); Edward J. DeBartolo Corp. v. Fla. Gulf Coast Bldg. & Constr. Trades Council, 485 U.S. 568, 575 (1988) (quoting United States ex rel. Attorney Gen. v. Del. & Hudson Co., 213 U.S. 366, 408 [1909]); Philip P. Frickey, Getting from Joe to Gene (McCarthy): The Avoidance Canon, Legal Process Theory, and Narrowing Statutory Interpretation in the Early Warren Court, 93 Calif. L. Rev. 397, 399 n. 6 (2005).

38 See Deborah Sontag, In a Homeland Far from Home, N.Y. Times, Nov. 16, 2003, at 48; Assoc. Press, Cambodia, U.S. Governments Sign Repatriation Agreement, May 3, 2002.

39 Zadvydas v. Davis, 533 U.S. 678 (2001). See also INS v. St. Cyr, 533 U.S. 289 (2001); Motomura, Phantom Norms.

40 See Bosniak, Membership, Equality, at 1056–57. See also Motomura, Immigration and Alienage, at 202–03.

41 Cal. Prop. 187 (West 1994) (approved by electors Nov. 8, 1994). See League of United Latin American Citizens v. Wilson, 997 F. Supp. 1244, 1261 (C.D. Cal. 1997); League of United Latin American Citizens v. Wilson, 908 F. Supp. 755 (C.D. Cal. 1995). The case settled while on appeal. See Patrick J. McDonnell, Prop. 187 Talks Offered Davis Few Choices, L.A. Times, July 30, 1999, at A3. On "self-deportation," see Janet Boss and Carol Kasel, Proposition 187 Feedback and Fallout, Rocky Mountain News, Nov. 21, 1994, at 3N.

42 Compare Schuck and Smith, Citizenship without Consent, with David A. Martin, Membership and Consent: Abstract or Organic?, 11 Yale J. Int'l L. 278, 291–96 (1987). For a proposed amendment, see H.J. Res. 46, 109th Cong. (2005); H.J. Res. 42, 108th Cong. (2003).

CHAPTER 6 *The Lost Story of Americans in Waiting*

1 See Smith, Civic Ideals, at 13.

2 See Act of Mar. 26, 1790, ch. 3, § 1, 1 Stat. 103. See generally Fox, Citizenship, Poverty, at 429–35; Frank George Franklin, The Legislative History of Naturalization in the United States: From the Revolutionary War to 1861, at 49–71, 167–68, 175–76, 215–300 (1906); Kettner, Development of American Citizenship, at 232–86; Neuman, Strangers to the Constitution, at 64; Pickus, True Faith and Allegiance, at 16–63; John P. Roche, The Early Development of United States Citizenship (Cornell Univ. Press 1949); Schuck and Smith, Citizenship without Consent, at 51; Smith, Civic Ideals, at 159–68; Tichenor, Dividing Lines, at 53–54; John S. Wise, A Treatise on American Citizenship 57–58 (Edward Thompson Co. 1906).

3 Act of Jan. 29, 1795, ch. 20, 1 Stat. 414.

4 Act of June 18, 1798, ch. 54, § 1, 1 Stat. 566, 566; Act of Apr. 14, 1802, ch. 28, § 1, 2 Stat. 153, 153; Act of May 26, 1824, ch. 186, §§ 1, 4, 4 Stat. 69, 69.

5 See Kettner, Development of American Citizenship, at 246; Maximilian Koessler, Rights and Duties of Declarant Aliens, 91 U. Pa. L. Rev. 321, 321 (1942–43); Gerald L. Neuman, "We Are the People": Alien Suffrage in German and American Perspective, 13 Mich. J. Int'l L. 259, 297, 325 (1992); Brian C. Riopelle, Note, Revitalization of the "Intending Citizen" Status: Rights of Declarant Aliens after IRCA, 28 Va. J. Int'l L. 987, 989–90 (1988); Frederick Van Dyne, A Treatise on the Law of Naturalization of the United States 54–84 (F. Van Dyne 1907).

6 See Virginia Harper-Ho, Noncitizen Voting Rights: The History, the Law and Current Prospects for Change, 18 Law & Inequality 271, 273–83 (2000); Kettner, Development of American Citizenship, at 102–03, 123; Neuman, Strangers to the Constitution, at 63–71; Jamin B. Raskin, Legal Aliens, Local Citizens: The

Historical, Constitutional, and Theoretical Meanings of Alien Suffrage, 141 U. Pa. L. Rev. 1391, 1401–17 (1993); Gerald M. Rosberg, Aliens and Equal Protection: Why Not the Right to Vote?, 75 Mich. L. Rev. 1092, 1093–1100 (1977).

7 See Mich. Const. of 1850, art. VII, § 1; Ind. Const. of 1851, art. II, § 2; Dakota Territorial Gov. Act, ch. 86, § 5, 12 Stat. 239, 241 (1861); Kansas-Nebraska Act, ch. 59, §§ 5, 23 (1854); Nevada Territorial Gov. Act, ch. 83, § 5, 12 Stat. 209, 211 (1861); Okla. Territorial Gov. Act, ch. 182, §§ 5, 26 Stat. 84 (1890); Wash. Territorial Gov. Act, ch. 90, § 5, 10 Stat. 172, 174 (1853); Wyoming Territorial Gov. Act, ch. 235, § 5, 15 Stat. 178, 179–80 (1868); Alexander Keyssar, The Right to Vote: The Contested History of Democracy in the United States 32–33, 104–05, 136–38, 371–73, app. table A.12 (Basic Books 2000); Higham, Strangers in the Land, at 214; Neuman, Alien Suffrage, at 297–99; Raskin, at 1406–08; Riopelle, Revitalization, at 995, 1098–99. For laws that limited voting by intending citizens to white men, see sources cited in chapter 9.

8 See Chambers, To Raise an Army, at 48–49, 53–54.

9 88 U.S. 162 (1874). On Virginia Minor, see Linda K. Kerber, No Constitutional Right to Be Ladies: Women and the Obligations of Citizenship 102–04 (Hill and Wang 1998). On citizenship rights, see Franklin, Legislative History, at 38. On voting qualifications, see Jacob Katz Cogan, The Look Within: Property, Capacity, and Suffrage in Nineteenth-Century America, 107 Yale L.J. 473 (1997); D.M. Dewey, The Naturalization Laws of the United States 77–86 (1855); Kettner, Development of American Citizenship, at 323. On disenfranchised citizens today, see Andrew L. Shapiro, Note, Challenging Criminal Disenfranchisement Under the Voting Rights Act: A New Strategy, 103 Yale L.J. 537, 538–39 (1993).

10 88 U.S. at 177 (emphasis added). See Ala. Const. of 1867, art. VII, § 2; Ark. Const. of 1868, art. VIII, § 2; Fla. Const. of 1868, art. XIV, § 1; Ga. Const. of 1868, art. II, § 2; Mo. Const. of 1865, art, II, § 18; Tex. Const. of 1876, art. VI, § 2. For other state laws to the same effect, see Idaho Territory Rev. Stat. § 1860 (1874); La. Const. of 1879, art. 185; N.D. Const. of 1889, art. 5, § 121; S.C. Const. of 1868, art. IV, § 2.

11 On intending citizens as noncitizens, see In re Kleibs, 128 Fed. 656, 656 (Cir. S.D.N.Y. 1897); In re Moses, 83 Fed. 995, 996 (Cir. S.D.N.Y. 1897); Maloy v. Duden, 25 Fed. 673, 673 (Cir. S.D.N.Y. 1885). On the Homestead Act, see 12 Stat. 392, 392 (1862); 7 Charles Gordon, Stanley Mailman, and Stephen Yale-Loehr, Immigration Law and Procedure § 96.02[02] (2005); Koessler, Rights and Duties, at 323. On naturalization of widows and children, see Act of Mar. 26, 1804, ch. 48, § 2, 2 Stat. 292, 293, cited in Minor v. Happersett, 88 U.S. at 168; Franklin, Legislative History, at 115. On military service, see Chambers, To Raise an Army, at 51, 59; Higham, Strangers in the Land, at 214; Neuman, Alien Suffrage, at 306; Riopelle, Revitalization, at 990. On passports, see Act of Mar. 2, 1907, ch. 2534, § 1, 34 Stat. 1228, 1228, discussed in 1 Charles Cheney Hyde, International Law Chiefly as Interpreted and Applied by the United States 688 (Little, Brown 1922); Neuman, Alien Suffrage, at 305–06; Van Dyne, Naturalization, at 74. On seamen, see Act of May 9, 1918, ch. 69, § 1, 40 Stat. 542, 544, discussed in 1 Hyde,

International Law, at 633; Van Dyne, Naturalization, at 74–77, repealed by Act of Oct. 14, 1940, subch. V, § 504, 54 Stat. 1172–73.

12 See Letter from Secretary of State William L. Marcy to Chevalier Hulseman, Sept. 26, 1853, H.R. Exec. Doc. No. 1, 33d Cong., 1st Sess., 30, 40 (1853), discussed in Alexander Porter Morse, A Treatise on Citizenship, by Birth and by Naturalization 68–71 (Little, Brown 1881); Frederick Van Dyne, Citizenship of the United States 70–73 (Lawyers' Co-operative Publishing Co. 1904); 1 Hyde, International Law, at 687 n. 2; Koessler, Rights and Duties, at 324–29; Neuman, Alien Suffrage, at 306; Riopelle, Revitalization, at 990–94. On U.S. government intervention in Mexico on behalf of a Mexican citizen who was an intending U.S. citizen, see Van Dyne, Naturalization, at 67–68.

13 On public employment, see Kansas Gas & Electric Co. v. City of Independence, 79 F.2d 32, 36 n. 3 (10th Cir. 1935) (citing National Industrial Recovery Act, 40 U.S.C. § 406). See Higham, Strangers in the Land, at 161–62, 248 (apparently referring to Revenue Act of 1918, Pub. L. No. 254, ch. 18, § 210, 40 Stat. 1057, 1062).

14 On voting only until intending citizens could naturalize, see Neuman, Alien Suffrage, at 297 (citing Mo. Const. of 1865, art, II, § 18 [five years after declaration]; N.D. Const. of 1889, art. 5, § 121 [six years after declaration]). For the seven-year rule, see Act of June 29, 1906, ch. 3592, §§ 4, 27, 34 Stat. 596, 596–97, 603–04. See also Act of Oct. 14, 1940, ch. 876, §§ 331–332, 54 Stat. 1137, 1153–54 (inexplicably with seven-year and ten-year limits); Charles Cheney Hyde, The Nationality Act of 1940, 35 Am. J. Int'l L. 314, 316 (1941).

15 263 U.S. 197, 218–19 (1923).

16 339 U.S. 763, 770 (1950).

17 342 U.S. at 585–86. See also Aleinikoff, Citizens, Aliens, at 16–17.

18 342 U.S. 524, 534, 541 (1952).

19 149 U.S. at 724. See also id. at 707.

20 441 U.S. 68, 80–81 (1979), upholding N.Y. Educ. Law § 3001(3).

21 441 U.S. at 74–80; 413 U.S. 634, 642, 646 (1973) (quoting Dunn v. Blumstein, 405 U.S. 330, 344 [1972]).

22 Cf. Nyquist v. Mauclet, 432 U.S. 1, 3–11 (1977) (invalidating a New York statute limiting college financial aid to citizens, naturalization applicants, and noncitizens who have declared their intent to naturalize).

23 See King, Making Americans, at 50–51.

24 See Madison Grant, The Passing of the Great Race, or, the Racial Basis of European History (Scribner 1916). See also Lothrop Stoddard, The Rising Tide of Color Against White World-Supremacy (Scribner 1920). On whiteness, see Jacobson, Whiteness, at 39–90. On the Nazi connection, see King, Making Americans, at 70, 167.

25 On eugenics and race, see Higham, Strangers in the Land, at 31–38, 151–52, 271–77; Jacobson, Whiteness, at 77–90; Johnson, Huddled Masses, at 113–14; King, Making Americans, at 50–81, 127–95; Ngai, Impossible Subjects, at 24–25; Alejandro Portes and Rubén G. Rumbaut, Immigrant America, A Portrait 159–64

(Univ. of California Press 2d ed. 1996); Salyer, Laws Harsh as Tigers, at 124, 130; Tichenor, Dividing Lines, at 42–43, 77–78, 115, 127–32, 140–44, 160.

26 Act of Feb. 5, 1917, ch. 29, § 3, 39 Stat. 874, 875–77. See Daniels, Golden Door, at 31–34, 46; Higham, Strangers in the Land, at 101, 112, 162–65, 191, 195, 202; 203; Hing, Asian America, at 32; King, Making Americans, at 78–79; Ngai, Impossible Subjects, at 37; Tichenor, Dividing Lines, at 81–83, 124–27, 133, 136–41.

27 Act of May 19, 1921, ch. 8, §§ 2(a)(6), 3, 42 Stat. 5, 5–6.

28 See Act of May 26, 1924, ch. 190, § 4(a), 43 Stat. 153, 155. On the period from 1921 through 1924, see Daniels, Golden Door, at 47–49, 54–57; Higham, Strangers in the Land, at 308–11; Edward P. Hutchinson, Legislative History of American Immigration Policy, 1798–1965, at 484 (Univ. of Pennsylvania Press 1981) (quoting H.R. Rep. No. 350, 68th Cong., 1st Sess. 13–14 [1924]); Jacobson, Whiteness, at 68–135; King, Making Americans, at 39–41, 138–65, 200–28; Ngai, Impossible Subjects, at 21–23, 25–27, 28–29; Tichenor, Dividing Lines, at 143–48. Johnson is quoted in King, Making Americans, at 74.

29 See Act of May 26, 1924, ch. 190, § 11, 43 Stat. 153, 159–60, 162.

30 See Ichioka, Issei, at 244–54; Ngai, Impossible Subjects, at 27. On Filipino immigration, see Daniels, Golden Door, at 67–68; Hing, Asian America, at 31, 33, 61–62.

31 See Act of May 26, 1924, ch. 190, § 11(d), 43 Stat. 153, 159.

32 See Francisco E. Balderrama and Raymond Rodriguez, Decade of Betrayal: Mexican Repatriation in the 1930s (Univ. of New Mexico Press 1995); Daniels, Golden Door, at 52, 61, 64–65; Johnson, Huddled Masses, at 25; Limerick, Legacy of Conquest, at 246–51; Massey, Durand, and Malone, Beyond Smoke and Mirrors, at 33–34; Ngai, Impossible Subjects, at 50, 54–55, 64, 70–75, 93–94; Tichenor, Dividing Lines, at 168–72; Reed Ueda, Postwar Immigrant America: A Social History 32 (St. Martin's Press 1994). On the Border Patrol, see Act of May 28, 1924, ch. 204, 43 Stat. 205, 240; Ngai, Impossible Subjects, at 57, 60, 68–70.

33 See id., at 75–90.

34 See Act of Dec. 17, 1943, ch. 344, §§ 1, 2, 3, 57 Stat. 600, 600–01 (China); Act of Mar. 24, 1934, ch. 84, § 8, 48 Stat. 456, 462 (Philippines); Proclamation No. 2696 (July 4, 1946), reprinted in 60 Stat. 1353 (1946) (Philippines).

35 See Act of June 27, 1952, ch. 477, §§ 101(a)(27), 202, 311, 66 Stat. 163, 169, 176–78, 239; S. Rep. 1137, 82d Cong., 2d Sess. at 17. On legislation up through 1952, see Daniels, Asian America, at 191–99; Daniels, Golden Door, at 91–97, 116–19, 123, 151; Hing, Asian America, at 38, 66–72, 36, 48–49; Hutchinson, Legislative History, at 473; King, Making Americans, at 245; Ngai, Impossible Subjects, at 203, 237–39; Tichenor, Dividing Lines, at 188–203. On black Caribbean immigration, see S. Rep. 1137, 82d Cong., 2d Sess. at 5–6, 15; King, Making Americans, at 237.

36 See Act of Sept. 22, 1922, ch. 411, § 3, 42 Stat. 1021, 1022 (race-based expatriation by marriage); Volpp, Divesting Citizenship.

37 See The President's Veto Message, in 6 Oscar M. Trelles and James F. Bailey, Immigration and Nationality Acts: Legislative Histories and Related Documents 275, 277, 278 (1979); President's Commission on Immigration and Naturalization,

Whom We Shall Welcome 52–56 (1953); Harry N. Rosenfield, The Prospects for Immigration Amendments, 21 Law & Contemp. Probs. 401, 409–18 (1956); S. Rep. No. 1515, at 455 (1951), quoted in Johnson, Huddled Masses, at 24.

38 See Act of Oct. 3, 1965, Pub. L. No. 89-236, §§ 2, 3, 8, 21(e), 79 Stat. 911–13, 916, 921.

39 Civil Rights Act of 1964, Pub. L. No. 88-352, 78 Stat. 241; Voting Rights Act of 1965, Pub. L. No. 89-110, 79 Stat. 437 (codified as amended at 42 U.S.C. § 1973–1973bb-1).

40 See John F. Kennedy, A Nation of Immigrants 75 (rev. & enl. ed. Harper and Row 1964).

41 Statement of Rep. de la Garza (Apr. 6, 1965), 10 Trelles and Bailey, Immigration and Nationality Acts, at 191, 192; Remarks at the Signing of the Immigration Bill, Liberty Island, New York, in Public Papers of the Presidents of the United States: Lyndon B. Johnson 1037, 1038–39 (1966). See also Statement of W. Willard Wirtz, Secretary of Labor (Mar. 18, 1965), 10 Trelles and Bailey, at 114; Letter From the President to the Speaker of the House, 111 Cong. Rec. 20,996 (daily ed. Aug. 25, 1965); Statement of Dean Rusk, Secretary of State (Mar. 11, 1965), 10 Trelles and Bailey, at 88; Statement of Rep. Fino (Apr. 6, 1965), id. at 193, 195. On the amendments, see Daniels, Golden Door, at 129–44; King, Making Americans, at 236–53; Massey, Durand, and Malone, Beyond Smoke and Mirrors, at 40; Ngai, Impossible Subjects, at 235, 243; Tichenor, Dividing Lines, at 196–216.

42 See 2003 Immigration Statistics, at 8, 14; Luke J. Larsen, U.S. Census Bureau, The Foreign-Born Population in the United States: 2003 (2004); Office of Policy and Planning, U.S. Immigration and Naturalization Service, Estimates of the Unauthorized Immigrant Population Residing in the United States: 1990 to 2000 (2003).

43 See Daniels, Golden Door, at 123, 137, 151; Hing, Asian America, at 66–72, 36, 48–49; Joppke, Nation-State, at 27; King, Making Americans, at 241–42.

44 See Ngai, Impossible Subjects, at 261–63. On the foreseeability of the rise in Asian immigration, compare Daniels, Golden Door, at 135; Hing, Asian America, at 39–41; David M. Reimers, Still the Golden Door: The Third World Comes to America 74–91 (2d ed. Columbia Univ. Press 1992); with Gabriel J. Chin, The Civil Rights Revolution Comes to Immigration Law: A New Look at the Immigration and Nationality Act of 1965, 75 N.C. L. Rev. 273 (1996). For occupational categories in prior law, see Act of June 25, 1948, ch. 647, § 6, 62 Stat. 1009, 1012.

45 On the Western Hemisphere limit, see Act of Oct. 3, 1965, Pub. L. No. 89-236, §§ 8, 21(e), 79 Stat. 911, 916, 921; Daniels, Golden Door, at 133; Select Commission on Immigration and Refugee Policy, U.S. Immigration Policy and the National Interest (Staff Report) 208 (1981); Johnson, Huddled Masses, at 25–26; Ngai, Impossible Subjects, at 254–61; John A. Scanlan, Immigration Law and the Illusion of Numerical Control, 36 U. Miami L. Rev. 819, 830 (1982).

46 On labor certification, see INA § 212(a)(5); Peter W. Rodino, Jr., The Impact of Immigration on the American Labor Market, 27 Rutgers L. Rev. 245, 250–56 (1974) (on the period from 1952 through 1965).

47 On informal crossing, see Daniels, Golden Door, at 53. The Bracero program ended on December 31, 1964, with the expiration of the authority granted by the Act of Dec. 13, 1963, Pub. L. No. 88-203, § 1, 77 Stat. 363, 363. See Kitty Calavita, Inside the State: The Bracero Program, Immigration, and the I.N.S. (Routledge 1992); Daniels, Golden Door, at 89–91, 142; Leonard Dinnerstein and David M. Reimers, Ethnic Americans: A History of Immigration 131–34 (4th ed. Columbia Univ. Press 1999); Massey, Durand, and Malone, Beyond Smoke and Mirrors, at 34–41; Ngai, Impossible Subjects, at 138–66.

48 On expectations, see Douglas S. Massey, Luin Goldring, and Jorge Durand, Continuities in Transnational Migration: An Analysis of Nineteen Mexican Communities, 99 Am. J. Sociology 1492, 1496–1503 (1994). On the increase in Mexican immigration, see Massey, Durand, and Malone, Beyond Smoke and Mirrors, at 41–47; Arthur F. Corwin and Johnny M. McCain, Wetbackism since 1964: A Catalogue of Factors, in Immigrants—and Immigrants: Perspectives on Mexican Labor Migration to the United States 67, 68 (Arthur F. Corwin ed., Greenwood Press 1978).

CHAPTER 7 *Transition at a Crossroads*

1 See H.R. Rep. No. 1365, 82d Cong., 2d Sess. at 27, reprinted in 1952 U.S. Code Cong. & Admin. News 1740; S. Rep. 1137, 82d Cong., 2d Sess. at 44; Riopelle, Revitalization, at 992. On the exceptions, see Act of Oct. 14, 1940, ch. 876, §§ 310, 311, 318, 324, 54 Stat. 1137, 1144–45, 1147, 1149; Dewey, Naturalization Laws, at 62–63; 1 Hyde, International Law, at 631–32; Van Dyne, Naturalization, at 61–64.

2 For current law, INA § 334(f); 8 C.F.R. § 334.11.

3 See Pub. L. No. 99-603, 100 Stat. 3359 (1986); INA §§ 101(a)(H)(ii)(a), 210, 245A, 274A.

4 See INA § 274B(a)(1); U.S. General Accounting Office, Immigration Reform—Employer Sanctions and the Question of Discrimination 5–7 (1990); Aleinikoff, Martin, and Motomura, Immigration and Citizenship, at 1132–35; Civil Rights Act of 1964, Pub. L. No. 88-352, Title VII, § 703, 78 Stat. 255 (codified as amended at 42 U.S.C. § 2000e-2).

5 See Act of Nov. 6, 1986, Pub. L. No. 99-603, § 102(a), 100 Stat. 3359, 3374–75.

6 See Pub. L. No. 101-649, § 533, 104 Stat. 4978, 5054–55 (1990); INA § 274B(a)(3)(B); Dhillon, 3 OCAHO 497 (1993) (construing requirement leniently); Southwest Marine, 3 OCAHO 429 (1992) (same).

7 See 30 U.S.C. § 22 (mineral rights), 17 Stat. 91 (1872); 48 U.S.C. § 1501 (territories), ch. 340, § 1, 24 Stat. 476 (1887); 43 U.S.C. § 315b (Taylor Grazing Act), ch. 865, § 3, 48 Stat. 1270 (1934); 15 C.F.R. § 734.2(b)(2)(ii) (technology transfer), 61 Fed. Reg. 12746 (1996); 31 C.F.R. § 560.418 (note 1(b)) (technology transfer), 64 Fed. Reg. 20173 (1999); 12 C.F.R. § 268.205 (Federal Reserve System), 68 Fed. Reg. 18093 (2003); 15 U.S.C. § 278g(d) (National Institute of Standards and Technology), Pub. L. No. 102-245, Title I, § 104(h)(2), 106 Stat. 11 (1992).

8 See Haw. Stat. § 201G-241(1)(A) (housing loans); Haw. Stat. § 206-9(c)(1) (purchasing or leasing state residential lots); Cal. Pub. Res. Code § 3900 (mining claims); Cal. Gov't. Code § 1031(a) (peace officers); Cal. Govt. Code § 68105 (court reporters); Cal. Mil. & Vet. Code § 550 (National Guard); Mass. Gen. Laws Ann. Ch. 146 § 50 (engineers); Ohio Rev. Stat. Code § 124.23 (civil service); N.J. Stat. Ann. § 18A:26-1 (teachers); N.Y. Educ. Law § 3001(3) (teachers); Okla. Stat. Ann. 5 § 1 (attorneys); Mass. Gen. Laws Ann. 221 § 38A (attorneys); Mass. Gen. Laws Ann. 112 § 45 (dentists); Mass. Gen. Laws Ann. 112 § 87TT (brokers); Ohio Stat. § 4731.292(A) (physicians); Utah St. § 34-30-1 (construction projects); Vt. Stat. Ann. 3 § 262 (civil service); Ore. Rev. Stat. § 166.291(1)(a)(B) (concealed handguns); State v. Hernandez-Mercado, 879 P.2d 283, 287 (Wash. 1994) (en banc).

9 Ambach v. Norwick, 441 U.S. 68, 80 (1979); N.Y. Educ. Law § 3001(3); N.J. Stat. Ann. § 18A:26-8.1(a).

10 See N.J. Stat. Ann. § 44:10-82c, d; Conn. Gen. Stat. Ann. § 17b-116(e); Wendy Zimmermann and Karen C. Tumlin, Patchwork Policies: State Assistance for Immigrants under Welfare Reform 28–29, 44, Urban Inst. Occasional Paper No. 24 (1999); Michael Wishnie, Laboratories of Bigotry? Devolution of the Immigration Power, Equal Protection, and Federalism, 76 N.Y.U. L. Rev. 493, 515–16 (2001). Statutes directing state agencies to encourage naturalization include Col. Rev. Stat. § 26-2-111.8(6); Wash. Rev. Code Ann. § 74.08A.130.

11 See 2003 Immigration Statistics, at 20.

12 Compare Guidelines for Naturalization (*Einbürgerungsrichtlinien*) § 2.3, July 1, 1977, reprinted in Kay Hailbronner and Günter Renner, Staatsangehörigkeitsrecht 623, 626 (C.H. Beck 1991) with Structuring Immigration, Fostering Integration: Report of the Independent Commission on Migration to Germany 13 (2001). On the classic country of immigration, see Roger Cohen, How Open to Immigrants Should Germany Be? An Uneasy Country's Debate Deepens, N.Y. Times, May 12, 2001, at 11.

13 See Gesetz zur Steuerung und Begrenzung der Zuwanderung und zur Regelung des Aufenthalts und der Integration von Unionsbürgern und Ausländern, §§ 7, 8, 9, 21, July 30, 2004.

14 See Dec. of 26 Sept. 1978, 1 BvR 525/77; Dec. of 18 July 1973, 1 BvR 23, 155/73; Joppke, Nation-State, at 71–73 (citing Gunther Schwerdtfeger, Welche rechtlichen Vorkehrungen empfehlen sich, um die Rechtstellung von Ausländern in der Bundesrepublik Deutschland angemessen zu gestalten?, Gutachten A zum 53. Deutschen Juristentag Berlin 1980, at 26–32 [1980]); Rubio-Marin, Democratic Challenge, at 12, 190, 210–12.

15 See Gesetz zur Steuerung und Begrenzung der Zuwanderung und zur Regelung des Aufenthalts und der Integration von Unionsbürgern und Ausländern, § 19, July 30, 2004. On pre-2005 law, see Joppke, Nation-State, at 66–67. See generally Rogers Brubaker, Citizenship and Nationhood in France and Germany 165–78 (Harvard Univ. Press 1992); Abraham, The Good of Banality? at 247, 248; David A. Martin, Graduated Application of Constitutional Protections for Aliens: The

Real Meaning of *Zadvydas*, 2001 Sup. Ct. Rev. 47, 95 (2002); Rainer Münz and Ralf Ulrich, Changing Patterns of Immigration to Germany, 1945–1995, in Migration Past, Migration Future: Germany and the United States 65 (Klaus J. Bade and Myron Weiner eds., Berghahn Books 1997).

16 See Nancy F. Rytina, Department of Homeland Security, U.S. Legal Permanent Residents: 2004, at 2 (2005); Wasem, Permanent Admissions, at 7–8; 2003 Immigration Statistics, at 20. See also INA § 245; Aleinikoff, Martin, and Motomura, Immigration and Citizenship, at 515–22; Douglas S. Massey and Katherine Bartley, The Changing Legal Status Distribution of Immigrants: A Caution, 39 Int'l Migration Rev. 469 (2005).

17 See INA § 101(a)(15)(S), (T), (U), (V). On earned legalization proposals, see Darryl Fears, Immigration Measure Introduced, Wash. Post, May 13, 2005, at A8.

18 533 U.S. 678, 693–94 (2001). On acknowledgment of presence, see Linda Bosniak, A Basic Territorial Distinction, 16 Geo. Immigr. L.J. 407 (2002); T. Alexander Aleinikoff, Detaining Plenary Power: The Meaning and Impact of *Zadvydas v. Davis*, 16 Geo. Immigr. L.J. 365 (2002); Michele R. Pistone, A Times Sensitive Response to Professor Aleinikoff's Detaining Plenary Power, 16 Geo. Immigr. L.J. 391 (2002).

19 See Martin, Graduated Application, at 101–09.

20 See INA §§ 101(f), 316, 319, 328, 329, 334(b).

21 For the first English requirement, see Act of June 29, 1906, ch. 3592, § 8, 34 Stat. 596, 599. For current law, see INA §§ 312, 316(a), § 337(a); Hmong Veterans' Naturalization Act of 2000, Pub. L. No. 106-207, § 2, 114 Stat. 316, 316; Aleinikoff, Martin, and Motomura, Immigration and Citizenship, at 53–89. On nineteenth-century proposals, see Higham, Strangers in the Land, at 97–105.

22 2003 Immigration Statistics, at 137. On the difficulty of the requirements, see Louis DeSipio and Rodolfo O. de la Garza, Making Americans, Remaking America: Immigration and Immigrant Policy 63–92 (Westview Press 1998); Peter J. Spiro, Questioning Barriers to Naturalization, 13 Geo. Immigr. L.J. 479, 485–516 (1999); Linda Kelly, Defying Membership: The Evolving Role of Immigration Jurisprudence, 67 U. Cin. L. Rev. 185, 197–209 (1998).

23 See Aleinikoff, Martin, and Motomura, Immigration (3d ed. 1995), at 1015; DeSipio and de la Garza, Making Americans, at 76–77; Susan Gonzalez-Baker, Luis F.B. Plascencia, Gary P. Freeman, and Manuel Orozco, The Making of Americans: Results of the Texas Naturalization Survey 9–10 (Tomas Rivera Policy Institute 2000); David S. North, The Long Grey Welcome: A Study of the American Naturalization Program, 21 Int'l Migration Rev. 311, 323–24 (1987).

24 See 2003 Immigration Statistics, at 134, 137, 138–41; Rytina, Estimates of the Legal Permanent Resident Population and Population Eligible to Naturalize in 2003; Rytina and Saeger, Naturalizations: 2004, at 1; Fix, Passel, and Sucher, Trends in Naturalization, at 1474–76. See also U.S. Immigration and Naturalization Service, 1997 Statistical Yearbook 141 (1999); The New Americans: Economic, Demographic, and Fiscal Effects of Immigration 378–82 (James P. Smith and Barry Edmonston eds., National Academy Press 1997).

25 On naturalization policies, see Gerald L. Neuman, Justifying U.S. Naturalization Policies, 35 Va. J. Int'l L. 237 (1994); Noah M. J. Pickus, To Make Natural: Creating Citizens for the Twenty-First Century, in Immigration and Citizenship in the Twenty-First Century 107 (Noah M.J. Pickus ed., Rowman and Littlefield 1998); Joseph H. Carens, Why Naturalization Should Be Easy: A Response to Noah Pickus, in Twenty-First Century, at 141. On naturalization as a government goal, see Hampton v. Mow Sun Wong, 426 U.S. 88, 105 (1976); City of Chicago v. Shalala, 189 F.3d 598, 608 (7th Cir. 1999); Campos v. FCC, 650 F.2d 890, 894 (7th Cir. 1981); Mow Sun Wong v. Campbell, 626 F.2d 739, 745 (9th Cir. 1980), cert. denied, 450 U.S. 959 (1981); William Branigin and Kathryn Wexler, INS Unveils Plan to Speed Naturalization Process, Wash. Post, Sept. 01, 1995, at A1. On the end of local administration, see Act of June 29, 1906, ch. 3592, §§ 1, 3, 34 Stat. 596, 596; S. Rep. 59-4373, at 1–2 (1906); DeSipio and de la Garza, Making Americans, at 73–78; Smith, Civic Ideals, at 446.

26 See Dilek Çinar, From Aliens to Citizens: A Comparative Analysis of Rules of Transition, in Bauböck, From Aliens to Citizens, at 49, 53–55; Hammar, Democracy, at 88; David Jacobson, Rights across Borders: Immigration and the Decline of Citizenship 23–26, 38–40 (Johns Hopkins Univ. Press 1997); Rubio-Marin, Democratic Challenge, at 63, 222–27; Sassen, Guests and Aliens, at 118–19, 146. On naturalization's function, compare Joppke, Nation-State, at 204–06 with Kay Hailbronner, Citizenship and Nationhood, in Brubaker, Politics of Citizenship, at 79.

27 See Guidelines for Naturalization (*Einbürgerungsrichtlinien*) §§ 2.2, 3.1, 3.1.1, July 1, 1977, reprinted in Hailbronner and Renner, Staatsangehörigskeitsrecht, at 626; Hammar, Democracy, at 87–88; Joppke, Nation-State, at 201; Gerald L. Neuman, Nationality Law in the United States and the Federal Republic of Germany: Structure and Current Problems, in Paths to Inclusion, at 247, 264–66.

28 On noncitizen children in *jus sanguinis* countries, see Brubaker, Citizenship and Nationhood, at 123; Neuman, Nationality Law, at 272; Wolfgang Seifert, Social and Economic Integration of Foreigners in Germany, in Paths to Inclusion, at 83, 98.

29 See United States v. Wong Kim Ark, 169 U.S. 649, 694–96 (1898). As chapter 5 explained, *jus soli* also has an affiliation-based rationale. On the U.S. second and third generation, see Joseph H. Carens, Who Belongs? Theoretical and Legal Questions about Birthright Citizenship in the United States, 37 U. Toronto L.J. 413, 414–30 (1987); Christopher Eisgruber, Birthright Citizenship and the Constitution, 72 N.Y.U. L. Rev. 54, 72–81 (1997); Hammar, Democracy, at 73–74; Neuman, Strangers to the Constitution, at 165–87. On reapportionment, see Garza v. County of Los Angeles, 918 F.2d 763, 773–76 (9th Cir. 1990), cert. denied, 498 U.S. 1028 (1991); H.J. Res. 53, 109th Cong. (2005).

30 See Rubio-Marin, Democratic Challenge, at 227. On German developments since 1990, Bauböck, Transnational Citizenship, at 71–86; Hailbronner, Citizenship and Nationhood, at 67–70; Joppke, Nation-State, at 96, 187, 203; Rubio-Marin, Democratic Challenge, at 12, 14, 216–22; Kay Hailbronner, Fifty Years of the Basic Law—Migration, Citizenship, and Asylum, 53 SMU L. Rev. 519, 530–31 (2000); Neuman, Nationality Law, at 266–68.

31 See Ausländergesetz §§ 85, 86 (1990).

32 Gesetz zur Reform des Staatsangehörigkeitsrechts, Bundesgesetzblatt, I 1618 (1999), amending Ausländergesetz § 85.

33 See Aleinikoff, Martin, and Motomura, Immigration and Citizenship, at 89–107; T. Alexander Aleinikoff and Douglas Klusmeyer, Plural Nationality: Facing the Future in a Migratory World, in Citizenship Today, at 63.

34 See Çinar, From Aliens to Citizens, at 49, 53–54; Joppke, Nation-State, at 205; Rubio-Marin, Democratic Challenge, at 127, 229–31.

35 On higher rates if naturalization does not mean loss of prior citizenship, see Hammar, Democracy, at 100; Rubio-Marin, Democratic Challenge, at 69–70, 111, 217; Peter J. Spiro, Dual Nationality and the Meaning of Citizenship, 46 Emory L.J. 1411, 1460–85 (1998). On Mexico, see Manual Becerra Ramirez, Nationality in Mexico, in From Migrants to Citizens 312, 328–38 (T. Alexander Aleinikoff and Douglas Klusmeyer eds., Carnegie Endowment for Int'l Peace 2000); Jorge A. Vargas, Dual Nationality for Mexicans, 35 San Diego L. Rev. 823 (1998); Louie Gilot, Mexico Revives Dual Nationality, El Paso Times, Aug. 16, 2004, at 1B; Angel Gonzalez, Mexico to Restart Dual Citizenship Plan, Dallas Morning News, Aug. 6, 2004, at 2B. On effects on perceptions, see Bauböck, Transnational Citizenship, at 109.

CHAPTER 8 *The Meaning of Transition*

1 On permanent residence as probationary, see Aleinikoff, Citizens, Aliens, at 15–16.

2 See Hammar, Democracy, at 1–6, 24–25, 109; Thomas A. Spragens, Jr., Civic Liberalism: Reflections on Our Democratic Ideals 252–53 (1999); Walzer, Spheres of Justice, at 31–63; Linda Bosniak, Universal Citizenship and the Problem of Alienage, 94 Nw. U. L. Rev. 963, 975–80 (2000).

3 See Universal Declaration of Human Rights, art. 25, G.A. Res. 217, U.N. GAOR, 3d Sess., pt. 1, U.N. Doc. A/810 (1948).

4 See International Covenant on Economic, Social and Cultural Rights, Dec. 16, 1966, art. 12, 993 U.N.T.S. 3 (entered into force Jan. 3, 1976).

5 Universal Declaration of Human Rights, art. 7, G.A. Res. 217, U.N. GAOR, 3d Sess., U.N. Doc. A/810 (1948); International Covenant for Civil and Political Rights, Dec. 16, 1966, art. 26, 999 U.N.T.S. 171, 179 (entered into force Mar. 23, 1976). See also Berta Esperanza Hernandez-Truyol and Kimberly A. Johns, Global Rights, Local Wrongs, and Legal Fixes: An International Human Rights Critique of Immigration and Welfare "Reform," 71 S. Cal. L. Rev. 547, 564, 570–80 (1998); cf. Linda Bosniak, Citizenship Denationalized, 7 Ind. J. Global Legal Studies 447, 467 (2000) (suggesting that international human rights do not strongly protect individuals).

6 See Joppke, Nation-State, at 64, 69, 143, 200–01; Hailbronner, Citizenship and Nationhood, at 78–79.

7 See Rubio-Marin, Democratic Challenge, at 105–07 (arguing for automatic naturalization or its equivalent).

8 For this argument against Proposition 187, see Sandra L. Jamison, Proposition 187: The United States May Be Jeopardizing Its International Treaty Obligations, 24 Denv. J. Int'l L. & Pol'y 229, 232–35 (1995). See also Joppke, Nation-State, at 272.

9 See Rubio-Marin, Democratic Challenge, at 22.

10 See Ngai, Impossible Subjects, at 82–90.

11 See INA § 312.

12 For the suggestion that naturalization becomes a matter of right for applicants who meet requirements, see Schneiderman v. United States, 320 U.S. 118, 120 (1943); United States v. Macintosh, 283 U.S. 605, 615 (1931); United States v. Ginsberg, 234 U.S. 472, 475 (1917). See also Rubio-Marin, Democratic Challenge, at 174–77.

13 On possible test revisions, see Citizenship Test Redesign, 82 Interpreter Releases 1348 (2005). On federal assistance, see USCIS Releases Guide for New Immigrants, 10-13 Bender's Immigr. Bull. 3 (2005); Department of Homeland Security, U.S. Citizenship and Immigration Services, Welcome to the United States: A Guide for New Immigrants 89–100 (2005); Abraham, The Good of Banality?, at 244. On state and local programs, see State of California Little Hoover Commission, We The People: Helping Newcomers Become Californians 23–26 (2002).

14 See Abraham, The Good of Banality? at 245; Rubio-Marin, Democratic Challenge, at 133.

15 See INA § 203(a)(2), (d); U.S. Dept. of State, 8 Visa Bulletin no. 93 (May 2006).

16 See INA §§ 201(b)(2)(A)(i), 203(a)(1), (a)(3), (a)(4); Aleinikoff, Martin, and Motomura, Immigration and Citizenship, at 277–80, 302–31.

17 See Moore v. City of East Cleveland, 431 U.S. 494, 499–500 (1977); Stanley v. Illinois, 405 U.S. 645, 651, 656–58 (1972).

18 430 U.S. 787, 797–800 (1977).

19 Cf. United States v. Virginia, 518 U.S. 515, 531 (1996) (gender classifications require an "exceedingly persuasive justification").

20 See Mark Krikorian, Legal Immigration: What Is to Be Done?, in Blueprints for an Ideal Legal Immigration Policy 47, 49 (Richard D. Lamm and Alan Simpson eds., Center for Immigration Studies 2001). On family immigration, see Hiroshi Motomura, The Family and Immigration: A Roadmap for the Ruritanian Lawmaker, 43 Am. J. Comp. L. 511 (1995). See also Rubio-Marin, Democratic Challenge, at 206–08 (discussing the German Constitutional Court case invalidating waiting periods).

21 See 2003 Immigration Statistics, at 27; George Borjas, Friends or Strangers: The Impact of Immigrants on the U.S. Economy 45–46, 49–53, 121–22, 231 (1990) (education at arrival); Roberto Suro, Strangers Among Us: How Latino Immigration Is Transforming America 158, 167 (Alfred A. Knopf 1998) (education after arrival).

22 457 U.S. at 222–23 (quoting Brown, 347 U.S. 483, 493 [1954]); 457 U.S. at 218–19, 226; id. at 234 (Blackmun, J., concurring). See also Becoming an American, at

36–45; Kenneth L. Karst, Paths to Belonging: The Constitution and Cultural Identity, 64 N.C. L. Rev. 303, 323–24 (1986); J.M. Balkin, The Constitution of Status, 106 Yale L.J. 2313, 2353–67 (1997).

23 On the meanings of citizenship, see T. H. Marshall, Citizenship and Social Class, in Thomas H. Marshall and Tom Bottomore, Citizenship and Social Class 8 (1992). See also Aleinikoff, Semblances of Sovereignty, at 44–46; Bosniak, Citizenship Denationalized, at 456–89.

24 On segmented assimilation, see Alejandro Portes and Min Zhou, Should Immigrants Assimilate? Public Interest 18, 22–26 (1994); Rubén G. Rumbaut, The Crucible Within: Ethnic Identity, Self-Esteem, and Segmented Assimilation Among Children of Immigrants, 28 Int'l Migration Rev. 748 (1994); Suro, Strangers Among Us, at 15. On a right to work, see William E. Forbath, Why Is This Rights Talk Different From All Others Rights Talk? Demoting the Court and Reimagining the Constitution, 46 Stan. L. Rev. 1771, 1790–91 (1994); Kenneth L. Karst, The Coming Crisis of Work in Constitutional Perspective, 82 Cornell L. Rev. 523, 553–59 (1997); Vicki Schultz, Life's Work, 100 Colum. L. Rev. 1881, 1886–92 (2000).

25 403 U.S. 365, 379–80 (1971); Foley v. Connelie, 435 U.S. 291, 295 (1978). See also Moving Phones Partnership v. FCC, 998 F.2d 1051, 1056 (D.C. Cir. 1993) (following Foley).

26 See Alan Wolfe, One Nation, After All 161–63 (Viking 1998); David A. Hollinger, Postethnic America: Beyond Multiculturalism 105–29 (Basic Books 1995).

27 See Hailbronner, Citizenship and Nationhood, at 79.

28 See 403 U.S. 365, 372 (1971); John Hart Ely, Democracy and Distrust 161–62 (Harvard Univ. Press 1980); Aleinikoff, Martin, and Motomura, Immigration and Citizenship, at 1027–28. On the importance of naturalization as deliberate and voluntary, see Bauböck, Transnational Citizenship, at 94, 105.

29 On these limitations of human rights, see Bosniak, Opposing Prop. 187, at 595–98; Richard Delgado and Jean Stefancic, Cosmopolitanism Inside Out: International Norms and the Struggle for Civil Rights and Local Justice, 27 Conn. L. Rev. 773, 775 (1995).

CHAPTER 9 *Race, Belonging, and Transition*

1 Higham, Strangers in the Land, at 234. See also id. at 120–23. Zangwill's play is reprinted in From the Ghetto to the Melting Pot: Israel Zangwill's Jewish Plays (Edna Nahshon ed., Wayne State Univ. Press 2005).

2 See Aleinikoff, Semblances of Sovereignty, at 54. See also Gary Gerstle, Liberty, Coercion, and the Making of Americans, 84 J. Am. Hist. 524 (1997); King, Making Americans, at 15–17, 81, 120–23. For a modern sanguine view, see Peter Salins, Assimilation, American Style (Basic Books 1997). For a classic analysis, see Milton Gordon, Assimilation in American Life (Oxford Univ. Press 1964).

3 Michael Omi and Howard Winant, Racial Formation in the United States 5 (2d ed. Routledge 1994).

4 See Peter Brimelow, Alien Nation: Common Sense about America's Immigration Disaster 9–11, 58–73, 264–65 (Random House 1995); Patrick J. Buchanan, The Death of the West: How Dying Populations and Immigrant Invasions Imperil Our Country and Civilization 125 (Thomas Dunne Books 2001); Samuel P. Huntington, Who Are We? The Challenges to America's National Identity 171–77 (Simon and Schuster 2004). For critiques, see Kevin R. Johnson and Bill Ong Hing, National Identity in a Multicultural Nation: The Challenge of Immigration Law and Immigrants, 103 Mich. L. Rev. 1347 (2005); Motomura, Whose Alien Nation?; Peter H. Schuck, Alien Rumination, 105 Yale L.J. 1963 (1996); Alan Wolfe, Native Son: Samuel Huntington Defends the Homeland, 83 Foreign Affairs 120 (May/June 2004).

5 See Oscar Handlin, The Uprooted 152–79 (2d ed. Little, Brown 1973); Joppke, Nation-State, at 149; King, Making Americans, at 117–18; Massey, Goldring, and Durand, Continuities, at 1496–1503; Alejandro Portes and Rubén G. Rumbaut, Legacies: The Study of the Immigrant Second Generation 46–49, 64–69 (Univ. of California Press 2001).

6 See Meyer v. Nebraska, 262 U.S. 390, 399–403 (1923). For cases striking down statutes against the use of other languages, see Farrington v. Tokushige, 273 U.S. 284 (1927); Bartels v. Iowa, 262 U.S. 404 (1923). See also Daniels, Coming to America, at 159–61; Higham, Strangers in the Land, at 195–99, 204–12, 235–36; King, Making Americans, at 88–90, 110–13; Juan F. Perea, Demography and Distrust: An Essay on American Languages, Cultural Pluralism, and Official English, 77 Minn. L. Rev. 269, 329–32 (1992); Scharf, Tired of Your Masses, at 140–42, 155–61.

7 See Portes and Rumbaut, Immigrant America, at 106 (quoting Roosevelt). On promoting English through immigration law, see Higham, Strangers in the Land, at 92; Ngai, Impossible Subjects, at 24; Portes and Rumbaut, Immigrant America, at 196–97.

8 See Angelo Ancheta, Race, Rights and the Asian-American Experience 104–26 (Rutgers Univ. Press 1998); Richard D. Lamm and Gary Imhoff, The Immigration Time Bomb: The Fragmenting of America 99–124 (Truman Talley Books 1985); David M. Reimers, Unwelcome Strangers: American Identity and the Turn Against Immigration 119–29 (Columbia Univ. Press 1998); Perea, Demography and Distrust, at 341–50. For the California initiatives, see Cal Const. art. III, § 6; 1998 Cal. Legis. Serv. Prop. 227 (codified at Cal. Educ. Code §§ 300–340).

9 For criticism of Proposition 227, see Kevin R. Johnson and George A. Martinez, Discrimination by Proxy: The Case of Proposition 227 and the Ban on Bilingual Education, 33 U.C. Davis L. Rev. 1227 (2000). On the 2000 Census, see Richard Alba, Language Assimilation Today: Bilingualism Persists More Than in the Past, But English Still Dominates (Center for Comparative Immigration Studies Nov. 2004). On English acquisition, see Richard Alba and Victor Nee, Remaking the American Mainstream: Assimilation and Contemporary Immigration 217–30 (Harvard Univ. Press 2003); Aleinikoff and Rumbaut, Terms of Belonging, at 12–14; Portes and Rumbaut, Immigrant America, at 192–231.

10 Neuman, Alien Suffrage, at 292–300, 307–08; Keyssar, The Right to Vote, at 137. See also Jacobson, Whiteness, at 12, 24–31; Rubio-Marin, Democratic Challenge, at 135; Raskin, Legal Aliens, at 1397–1417; Rosberg, Equal Protection, at 1093–1100. For laws limiting intending citizen voting to white males, see Ind. Const. of 1851, art. II, § 2; Mo. Const. of 1865, art, II, § 18; Dakota Territorial Gov. Act, ch. 86, § 5, 12 Stat. 239, 241 (1861); Kansas-Nebraska Act, ch. 59, §§ 5, 23 (1854); Nevada Territorial Gov. Act, ch. 83, § 5, 12 Stat. 209, 211 (1861); Wash. Territorial Gov. Act, ch. 90, § 5, 10 Stat. 172, 174 (1853).

11 United States v. Wong Kim Ark, 169 U.S. 649, 712 (1898) (Fuller, C.J., dissenting). Thanks to Lucy Salyer for directing me to this passage.

12 See Bauböck, Transnational Citizenship, at 99, 111. On the perpetual foreigner syndrome, see Neil Gotanda, "Other Non-Whites" in American Legal History: A Review of Justice at War, 85 Colum. L. Rev. 1186, 1188–92 (1985) (book review). On the Catch-22 for Japanese-Americans who were discriminated against, then called understandably disloyal by the Supreme Court, see Jerry Kang, Denying Prejudice: Internment, Redress, and Denial, 51 UCLA L. Rev. 933, 947–48 (2004).

13 See Robin Toner and Janet Elder, Public Is Wary but Supportive on Rights Curbs, N.Y. Times, Dec. 12, 2001, at A1.

14 See Rasul v. Bush, 542 U.S. 466 (2004).

15 See Viet D. Dinh, Law and the War on Terrorism: Freedom and Security After September 11, 25 Harv. J.L. & Pub. Pol'y 399, 400–01 (2002). For overviews of post–September 11 immigration law measures, see Aleinikoff, Martin, and Motomura, Immigration and Citizenship, at 1243–49; Donald Kerwin, Counterterrorism and Immigrant Rights Two Years Later, 80 Interpreter Releases 1401 (2003).

16 See Office of the Inspector General, Department of Justice, The September 11 Detainees: A Review of the Treatment of Aliens Held on Immigration Charges in Connection with the Investigation of the September 11 Attacks 21 (2003).

17 Memorandum from Chief Immigration Judge Michael Creppy, to All Immigration Judges (Sept. 21, 2001). On deportation priorities, see DOJ Focusing on Removal of 6,000 Men from Al Qaeda Haven Countries, 79 Interpreter Releases 115 (2002); Mark Bixler, U.S. Deportations to Muslim Nations Soar, Atlanta Journal-Constitution, Jan. 15, 2003, at 1A; 2003 Immigration Statistics, at 161–68, 171–78. On entry-exit and visa processing, see 67 Fed. Reg. 52,584 (2002). On collateral harms to other noncitizens, see Steven W. Bender, Sight, Sound, and Stereotype: The War on Terrorism and Its Consequences for Latinas/os, 81 Or. L. Rev. 1153 (2002); Kevin R. Johnson, September 11 and Mexican Immigrants: Collateral Damage Comes Home, 52 DePaul L. Rev. 849 (2003). On the interviews, see General Accounting Office, Justice Department's Project to Interview Aliens after September 11, 2001 (2003).

18 On special registration, see Rachel L. Swarns, Special Registration for Arab Immigrants Will Reportedly Stop, N.Y. Times, Nov. 22, 2003, at A16; Maia

Jachimowicz and Ramah McKay, "Special Registration" Program, Migration Information Source, Migration Policy Institute, Apr. 1, 2003; U.S. Detains Nearly 1,200 During Registry, Wash. Post, Jan. 17, 2003. On Iraq war measures, see U.S. Immigration and Customs Enforcement, Fact Sheet: Operation Liberty Shield, Mar. 17, 2003; Danny Hakim and Nick Madigan, A Nation at War: Iraqi-Americans: Immigrants Questioned by FBI, N.Y. Times, Mar. 22, 2003, at B12.

19 See Samuel R. Gross and Debra Livingston, Racial Profiling Under Attack, 102 Colum. L. Rev. 1413, 1413-14 (2002).

20 See Uniting and Strengthening America by Providing Appropriate Tools Required to Intercept and Obstruct Terrorism (USA PATRIOT) Act of Oct. 26, 2001, Pub. L. No. 107-56, 115 Stat. 272.

21 See Act of June 27, 1952, ch. 477, § 274(a), 66 Stat. 163, 229; Daniels, Golden Door, at 121; Tichenor, Dividing Lines, at 194.

22 See Aleinikoff, Martin, and Motomura, Immigration and Citizenship, at 1130-51; Kitty Calavita, Employer Sanctions Violations: Toward a Dialectical Model of White-Collar Crime, 24 Law & Society Rev. 1041, 1046-55, 1057, 1060 (1990); Wayne A. Cornelius, The U.S. Demand for Mexican Labor, in Mexican Migration to the United States: Origins, Consequences, and Policy Options 25, 43-44 (Wayne A. Cornelius and Jorge A. Bustamante eds., Center for U.S.-Mexican Studies 1989); Massey, Durand, and Malone, Beyond Smoke and Mirrors, at 118-21; Tichenor, Dividing Lines, at 243.

23 See Aleinikoff, Martin, and Motomura, Immigration and Citizenship, at 1140, Table 10.3; Miriam Jordan, As Border Tightens, Growers See Threat to "Winter Salad Bowl," Wall St. J., Mar. 11, 2005, at A1; Douglas Holt, INS Is Scaling Back Its Workplace Raids, Chicago Tribune, Jan. 17, 1999, at C1. On tax law enforcement, see Shereen C. Chen and Stephanie Wisdo, The Interplay between the IRS and the USCIS, New Jersey L.J. Mar. 28, 2005; House Holds Hearings on Social Security Numbers/ITINs, Operation Predator, US-VISIT, 81 Interpreter Releases 382 (2004); Elena Gaona, Illegal Immigrants Paying Taxes as Example of Good Citizenship, San Diego Tribune, Apr. 15, 2004, at A1.

24 See Estimates of the Unauthorized Immigrant Population, at 1. On discretionary relief, see Ngai, Impossible Subjects, at 55, 63.

25 On the Bracero roots of today's flow, see Kitty Calavita, The Immigration Policy Debate: Critical Analysis and Future Options, in Mexican Migration, at 151, 155-60; Gerald P. López, Undocumented Mexican Migration: In Search of a Just Immigration Law and Policy, 28 UCLA L. Rev. 615, 664-72, 707-08 (1981); Massey, Durand, and Malone, Beyond Smoke and Mirrors, at 34-51; Ngai, Impossible Subjects, at 147-52. On Mexican labor recruitment, see Tichenor, Dividing Lines, at 168-75, 202, 211. For temporary farmworker admissions, see INA § 101(a)(15)(H).

26 See Massey, Durand, and Malone, Beyond Smoke and Mirrors, at 45-47, 84-98; Peter Andreas, Border Games: Policing the U.S.-Mexico Divide 85-87, 89-96,

106–12 (2000); Calavita, Immigrants at the Margins; Bill Ong Hing, The Dark Side of Operation Gatekeeper, 7 U.C. Davis J. Int'l L. & Pol'y 121 (2001).

27 On deportations based on convictions, see Peter H. Schuck and John Williams, Removal Criminal Aliens: The Pitfalls of Federalism, 22 Harv. J. L. & Pub. Pol'y 367, 375–85 (1999). On the address reporting, see INA § 265(a); Mark Bixler, High Response to Address Law Swamps INS, Atlanta Journal-Constitution, Sept. 18, 2002, at 3F.

28 *Plyler*, 457 U.S. at 226. See Darryl Fears, Immigration Measure Introduced, Wash. Post, May 13, 2005; at A8; Anne E. Kornblut, Bush Cites Political Hurdles In Plan for "Guest Workers," N.Y. Times, Mar. 24, 2005, at A6; Pres. Bush Renews Call for a Temporary Worker Program, 82 Interpreter Releases 274 (2005).

29 On migration patterns, see Massey, Goldring, and Durand, at 1496–1503. On attractions of undocumented labor, see Wayne A. Cornelius, Mexican Migration to the United States: Introduction, in Mexican Migration to the United States, at 1, 4–8.

30 See Little Hoover Commission, We The People, at 28; Int'l Ass'n of Chiefs of Police, Press Release, Police Chiefs Announce Immigration Enforcement Policy, Dec. 1, 2004.

31 See Daniels, Golden Door, at 73–80. On refugees, see Aleinikoff, Martin, and Motomura, Immigration and Citizenship, at 506–09, 805–08.

32 See Department of Justice, Attorney General Ashcroft Outlines Foreign Terrorist Task Force, Oct. 31, 2001; Amy Goldstein, A Deliberate Strategy of Disruption; Massive, Secretive Detention Effort Aimed Mainly at Preventing More Terror, Wash. Post, Nov. 4, 2001, at A1. On nationality-based student visa enforcement, see David Morgan, U.S. Plans Search for Student-Visa Violators, Reuters, May 29, 2003.

33 See Wasem, Permanent Admissions, at 13–14.

34 On convictions, see Mary Beth Sheridan, Immigration Law as Anti-Terrorism Tool, Wash. Post, June 13, 2005, at A1; Dan Eggen and Julie Tate, U.S. Campaign Produces Few Convictions on Terrorism Charges: Statistics Often Count Lesser Crimes, Wash. Post, June 12, 2005, at A1. On mistrust, see David A. Harris, The Stories, the Statistics, and the Law: Why "Driving While Black" Matters, 84 Minn. L. Rev. 265, 294–309 (1999); Nelson Lund, The Conservative Case Against Racial Profiling in the War on Terrorism, 66 Albany L. Rev. 329, 335–41 (2003).

35 See Frank H. Wu, Yellow: Race in America Beyond Black and White 173–213 (Basic Books 2002). On rational truth and other values, see Charles Nesson, The Evidence or the Event? On Judicial Proof and the Acceptability of Verdicts, 98 Harv. L. Rev. 1357, 1376 (1985).

36 See David Cole, Enemy Aliens: Double Standards and Constitutional Freedoms in the War on Terrorism 91–100 (2003).

37 Brimelow, Alien Nation, at 5.

38 On nondiscrimination, see Jean v. Nelson, 472 U.S. 846, 852 (1985); Tichenor, Dividing Lines, at 249–50; Refugee Act of 1980, Pub. L. No. 96-212, § 101(b), 94 Stat. 102, 102; Arthur C. Helton, Political Asylum Under the 1980 Refugee Act: An Unfulfilled Promise, 17 U. Mich. J.L. Ref. 243, 250–62 (1984). For less sanguine views of the Refugee Act, see Johnson, Huddled Masses, at 26 (citing Hing, Asian America, at 121–38); Harvey Gee, The Refugee Burden: A Closer Look at the Refugee Act of 1980, N.C. J. Int'l L. & Comm. Reg. 559, 573–651 (2001); Gil Loescher and John A. Scanlan, Calculated Kindness: Refugees and America's Half-Open Door, 1945 to the Present 102–69 (Free Press 1986). On apparently neutral laws, see Johnson, Huddled Masses, at 26, 42–46; Ngai, Impossible Subjects, at 245. On the income gap, see Nathan Glazer, The New Immigration: A Challenge to American Society 17 (San Diego State Univ. Press 1988); Borjas, Friends or Strangers, at 13. On the per-country limit, see Massey, Durand, and Malone, Beyond Smoke and Mirrors, at 41–47; Ngai, Impossible Subjects, at 227–28.

39 See INA § 203(c); Pub. L. No. 101-649, §§ 131–133, 104 Stat. 4978, 4997–5001 (1990); Pub. L. No. 100-658, §§ 2, 3, 102 Stat. 3908, 3908–09 (1988); Pub. L. No. 99-603, § 314, 100 Stat. 3359, 3439 (1986); H.R. Rep. 100-1038, 100th Cong., 2d Sess. (1988); Aleinikoff, Martin, and Motomura, Immigration and Citizenship, at 282–84; Stephen H. Legomsky, Immigration, Equality, and Diversity, 31 Colum. J. Transnat'l. L. 319, 329–33 (1993); Johnson, Huddled Masses, at 27.

40 See Whose Alien Nation? at 1948–50; Cox, Citizenship, Standing, and Immigration Law, at 396–402. On finding a baseline, see T. Alexander Aleinikoff and Samuel Issacharoff, Race and Redistricting: Drawing Constitutional Lines After Shaw v. Reno, 92 Mich. L. Rev. 588, 620 (1993). Compare Rosberg, Protection of Aliens, at 324–25 (immigration), with Miller v. Johnson, 515 U.S. 900, 915–16 (1995) (redistricting).

41 On intent, see Village of Arlington Heights v. Metro. Hous. Dev. Corp., 429 U.S. 252, 265–66 (1977); Johnson, Immigration Politics, at 662–69.

42 See Ronald Dworkin, Taking Rights Seriously 227 (Harvard Univ. Press 1977).

43 See INS Announces Second Cuban Migration Program, 73 Interpreter Releases 319 (1996); U.S., Cuba Reach Important Migration Agreement, 71 Interpreter Releases 1213, 1236–37 (1994); Cuban Adjustment Act, Pub. L. No. 89-732, 80 Stat. 1161, 1161 (1966).

44 On discrimination, see Brief of the National Association for the Advancement of Colored People, Transafrica, and the Congressional Black Caucus as Amici Curiae in Support of Respondents 11, in Sale v. Haitian Centers Council, Inc., 509 U.S. 155 (1993); Malissia Lennox, Note, Refugees, Racism, and Reparations: A Critique of the United States' Haitian Immigration Policy, 45 Stan. L. Rev. 687, 714–23 (1993).

45 On remittances, see Kevin O'Neil, Remittances from the United States in Context, Migration Policy Institute, June 1, 2003.

46 See Susan M. Akram and Kevin R. Johnson, Race, Civil Rights, and Immigration After September 11, 2001: The Targeting of Arabs and Muslims, 58 N.Y.U. Ann. Surv. Am. L. 295, 338 (2002).

47 On Asian-American communities, see Daniels, Coming to America, at 246; Daniels, Golden Door, at 50; Hing, Asian America, at 45, 190; Leti Volpp, American Mestizo: Filipinos and Antimiscegenation Laws in California, 33 U.C. Davis L. Rev. 795, 830 (2000). On attitudes toward Arabs and Muslims, see Akram and Johnson, Race, Civil Rights, at 301–02; Susan M. Akram and Maritza Kennedy, Immigration and Constitutional Consequences of Post–9/11 Policies Involving Arabs and Muslims in the United States: Is Alienage a Distinction without a Difference? 38 U.C. Davis L. Rev. 609, 612–20 (2005); Susan M. Akram, Scheherezade Meets Kafka: Two Dozen Sordid Tales of Ideological Exclusion, 14 Geo. Immigr. L.J. 51, 70–113 (1999); Leti Volpp, The Citizen and the Terrorist, 49 UCLA L. Rev. 1575, 1586–95 (2002). On effects on communities, see Tatsha Robertson, Deportation Surge Leaves Void in Brooklyn's Little Pakistan, Boston Globe, Aug. 14, 2005, at A1; American-Arab Anti-Discrimination Committee, Press Release/Action Alert, Immigration and Customs Enforcement (ICE) Plans Immigration Sweeps (Sept. 30, 2004); David Runk, Crackdown Affects Michigan Arab Community, Assoc. Press, June 4, 2003; Michael Powell, An Exodus Grows in Brooklyn: 9/11 Still Rippling Through Pakistani Neighborhood, Wash. Post, May 29, 2003, at A1.

48 347 U.S. 483, 494 (1954). See also Shaw v. Reno, 509 U.S. 630, 643 (1993); Strauder v. West Virginia, 100 U.S. 303, 307–08 (1880); Kevin R. Johnson, The Case Against Race Profiling in Immigration Enforcement, 78 Wash. U. L. Q. 675, 711–16 (2000); Paul Brest, Foreword: In Defense of the Antidiscrimination Principle, 90 Harv. L. Rev. 1, 8–36 (1976); Kenneth L. Karst, Foreword: Equal Citizenship Under the Fourteenth Amendment, 91 Harv. L. Rev. 1, 48–53 (1977); R.A. Lenhardt, Understanding the Mark: Race, Stigma, and Equality in Context, 79 N.Y.U. L. Rev. 803 (2004); Rosberg, Protection of Aliens, at 304, 326–27. On hate crimes, see Muneer Ahmad, A Rage Shared By Law: Post-September 11 Racial Violence as Crimes of Passion, 92 Calif. L. Rev. 1259 (2004); Remarks of President George W. Bush at the Islamic Center, Sept. 17, 2001; U.S. Department of Justice, Civil Rights Division, Enforcement and Outreach Following the September 11 Terrorist Attacks (Sept. 9, 2004); Federal Bureau of Investigation Uniform Crime Reporting Program, Hate Crimes Statistics, 2001; Curt Anderson, FBI: Hate Crimes v. Muslims Rise, Assoc. Press, Nov. 25, 2002; Mary Beth Sheridan, Bias Against Muslims Up 70%, Wash. Post, May 3, 2004, at A12.

49 See Aleinikoff and Rumbaut, Terms of Belonging, at 2. See also Johnson, Huddled Masses, at 38–39; Rumbaut, Crucible Within, at 789; Marcelo M. Suarez-Orozco, Everything You Ever Wanted to Know About Assimilation But Were Afraid to Ask, 129 Daedalus 1 (Fall 2000). See also Rubio-Marin, Demo-

cratic Challenge, at 102–29 (arguing for automatic naturalization in part by considering immigrants as future citizens).

CHAPTER 10   *Taking Transition Seriously*

1 INA § 334 (on timing). For the seven-year rule, see 8 U.S.C. § 1612(a)(2)(A); H.R. Rep. 105-149, 105th Cong., 1st Sess. (1997).

2 See Francis Fukuyama, Immigrants and Family Values, 95 Commentary 26, 30 (1993).

3 See 88 U.S. 162 (1874). On the end of noncitizen voting and modern practice, see Higham, Strangers in the Land, at 214; Keyssar, Right to Vote, at 136–38, 310–11; Neuman, Strangers to the Constitution, at 70; Raskin, Legal Aliens, at 1415–17, 1461–66.

4 See Tara Kini, Comment, Sharing the Vote: Noncitizen Voting Rights in Local School Board Elections, 93 Cal. L. Rev. 271, 273–78 (2005); Ron Hayduk and Michele Wucker, Immigrant Voting Rights Receive More Attention, Migration Information Source (Migration Policy Institute 2004).

5 191 Colo. 399, 553 P.2d 830 (1976), appeal dismissed, 430 U.S. 961 (1977); *Sugarman,* 413 U.S. 634, 642, 646 (1973) (quoting Dunn v. Blumstein, 405 U.S. 330, 344 [1972]). See also Rosberg, Equal Protection, at 1100–04.

6 454 U.S. 432, 438–39 (1982).

7 See Kathleen Hennessey, Rare Town Where Voters Don't Have to Be Citizens, L.A. Times, July 22, 2004, at A23; Raskin, Legal Aliens, at 1441–45.

8 Woodcock v. Bolster, 35 Vt. 632, 640 (1863) (quoted in Neuman, Alien Suffrage, at 302; Raskin, Legal Aliens, at 1454). See also Harper-Ho, Noncitizen Voting Rights, at 280, 297; Pickus, True Faith and Allegiance, at 68; Raskin, Legal Aliens, at 1406–07; Marta Tienda, Demography and the Social Contract, 39 Demography 587, 603–05 (2002).

9 See Rodolfo O. de la Garza and Louis DeSipio, Save the Baby, Change the Bathwater, and Scrub the Tub: Latino Electoral Participation After Seventeen Years of Voting Right Act Coverage, 71 Tex. L. Rev. 1479, 1522–23 (1993); DeSipio and de la Garza, Making Americans, at 99–100. See also Aleinikoff, Citizens, Aliens, at 29 n. 77; Rubio-Marin, Democratic Challenge, at 76–77, 120.

10 See Aleinikoff, Semblances of Sovereignty, at 61.

11 Invalidating state laws: Bernal v. Fainter, 467 U.S. 216, 219–28 (1984); Examining Bd. v. Flores de Otero, 426 U.S. 572, 601–06 (1976); Matter of Griffiths, 413 U.S. 717, 718 (1973). Upholding state laws: Cabell v. Chavez-Salido, 454 U.S. 432, 438–47 (1982); Ambach v. Norwick, 441 U.S. 68, 69–72 (1979); Foley v. Connelie, 435 U.S. 291, 297–300 (1978).

12 *Cabell,* 454 U.S. at 438–41, 455; *Flores de Otero,* 426 U.S. at 604 (quoting Truax v. Raich, 239 U.S. 33, 41 [1915]). See also *Griffiths,* 413 U.S. at 719–22; *Ambach,* 441 U.S. at 81–82 (Blackmun, J., dissenting).

13 See INA § 240A(a).

14 See Martin, Graduated Application, at 115–19 (based on contract and affiliation as well as transition).

CONCLUSION   *The Idea of Americans in Waiting*

1 See Building the New American Community: Newcomer Integration and Inclusion Experiences in Non-Traditional Gateway Cities (Migration Policy Institute 2004); Little Hoover Commission, We The People, at 23–26. See also Governor Rod R. Blagojevich, Exec. Order 2005-10, Creating New Americans Immigrant Policy Council (Ill. Nov. 19, 2005). Other models include the Maryland Office for New Americans and the Los Angeles Mayor's Office of Immigrant Affairs.

INDEX